Preferred Stocks
The Art of Profitable Income Investing

Kenneth G. Winans

A Wealth of Wisdom LLC
Keauhou Hawaii

Published by A Wealth of Wisdom LLC, Hawaii USA
AWealthOfWisdom.com
Printed in the United States of America

The amounts and percentages shown in the exhibits are for illustration purposes only and do not reflect actual securities or performance. See disclaimer on page 216.

ISBN: 978-0-9843125-1-1
Library of Congress Control Number: 2010914055

Book Design: Renée Robinson of A Wealth of Wisdom LLC
Copyeditor: John Maybury of goofbuster.com
Author Portrait: © 2007 Jeanette Vonier

The investment certificates and magazines used to accent the book are from the author's extensive collection of rare financial artifacts. Many are on display in The Museum of American Finance of New York (moaf.org).

Front Cover
Preferred stock certificate of The Edison Portland Cement Company issued to Thomas A. Edison in 1906.

The past few years have been financially devastating to many people. While I escaped that fate, I did suffer a loss in many respects far worse—the death of my stepmother and dear friend Joyce A. Winans.

When my beloved mother unexpectedly died during my 12th year, Joyce soon stepped into some very "big shoes" and became my second mom.

Her love and kindness has had a lasting effect on our entire family. She will always be remembered!

Thank you, Joyce, for always supporting my efforts and dreams; this book is dedicated to you.

Love, Ken

Winans Coat of Arms – 1098 AD

Acknowledgments

Authors don't write books entirely by themselves. It takes hundreds of hours of intense work. A special "thank you" to the following people for their help on this project.

Karen Blair
Elizabeth Boaz
Michael Carr, CMT
Marc G. Edwards
Stephane Fitch
Justin Gularte, CMT
Mathew Krantz
John Maybury
Vassilis Popotas, CMT
Renée Robinson
Deborah Wreyford

Preface

What should a reader get from *Preferred Stocks: The Art of Profitable Income Investing*? A logical assumption is that this is merely a second edition of my 2007 award-winning book *Preferreds: Wall Street's Best-Kept Income Secret*. And yet this is incorrect!

Before *Preferreds* was written, the modern investing world was flying blind when it came to preferred stocks.

That was the first book written on preferred stocks since the 1930s, and until the development of the *Winans International Preferred Stock Index (WIPSI)*, there wasn't a current benchmark to evaluate the $200 billion preferred-stock market.

This was "uncharted territory" for investment analysis. The superior overall performance of preferred stocks was revealed. *Preferreds* also proved that popular technical indicators (such as the 200-day moving average) worked in identifying changes in the long-term price trends of preferred stocks from 1900-2005.

Although it was a winner of the 2007 USA Book News Awards in the Business: Investing category, many critics have attacked the book "for having too many charts." Or as written in the 2009 book *Investing in Preferred Stock* by Paul Josephs, "There is little one can say to discourage the large world of investors who are enamored of technical analysis and momentum trading. Investors interested in applying short-term technical methods may find *Preferreds* to be useful."

It appears that the classic battle between technical and fundamental investors is alive and well when it comes to this security!

Needless to say, these readers missed the key points to my research. Much of what I forecasted in 2007 came true, and many of the long-term research tools discussed performed brilliantly on signaling that a new bear market arrived in preferred stocks in May 2007 (seven months prior to the financial free fall of 2008) as well as the new uptrend in preferred stocks in April 2009. In fact, my company, Winans International Investment

Management and Research, put this knowledge to work and navigated the worst investment climate since the Great Depression. Our track record can be reviewed at winansintl.com.

Why write a new book on preferred stocks? Answer: 2008 dramatically changed everything for preferreds!

The once-orphaned preferred security, with a total market capitalization of only 7% the size of the massive corporate bond market, was one of the key tools used by the U.S. government in its intervention efforts (i.e., TARP) to stabilize the world economy during the fall of 2008.

Since then, preferred stocks have been the best-performing U.S. investment medium in 2009 (and so far in 2010) and the darlings of the financial media.

It is rare to read anything new about investing. *Preferred Stocks: The Art of Profitable Income Investing* builds upon my past historical research from my previous books with the addition of new research (market analysis, investment analysis, etc.) as well as revised methodologies in portfolio management for successful income investing in today's environment.

It is a mystery why preferred stocks, one of the oldest exchange-listed investments in existence, had "fallen between the cracks" in a global investment industry fixated on offering as many investment products as possible. *Preferred Stocks: The Art of Profitable Income Investing* has shown that an unpolished investment gem has been rediscovered.

The rebirth of income investing is here to stay. Why? America's aging population has lost much of its appetite for financial volatility and has chosen the same fiscal course as its ancestors, where investment income matters as much as capital appreciation.

Ken Winans

Table of Contents

Chapter 1

2008 and the Mistakes Made

"Except under the worst depression conditions of the early '30s, dividends were regularly paid for many years and all Depression arrears were paid off in 1936-1937 to patient investors."
THE MAGAZINE OF WALL STREET (2/5/1944)

"Yes, you can get high yield, if you're willing to take the risk of losing your entire principal as investors go for junk-rated preferreds."
FORBES (6/7/2004)

Boy, how the investment climate has changed in only a few years!

With the popping of financial bubbles in real estate, stocks, and bonds (that nearly collapsed the world financial system in 2008), Wall Street, government, and academia quickly "circled the wagons" to explain their rationale and actions. They claim in unison that this was a "one-of-a-kind" global economic contraction that no one could have predicted or prevented. The truth is that the warning signs were there.

When I wrote *Preferreds* in 2007, the first chapter was titled "The Bulls Are Running—But There Is a Problem." In it I warned, "A future market correction in income investments could cause even more damage than the burst of the dot-com bubble."

Sadly, that is exactly what happened!

As the housing market gravy train abruptly halted, "risk free" illiquid, mortgage-backed securities brought down many of the long-standing giants of global finance. The bigger surprise was that preferred stocks played a key role in the demise and salvation of the world economy. Considered an orphan security by Wall Street, with a total market capitalization of only 7% the size of the massive corporate bond market, "preferreds" were issued by financial institutions to prop up their failing finances, and were one of the key tools used by the U.S. government in its intervention efforts, better known as TARP, to stabilize the world economy during the fall of 2008. Since then, preferreds have rapidly grown in popularity with investors and have been one of the best-performing investments since the Great Recession ended.

THE FINANCIAL HURRICANE OF 2008

Like natural hurricanes that frequently strike our nation, cliff-dropping financial bear markets are unique but not uncommon. Since 1900, the Dow Jones Industrial Average declined more than 20% in a single year 11 times. Worse yet, there was very little "shelter" to escape to as bonds, preferred stocks, and housing also suffered declines during most of these periods.

FINANCIAL HURRICANES SINCE 1900

TABLE 1: Financial Hurricane Years Total Returns

	Common Stocks	Corporate Bonds	Preferred Stocks	90-day T-Bills	Real Estate
1903	(24%)	(5%)	(11%)	5%	13%
1907	(38%)	(5%)	(23%)	5%	(16%)
1914	(31%)	(1%)	7%	4%	(5%)
1917	(22%)	(8%)	(6%)	3%	(10%)
1920	(33%)	0%	(3%)	6%	25%
1930	(34%)	7%	6%	2%	(11%)
1931	(53%)	(14%)	(11%)	3%	(10%)
1932	(23%)	8%	8%	0%	(44%)
1937	(33%)	(8%)	0%	0%	(4%)
1974	(28%)	(1%)	(3%)	7%	5%
2008	(35%)	1%	(19%)	0%	(8%)
Average	(32%)	(2%)	(5%)	3%	(6%)
Worst	(53%) **1931**	(14%) **1931**	(23%) **1907**	0% **1932**	(44%) **1932**

Common Stocks—Dow Jones Industrial Average Total Return
Corporate Bonds—Dow Jones Corporate Bond Average Total Return
Preferred Stocks—Winans International Preferred Stock Index Total Return
Real Estate—Winans International Real Estate Index (Residential)

As the above table shows, average declines in most assets classes were severe, and 1931-2 still holds the record as the worst period. The only "high ground" was the 90-day T-bill that produced a positive 3% average return during these fiscal free falls.

Common factors in these market meltdowns were:

- The combination of over-leverage and illiquidity burst bubbles in all financial instruments.
- Many Wall Street innovations went awry.
- Investments responded negatively to failed government actions and inept regulation.
- Military conflicts and the national costs associated with them scared investors to the sidelines.

All these issues played a role in 2008. Why did the investment community overlook obvious warning signs? As Mark Twain said, "History doesn't repeat itself; it just rhymes." This might explain why historic comparisons are often misunderstood or blatantly ignored, by even experienced investors, in the run-up of a financial bubble.

The financial hurricane of 2008 was a classic financial bubble and had much in common with past economic calamities. While the names and dates have changed throughout history, the causes were similar to past situations.

TRAGIC CHAIN OF EVENTS

To fully understand what happened, it's important to look at the chronology of events from 2007 through 2009, and its effect on all investments (not just common stocks). I had an interesting vantage point during the crisis due to my "expert" status with the media. I had written what many consider "the book" on preferred stocks and pioneered the development of key indices in preferred stocks and real estate. On the other hand, as president of Winans International, an investment management firm, I daily provided calm, disciplined leadership to our clients, as the tragedy unfolded.

REVIEW OF 2007

"In 2007, investors in preferred stock had one of the worst years in memory, with a credit crunch, oversupply and a tax-related sell-off."
INVESTOR'S BUSINESS DAILY (2/6/08)

Market Overview, total returns (CHARTS 1-4)
S&P 500 Index = 5.3%, Dow Jones Corporate Bonds Avg = 4.8%,
WI Preferred Stock Index = (9.6%), WI Real Estate Index = (5.8%)

- Residential real estate prices reached an all-time high in March. This brought an end to a 14-year bull market in housing, the second-longest housing expansion since 1850. During this real estate run-up, Wall Street constructed Collateralized Debt Obligations (CDO) by packaging mortgages of various quality into a security and coupled it with a form of default insurance called Credit Default Swaps (CDS). Banks estimate that $450 billion of these highly rated, popular securities were sold globally from 2005 to 2007.

- Mortgage rates rose by 28% to a five-year high of 6.7%. Financing became difficult as the average time it took to sell a new house rose from 4 to 7 months. Since adjustable rate mortgages were popular among new homeowners, because they could qualify for a mortgage more easily, the increase in interest rates had suddenly disqualified many prospective buyers.

- Housing sales quickly contracted and by year-end were down 38% to levels not seen since the early 1990s.

- Preferred stocks entered into a new bear market. The Winans Preferred Stock Index (WIPSI) broke below its 200-day moving average in May, and WIPSI's dividend yield soon reached a 13-year high of 8%. Particularly hard hit were preferred stocks in large financial companies (CHARTS 5 AND 6).

2007

Chart 1: S&P 500 Index 5.3%

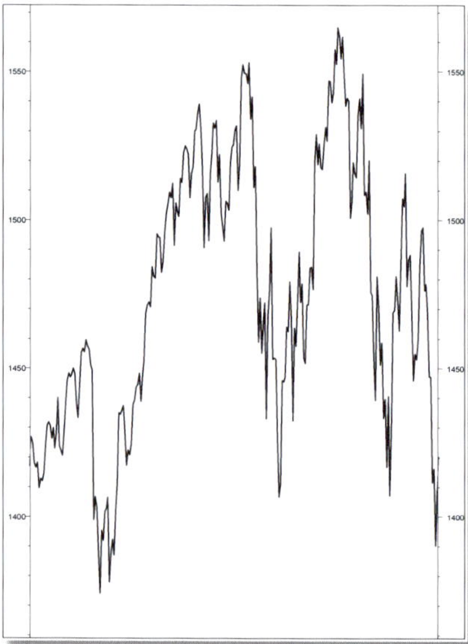

Chart 2: Winans International Real Estate Index, WIREI (5.8%)

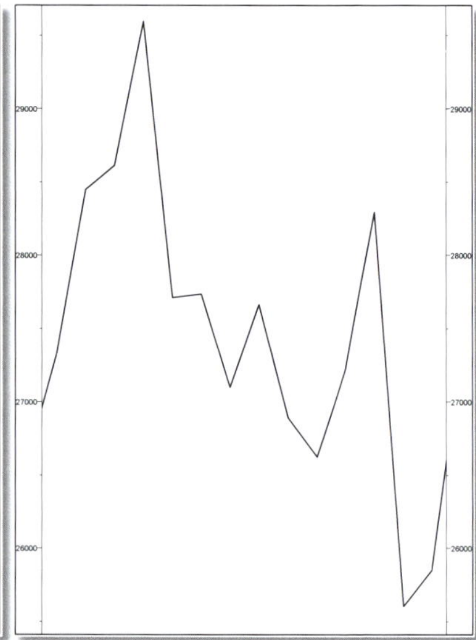

Chart 3: Winans International Preferred Stock Index, WIPSI (9.6%)

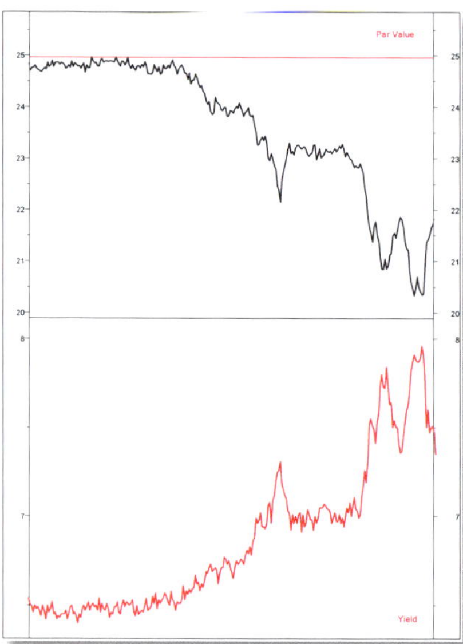

Chart 4: Dow Jones Corporate Bonds Average 4.8%

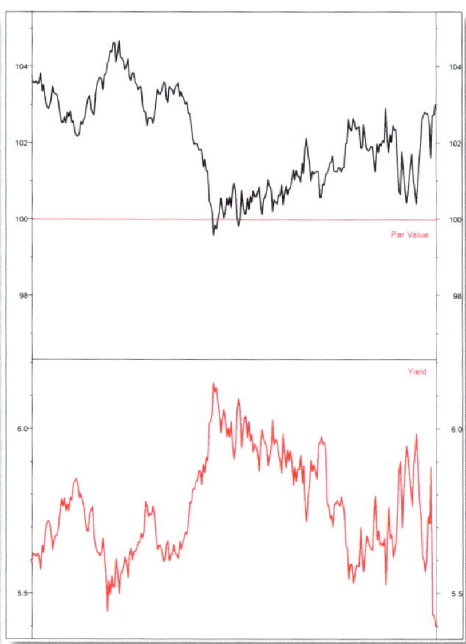

Chart 5:
Bank of America
Capital 6%
Series Z
2007

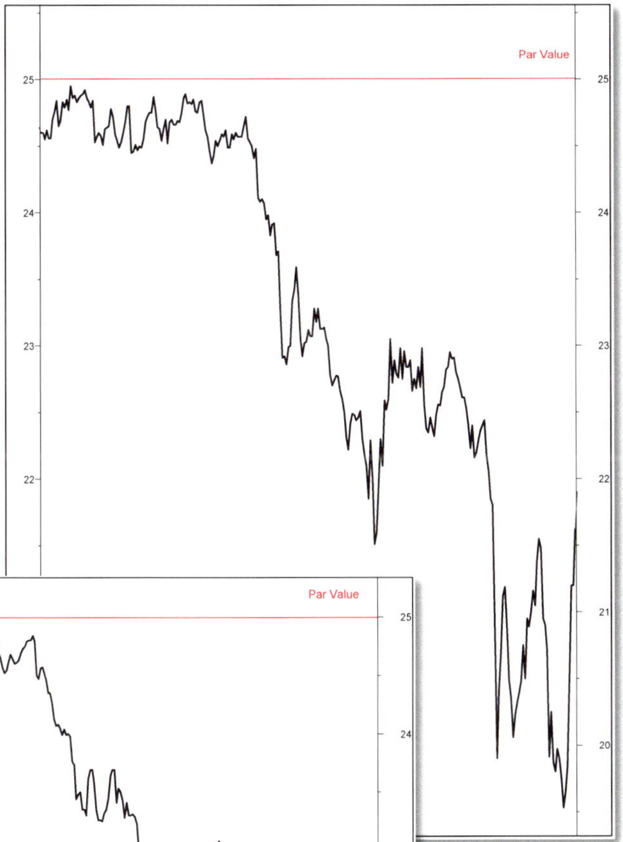

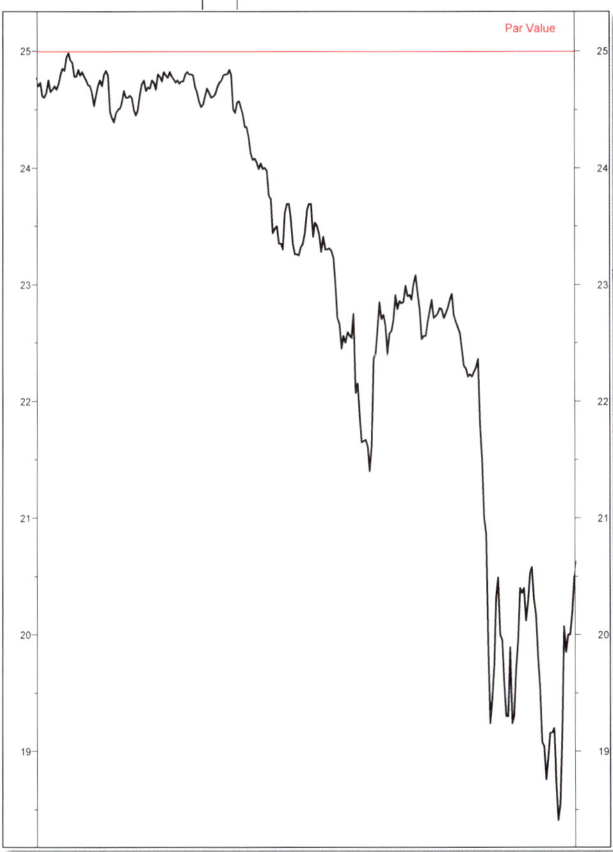

Chart 6:
Citigroup
CAP IX 6%
2007

Charts created in
MetaStock from
Equis International

Chart 7:
Bank of America
Common Stock
2007

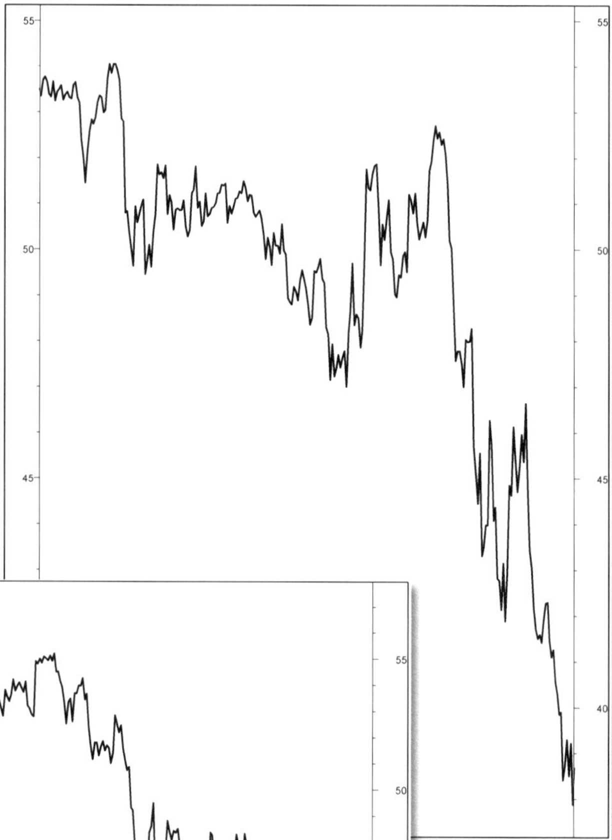

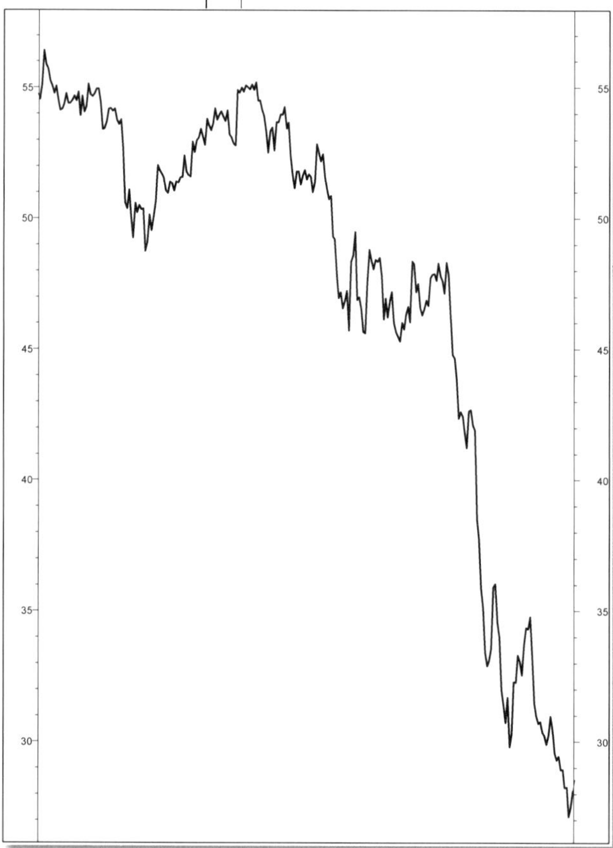

Chart 8:
Citigroup
Common Stock
2007

Charts created in
MetaStock from
Equis International

- A major divergence occurred as most major stock market indices reached all-time highs in the fall, while financial common stocks, which began their long slide early in the year, continued to rapidly decline (Charts 7 and 8).

- Bank regulators require banks to have enough capital on hand to meet liabilities, as well as meeting certain reserve requirements. As the credit crunch squeezed banks, issuing preferreds became a cheap way to raise capital without altering their balance sheets. New issues of preferred stock reached a record of $120 billion (vs. $74 billion in 2006) as Fannie Mae sold $7 billion (S&P Rating AA-), Freddie Mac sold $6 billion (S&P Rating AA-), and Citigroup sold $6 billion (S&P Rating A+).

- Eager investors purchased these investments, as financial advisors at major investment firms pitched preferred shares in Fannie Mae and Freddie Mac to more than 1 million investors nationwide as ultra-safe investments that were appropriate and suitable for conservative clients.

- Many equity and fixed income mutual funds (that are not traditional investors in preferred stocks) bought the preferreds to diversify their financial holdings. In fact, many of the preferred-stock mutual funds concentrated more than 65% of their holdings in financial preferreds.

- At year-end, tax loss selling and reallocation into better-performing fixed-income securities accelerated selling of financial common and preferred stocks.

- Most financial ratings on common stocks, preferred stocks, and bonds of major financial institutions were unchanged throughout 2007.

2008

Chart 9: S&P 500 Index (35.4%)

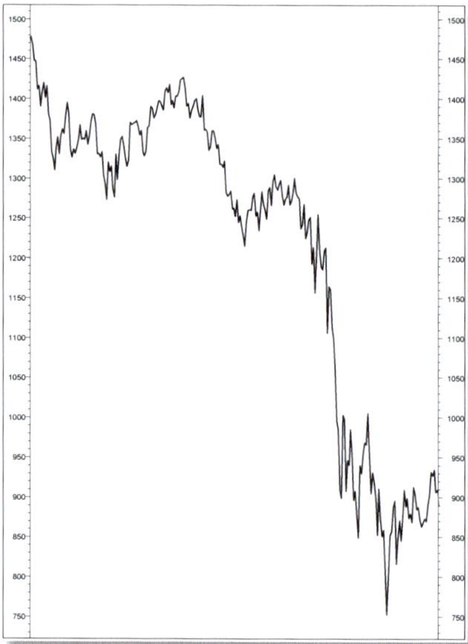

Chart 10: Winans International Real Estate Index, WIREI (7.5%)

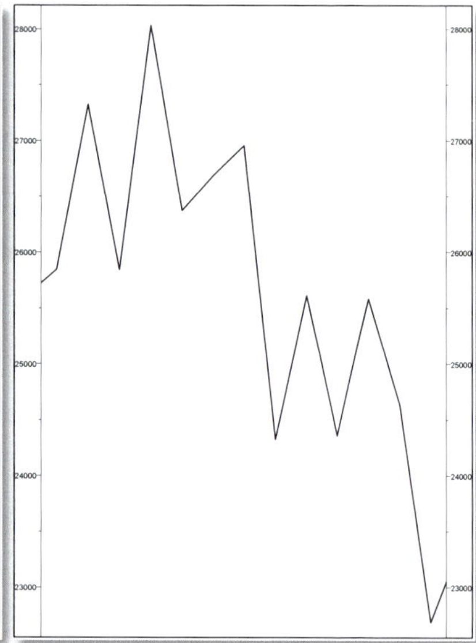

Chart 11: Winans International Preferred Stock Index, WIPSI (19.4%)

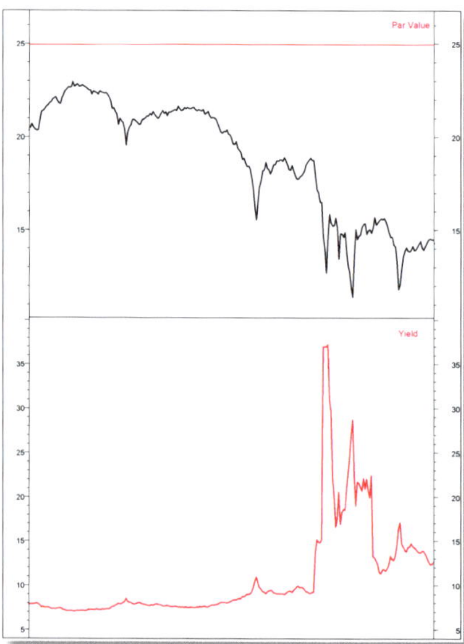

Chart 12: Dow Jones Corporate Bonds Average 1.3%

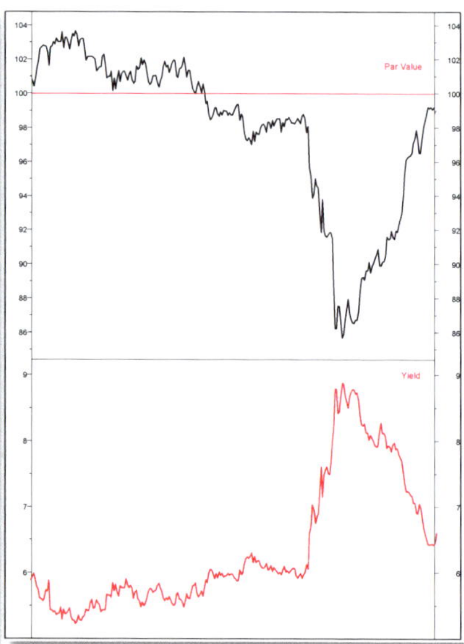

Charts created in MetaStock from Equis International

REVIEW OF 2008

"The reason yields have gotten so high is the share prices of many financial companies' preferred stocks have been punished. They're continuing to be punished because investors suspect there's more trouble ahead in the financial industry."
USA Today (7/23/2008)

Market Overview, total returns (Charts 9-12)
S&P 500 Index = (35.4%), Dow Jones Corporate Bonds Ave = 1.3%, WI Preferred Stock Index = (19.4%), WI Real Estate Index = (7.5%)

- Common stocks start off the year badly as most major indices crossed below their 200-day moving average, thus ushering in a new bear market. By November, the S&P 500 had declined approximately 50% and came close to setting a one-year record as the worst since 1900.

- Housing continued to implode. The Winans International Real Estate Index posted a price decline of (7.5%) as sales nose-dived by 41%. This was the worst annual drop in U.S. housing prices and sales since the 1970s. The CDO and CDS securities became illiquid. By year-end they were priced as low as 5 cents on the dollar.

- Corporate bonds went into a severe decline from February to October and rivaled the 1931 bond bear market. The price component of the Dow Jones Corporate Bond Average fell –17%, and its yield shot up to nearly 9%, an interest rate not seen since 1991.

- Preferred stocks started 2008 in positive territory, as many of the Bear Stearns preferred shares were treated well in the shotgun marriage with JP Morgan Chase. Financial institutions managed to raise $72 billion through new preferred issues in Q1. This access to cheap private funds was short-lived, as the Q1 earnings showed deteriorating problems in the financial sector.

CHART 13: Fannie Mae Common Stock
2008

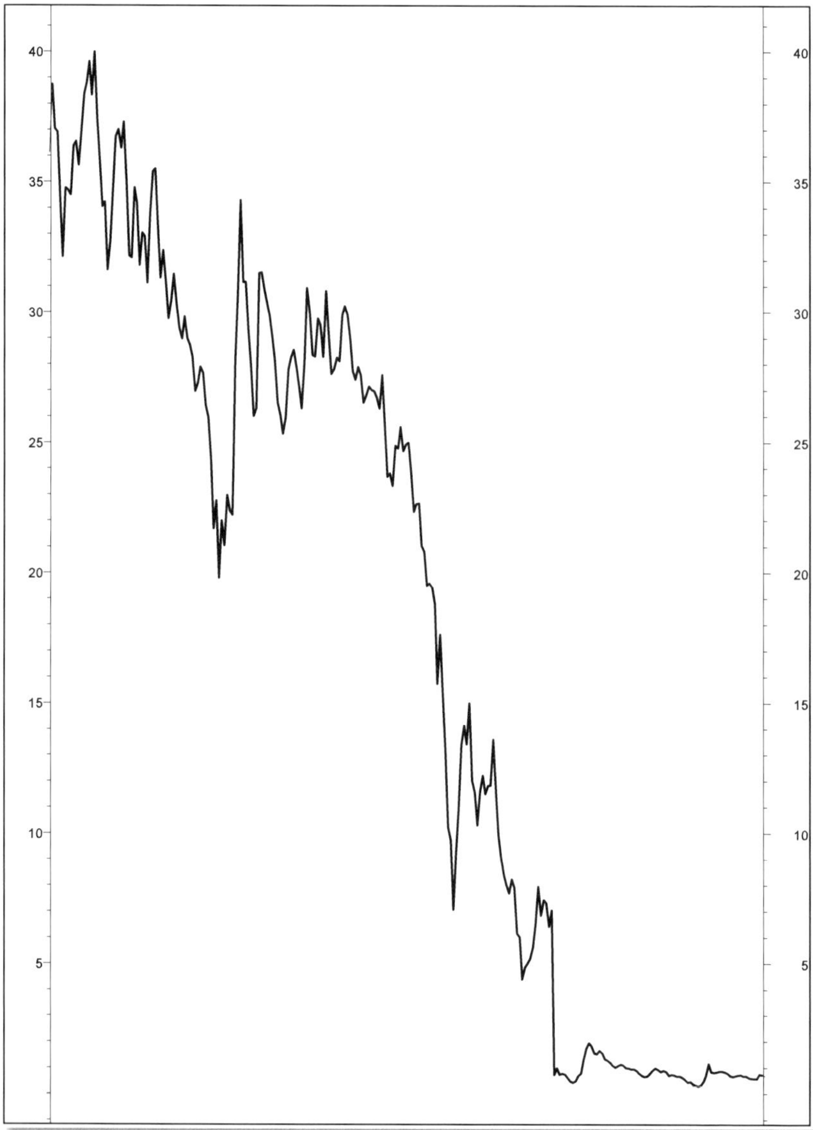

Created in MetaStock from Equis International

- In July, Bank of America completed the purchase of distressed Countrywide Credit (a leader of subprime mortgage originations) and absorbed its preferred issues.

- The government-created mortgage giants Fannie Mae and Freddie Mac were taken over by the federal government on 9/8. The dividends of both common and $36 billion in preferred shares (with an S&P rating of AA- and roughly 10% of the preferred market) were immediately suspended (Chart 13).

- Lehman Brothers filed for bankruptcy on 9/15 and became one of the largest financial failures in U.S. history. Tragically, S&P had investment grade ratings on its common, preferred, and bonds as late as August. These securities were deemed worthless a week after the firm's collapse (Chart 14). The preferred hybrid securities (e.g., PINES, QUICS, SATURNS, etc.) also suffered a huge blow, because Lehman Brothers was one of the creators and major market makers of these securities.

- The Winans International Preferred Stock Index (WIPSI) declined 21% in September as fear spread market-wide that preferred investments in other financial companies would share a similar fate to that of Fannie, Freddie, and Lehman Brothers. This was one of the worst monthly declines in preferred shares since the 1930s. The current dividend yield of WIPSI reached a 108-year record of 37%!

- In early October, legendary value investor Warren Buffett bought $5 billion in Goldman Sachs and $3 billion in General Electric preferred stock that pay a 10% dividend yield in perpetuity.

- On 10/14, thc U.S. Trcasury and Federal Reserve started the controversial "Wall Street Bailout" and agreed to buy $250 billion in preferred stocks of major financial institutions such as Bank of America and Citigroup. The shares would pay a 5% dividend yield and were convertible into common shares. A key difference

CHART 14: Lehman Brothers Preferred Series K 6%
2008

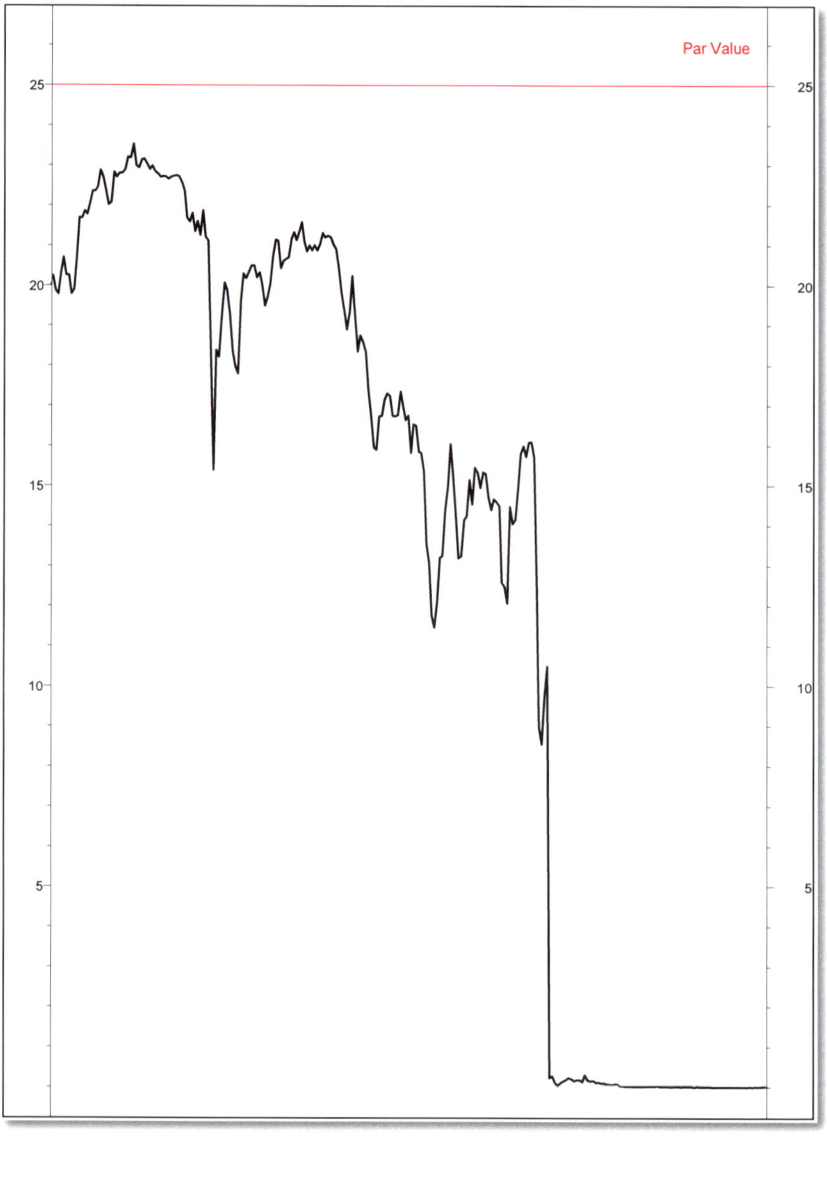

Created in MetaStock from Equis International

from the Fannie Mae and Freddie Mac takeover was that existing preferred shareholder rights would be honored.

- Although still highly volatile, the Winans International Preferred Stock Index and Dow Jones Corporate Bond Average staged powerful year-end rallies as investors bought quality issues at bargain prices.

REVIEW OF 2009

"Preferred Stock represents an upper notch in the investor pecking order and receives the most notoriety when economic times turn bad."
The Chicago Tribune (3/2/2009)

Market Overview, total returns (Charts 15-18)
S&P 500 Index = 26.0%, Dow Jones Corporate Bonds Ave = 17.9%,
WI Preferred Stock Index = 39.4%, WI Real Estate Index = 5.8%

There is always light at the end of a dark tunnel. History has shown financial hurricanes are followed by powerful rallies over the following 12 months, and long before the media's headlines become bullish.

2009

Chart 15: S&P 500 Index
26.0%

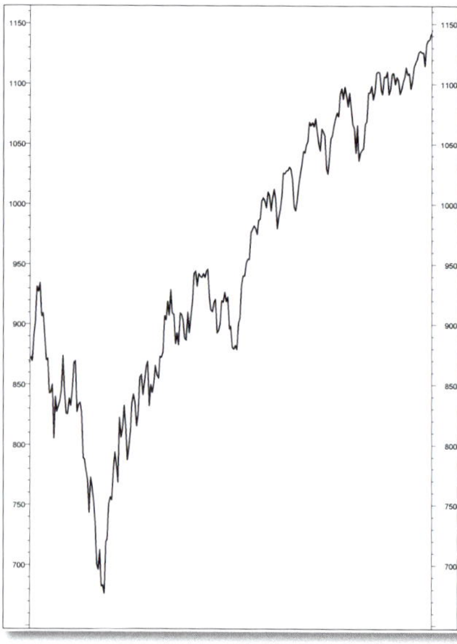

Chart 16: Winans International Real Estate Index, WIREI 5.8%

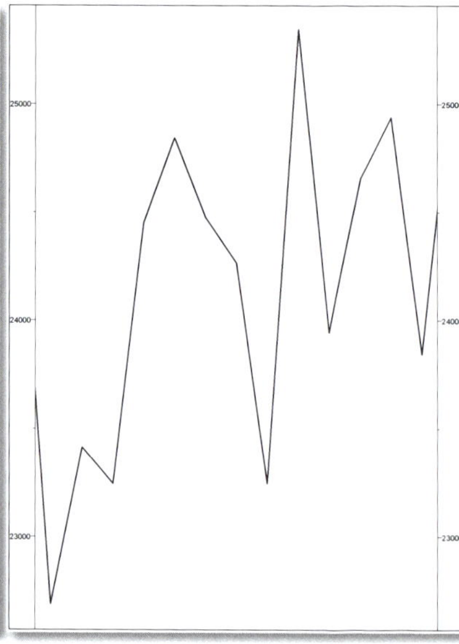

Chart 17: Winans International Preferred Stock Index, WIPSI 39.4%

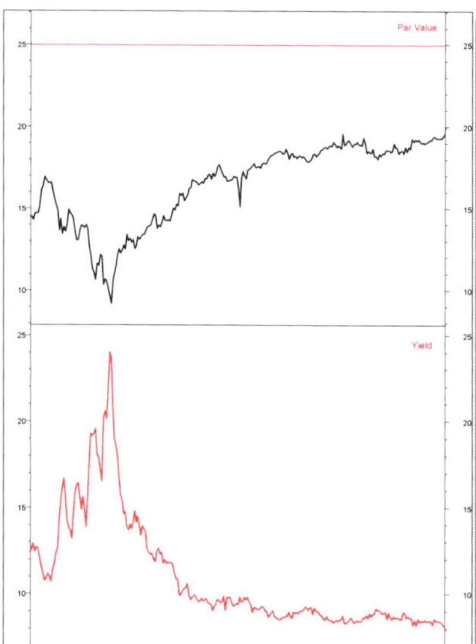

Chart 18: Dow Jones Corporate Bonds Average 17.9%

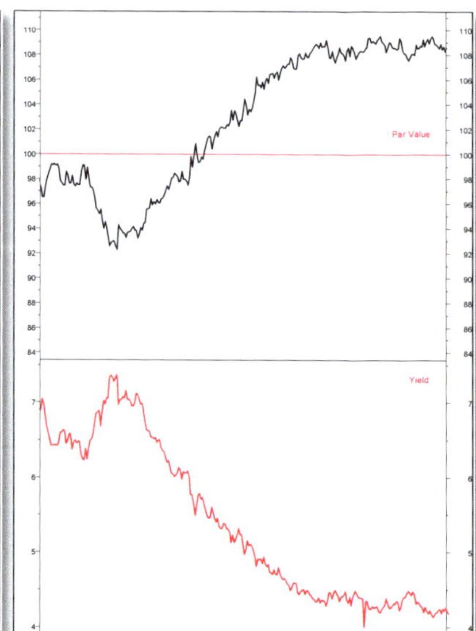

Charts created in MetaStock from Equis International

The Rebound!

Table 2: The Rebound Total Returns

	Common Stocks	Corporate Bonds	Preferred Stocks	90-day T-Bills	Real Estate
1904	46%	18%	25%	4%	22%
1908	52%	15%	37%	4%	(10%)
1915	88%	13%	13%	3%	5%
1918	18%	9%	14%	5%	(9%)
1921	19%	18%	15%	4%	12%
1931	(53%)	(14%)	(11%)	3%	(10%)
1932	(23%)	8%	8%	0%	(44%)
1938	30%	3%	12%	0%	(14%)
1975	36%	14%	13%	6%	14%
2009	26%	18%	39%	0%	6%
Average	24%	10%	17%	3%	(3%)
% of Time Positive	80%	90%	90%	100%	50%
Best	88% **1988**	18% **2009**	39% **2009**	6% **1975**	22% **1904**

Common Stocks = Dow Jones Industrial Average Total Return
Corporate Bonds = Dow Jones Corporate Bond Average Total Return
Preferred Stocks = Winans International Preferred Stock Index Total Return
Real Estate = Winans International Real Estate Index (Residential)

As the table above shows, with the exception of 1931, most asset classes posted powerful rallies a high percentage of the time immediately after financial hurricanes.

From a historical perspective, 2009 was a "textbook" recovery.

- Common stocks, preferreds, and corporate bonds continued to be volatile as common and preferred stock indices reached low levels not seen since the mid-1990s in Q1, then posted powerful rallies for the rest of the year.

- Residential real estate prices continued to be volatile. By January, the high to low percentage drop of the housing bear market was 26%. This was the worst housing market since World War II. In February, the government implemented the Homeowners Affordability and Stability Plan to help 9 million homeowners avoid foreclosure. By year-end, home prices were up 6% although on low sales activity caused by continued tight credit conditions.

- The Federal Reserve continued to keep interest rates low. This had been the longest period, since the mid-1930s, that the 90-day T-bill yield was effectively 0%.

- The new presidential administration of Barack Obama accelerated direct government "bailouts" in other industries (such as automotive). In April, the federal government provided direct financial support, and by June, GM and Chrysler both filed Chapter 11 bankruptcy. In a controversial move, the government effectively bypassed bankruptcy law that negatively affected $43 billion of existing bondholders in General Motors.

- Fears of an unprecedented level of municipal bond defaults across the country caused an 11% decline in the Bond Buyer Municipal 20 Index during October.

- By year-end, the average price in the Dow Jones Corporate Bond Index had not only made up all losses from the financial disaster but had advanced to a level last seen in 2005. The Winans International Preferred Stock Index had staged an 81% rally from its February low and outperformed the 67% rally in the S&P 500 Index. Preferred stocks were the best-performing U.S. investment medium in 2009!

INVESTOR MISTAKES

How did the majority of investors, the most knowledgeable and technologically advanced in history, mishandle this classic bubble? Some claim that this was a "one-of-a-kind" global economic contraction that no one could have predicted or prevented. This might explain why historic comparisons are often dismissed as "interesting" facts but not seriously acted on during a financial bubble.

As I pointed out in my book *Preferreds*, the warning signs were obvious to the student of financial history. While the names and dates might have changed throughout history, the causes were similar to past situations.

An ex post facto stroll down "memory lane" might help us better understand the mistakes made by investors.

As the "baby boom" generation enters retirement, they are told in unison by most financial advisors that they must reallocate a significant portion of their portfolios into income-producing investments to generate the earnings they will need to live on during retirement. This investment shift has also been traditionally recommended to better secure the value of a retirement portfolio due to the protections offered by the issuers of these income investments.

It was easy to see the massive rush toward income investments from their strong performance since the stock market's dot.com bubble burst in 2000.

By 2007, common stocks had barely made up the ground lost in the 2000-2002 bear market, yet both the Dow Jones Corporate Bond Index and Winans International Preferred Stock Index staged impressive rallies as record numbers of consumers had been buying these little-understood investments, which many past investors considered to be downright boring (Charts 19 and 20).

Regrettably, many of these seasoned stockholders and real estate owners rushed into this sector of investing, failed to learn the time proven rules of income investing, and made dangerous mistakes.

Blunders like chasing high-yield investments regardless of liquidity or maturity, believing that bonds and bond mutual funds are identical investments, grossly misusing performance statistics and ratings, and subscribing to a stubborn conviction that income investments are "always" safe had grave consequences.

No help came from media "talking heads." They remained focused on educating the public about investing in stocks and real estate for capital appreciation, while many important problems surrounding income investing had been virtually overlooked.

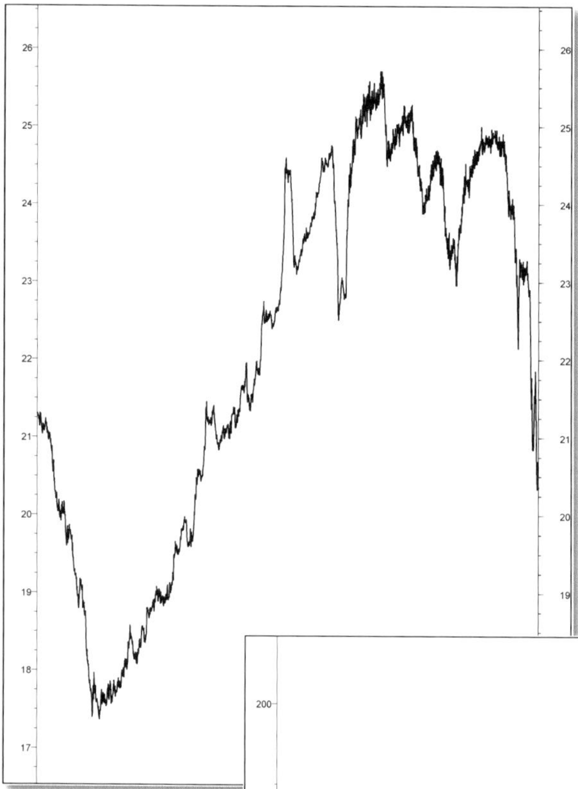

Chart 19:
Winans International
Preferred Stock Index
1999-2007

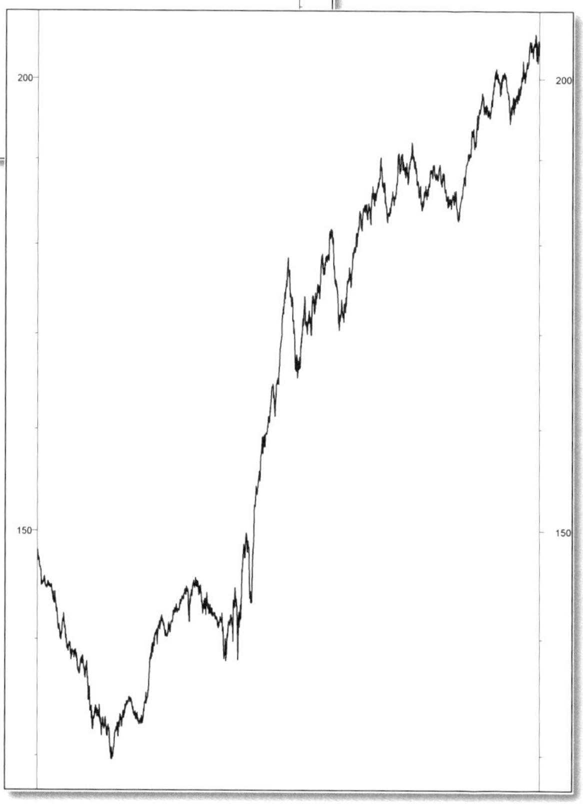

Chart 20:
Dow Jones Corporate
Bond Average
1999-2007

Charts created in
MetaStock from
Equis International

Financial institutions, government agencies, and even academics are also to blame for ignoring the problems that ultimately harmed older, retired investors who could least afford to take the risks in investments such as Fannie Mae and Freddie Mac.

Let's look at the key mistakes made by income investors leading up to the 2008 financial meltdown:

Mistake 1: Income Investing Is Always Safe!

Unlike other investment mediums, income investors had fewer alternatives than in the past; the once ample supply of corporate bonds from exchanges and brokerage house inventories had "dried up." For example, during 1988, 1,127 exchange-listed bond issues actively traded. By 2006, the number had dropped to 131 issues—an 88% decline in supply (CHART 21).

This scarcity of exchange-listed bonds coincided with an increase in the availability of other types of income investments, such as bond mutual funds, an assortment of new preferred stock issues, and bond hybrid securities inaccurately listed as preferred stocks in most newspapers. According to Standard & Poor's, by 2006 the size of the preferred-stock market has quadrupled over 15 years to nearly $200 billion.

While equity income investments possess many advantages; they are not conventional bonds and don't posses the greatest advantage of a fixed-income investment—a maturity date and the knowledge of an exact return, if the investment is held to maturity.

In the "old days," many income investors constructed portfolios of mainly bonds diversified by issuer, industry, rating, and evenly spaced by year (i.e., laddered), with each investment intended to be held to maturity. During the horrible bond bear markets of the early 1980s and mid-1960s, investors could maintain their discipline because they knew that, even though solvent bond holdings had significantly fallen in market value, they would get their principal back, as well as their expected interest payments, if they held the bonds to maturity.

Investors mistakenly embraced the other kinds of income investments as "apples to apples" substitutes for conventional bonds. The simple fact is that many of these investments don't mature. Open-ended mutual funds rarely hold their bond investments to maturity. As was discovered during the financial hurricane of 2008, these volatile income securities

CHART 21: NYSE Listed Corporate Bonds Issues Traded
1988-2005

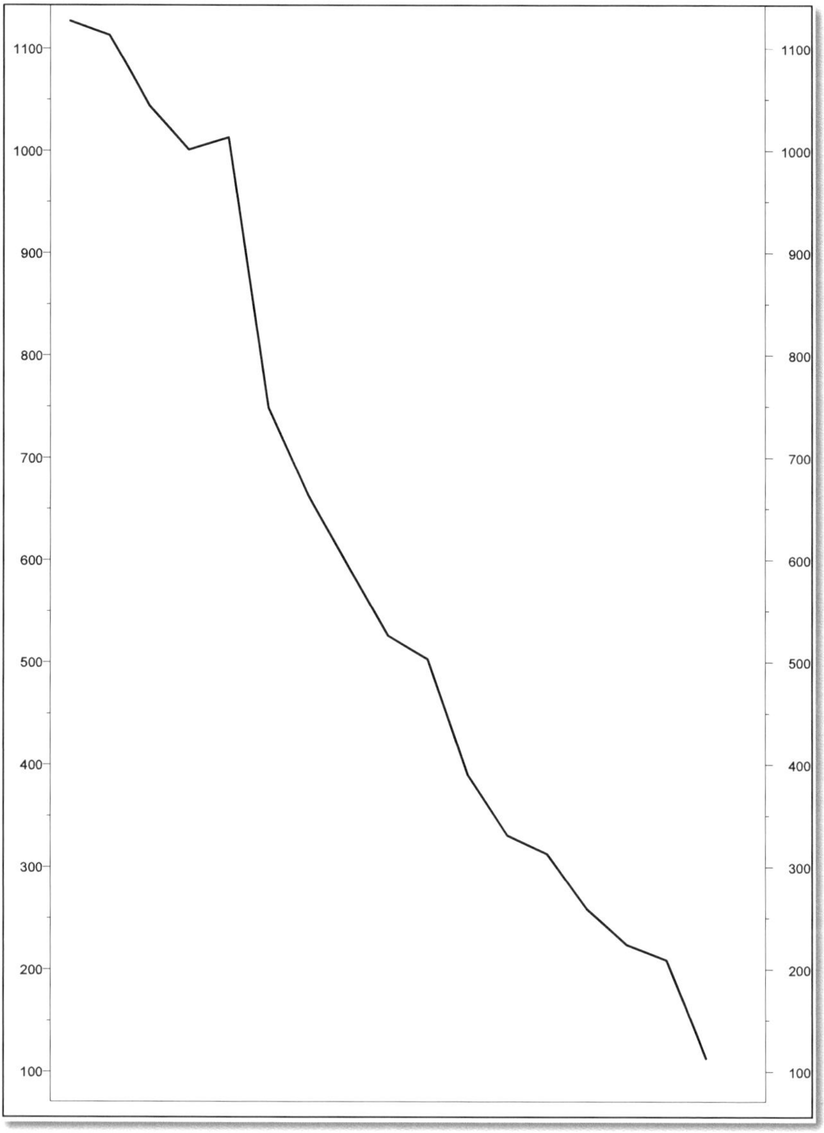

Created in MetaStock from Equis International

turned out to be more like common stocks than corporate bonds held to maturity.

Mistake 2: Income Statistics Were Badly Misused

When novice investors buy income investments, they are immediately exposed to new statistics, which they often don't know how to interpret. Yield to Maturity (YTM) is one of the oldest, most widely followed fixed-income statistics used. Unfortunately, many investors believe that YTM is an absolute, perfect gauge of return. In truth, YTM is really a theoretical total return projection not based on reality. Instead, its projections tend to be too low when future interest rates increase and too high when future interest rates decline.

The problem lies in YTM's primary assumptions:

- All interest is reinvested.
- The reinvested funds earn interest at the same rate as the original YTM.

This is not realistic because:

- Most investors who buy bonds are older investors who eventually use some or all the income generated (i.e., little or no income reinvestment).
- Very few times in the past 50 years have interest rates been stable enough to allow interest received to be reinvested at the same rate over the entire life of even a medium-term bond.

To make matters even worse, many financial institutions provide inconsistent information without descriptions or explanations:

- On most brokerage house trade confirmations for bond purchases, the bond's yield-to-maturity (YTM) calculation is posted prominently (Exhibit 1).
- On most monthly brokerage house statements, only current yield percentages are used. This yield is based on the monthly closing price of the security, and is generally useless to the investor who has purchased the investment at a different price and at a different time (Exhibit 2).

Exhibit 1: Bond Transaction Confirmation Sheet (sample)

ABC BROKERAGE HOUSE

SAMPLE CONFIRMATION

Account Number:
Financial Consultant:

Summary For Settlement Date	01/22/2003	
Total Purchases	$ 14,879.27	
Net Amount	$ 14,879.27	Debit

You Bought 15,000 at a price of 96 ROYAL CARIBBEAN CRUISES LTD SR NOTES – BK/ENTRY-DTD 8/12/96 YTM 8.573 7.2500% FA-15 DUE 08/15/2006 SEE CORP/MUNI BOND NOTE BELOW SEE HIGH YIELD BOND NOTE BELOW			Gross Amount Accrued Bond Int Transaction Fee Amount Settlement Date	$14,400.00 474.27 5.00 **$14,879.27** **01/22/2003**
Trade Date: 01/16/2003 Market: Other Markets	CUSIP#: 780153-AE-2 Symbol: RCL.GD	Solicited Order Cash Acct. Ref #: xxxx	HOLD SECURITIES	
We acted as principal in this transaction.				

This is a sample of a brokerage house confirmation.

- Accrued interest is included in the cost basis of a bond on many brokerage statements and 1099 tax forms, when in fact it is a temporary transaction adjustment that is corrected during the next payment of interest to the current bondholder (Exhibits 1, 3).

Exhibit 2: Brokerage Statement (sample)

XYZ BROKERAGE HOUSE

SAMPLE STATEMENT

July 28 – August 31, 2003

Corporate bonds

Amount	Description	Date acquired	Cost/ Adjusted cost	Share cost/ Adjusted share cost	Current share price/ Accrued interest	Current value	Unrealized Gain/(loss) Original/ Adjusted	Current % Yield/ Anticip. Income (annualized)	Ordinary Income/ Capital gain/(loss)
15,000	TENET HEALTHCARE CORP SR NOTES BK/ENTRY-DTD 1/30/1997 INT 08.000% MATY 01/15/2005 Exchange NYSE Rating BA3/BB	11/1/00	$ 14,986.25 **$ 14,986.25**	$ 99.375 $ 99.375	103.438 **$146.66**	**$ 15,515.70**	$ 529.45 LT **$ 529.45 LT**	7.734 **$ 1,200.00**	**$ 0.00** **$ 529.45**
15,000	AT&T CORP NOTES B/E DTD 6/1/1994 INT 07.500% MATY 06/01/2006 Rating BAA2/BBB	11/07/00	$ 15,023.75 **$ 15,023.75**	$ 99.375 $ 99.375	109.875 **$ 274.99**	**$ 16,481.25**	$ 1,457.50 LT **$ 1,457.50 LT**	6.825 **$ 1,125.00**	**$ 0.00** **$ 1,457.50**
15,000	ROYAL CARIBBEAN CRUISES LTD SR NOTES BK/ENTRY-DTD 8/12/1996 INT 07.250% MATY 08/15/2006 Rating BA2/BB+	01/16/03	$ 14,405.00 **$ 14,405.00**	$ 96.00 $ 96.00	102.00 **$ 42.29**	**$ 15,300.00**	$ 895.00 ST **$ 895.00 ST**	7.107 **$ 1,087.50**	**$ 89.55** **$ 805.45**

This is a sample of the bond portion of a brokerage house statement

- The current values of income investments posted on monthly brokerage statements or daily websites can be estimated only when there was no trading activity for an investment on the date shown. This can cause investors to think that there are "wild" swings in the value of an investment that never really happen! This problem

EXHIBIT 3: 1099 Tax Form (sample)

Page 1 of 2

XYZ BROKERAGE HOUSE

SAMPLE FORM 1099 for 2005

This is important tax information and is being furnished to the Internal Revenue Service. If you are required to file a return, a negligence penalty or other sanction may be imposed on you if this income is taxable and the IRS determines that it has not been reported.

1099-INT Interest Income 2005

Interest income not I ncluded in box 3	Early withdrawal penalty	Interest on US Savings Bonds and Treas. obligations	**Federal income tax withheld**	Investment expenses	Foreign tax paid	Foreign country or US possession
$ 15,968.10 Box 1	Box 2	Box 3	Box 4	Box 5	Box 6	Box 7

1099-DIV Dividends and Distributions 2005

Total ordinary dividends	Qualified dividends	Total capital gain distributions	Unrecaptured Sec. 1250 gain	Section 1202 gain	Collectibles (28%) gain
$ 8,582.46 Box 1a	$ 2,636.46 Box 1b	$ 2,147.33 Box 2a	$ 320.33 Box 2b	Box 2c	Box 2d

Nondividend distributions	Federal income tax withheld	Investment expenses	Foreign tax paid	Foreign country or US possession	Cash liquidation distributions	Non cash liquidation distributions
Box 3	Box 4	Box 5	Box 6	Box 7	Box 8	Box 9

Page 2 of 2

This is important tax information and is being furnished to the Internal Revenue Service. If you are required to file a return, a negligence penalty or other sanction may be imposed on you if this income is taxable and the IRS determines that it has not been reported.

1099-B Proceeds from Broker and Barter Exchange Transactions 2005

Reference number	Date of sale or exchange (Box 1a)	CUSIP number (Box 1b)	Quantity	Description (Box 7)	Price	Gross proceeds less commissions (Box 2)	Federal income tax withheld (Box 4)
	06/15/05	527288AJ30R0	26,000	LEUCADIA NATL CORP SR SUB NTS REG-DTD 6/13/95 DUE 06/15/2005 RATE 8.250		$ 26,000.00	
	08/01/05	612448GE40B0	10,000	MONTEREY CNTY CALIF CTFS PARTN NATIVIDAD M/C IMPT PJ-C MBIA B/E DTD 10/15/94 F/C8/1/95 PREF DUE 08/01/2023 RATE 6.600		10,200.00	
	12/08/05	872384102000	165	TEPPCO PARTNERS L P UNIT L.P.	36.28	5,924.83	
	01/15/05	88033GAF70B0	25,000	TENET HEALTHCARE CORP SR NOTES BK/ENTRY-DTD 1/30/1997 DUE 01/15/2005 RATE 8.000		25,000.00	
	11/17/05	885218107000	444	THORNBURG MTG INC	25.46	11,195.74	
	12/08/05	902911106000	437	UST INC	39.54	17,137.07	
Totals						**$ 182,765.42**	

This is an exact replication of a 1099 from a brokerage house.

was particularly severe in October 2008 when bond prices in stable companies posted incredibly low daily prices on websites due to the temporary illiquidity.

- Mutual funds provide yet another set of figures, such as Average Weighted Coupon, 12-Month Yield, and 30-day SEC Yield that make comparisons with other income investments complicated.

Sadly, the one simple figure that would be useful to most investors of preferred stocks and bonds is "Annual Yield" (Annual Income/Original Cost Basis). Yet it is not found on any information sent to clients by most brokerage houses.

Knowing how to filter the information that is truly important for successful investing from random, useless data is a critical skill set—especially in today's information-driven environment.

Mistake 3: Agency Ratings Give a False Sense of Security

Integrated into discussions on bonds are terms, such as "investment grade" and "junk bonds," which are based on ratings issued by independent firms. Many investors misunderstand how to interpret and use the ratings on bonds, stocks, and mutual funds provided by firms like Standard & Poor's, Moody's, and Morningstar. They often treat this information as "manna from heaven," without seeing the need to do any more research.

As stated in *Standard & Poor's Bond Guide*, "The issue credit rating is not a recommendation to purchase, sell or hold a financial obligation inasmuch as it does not comment as to market price or suitability for a particular investor."

It is not uncommon to find companies that have good financials and that have never missed a dividend or interest payment, yet receive a non-investment grade rating. On the other end of the spectrum, ratings can be "sticky" and not decline as fast as a troubled company's or municipality's financial condition warrants. It is not uncommon to see the price of a distressed investment plummet long before its ratings do! In fact, many of the financial institutions that went bankrupt in 2008 had investment grade ratings in 2007.

History has shown that bear markets don't discriminate between income investments of different ratings. In tough market conditions, most bonds and preferred stocks decline together regardless of their ratings.

Mistake 4: Misuse of Market Benchmarks

All too often the investing public blindly makes daily head-to-head comparisons between the performance of income investment indices and those of more liquid common stock investments. Many investors then quickly change their asset allocations, based on the "race" that they somehow think is going on between these investments.

As someone who has constructed investment indices, I can tell you that income investment indices are as different as night and day, when compared to broader stock market benchmarks, such as the S&P 500. After all, many of the income issues used in these indices don't trade every day, so price distortions can occur. It's also important to note that most bond indices incorporate interest only when it is paid, rather than the total interest due by the end of the year.

While indices of income investments are useful in showing overall price trends needed in market analysis, they are not useful as a daily performance gauge unless you first understand the composition of a particular index and what practical adjustments need to be made (such as adding all bond interest earned). Not knowing the index's assumptions can lead to false conclusions or misconceptions about performance that are costly.

Since income benchmarks are unusual, it is wise to monitor several different types and from different sources to reach realistic conclusions about the trends of income investments. For example, The Winans International Preferred Stock Index and the S&P Preferred Stock Index both track preferred stocks, but they use different components and calculation methods.

It is also recommended to use indices that cover long periods of time for accurate historical comparisons, as well as short-term market analysis. I recommend using the Dow Jones Corporate Bond Average and the Winans International Preferred Stock Index since both have data going back to 1900 (Chart 22).

INVESTING 2010 AND BEYOND

It has taken two 50% corrections in the S&P 500 Index over the past 10

CHART 22: WIPSI Price and Yield
1900-2009

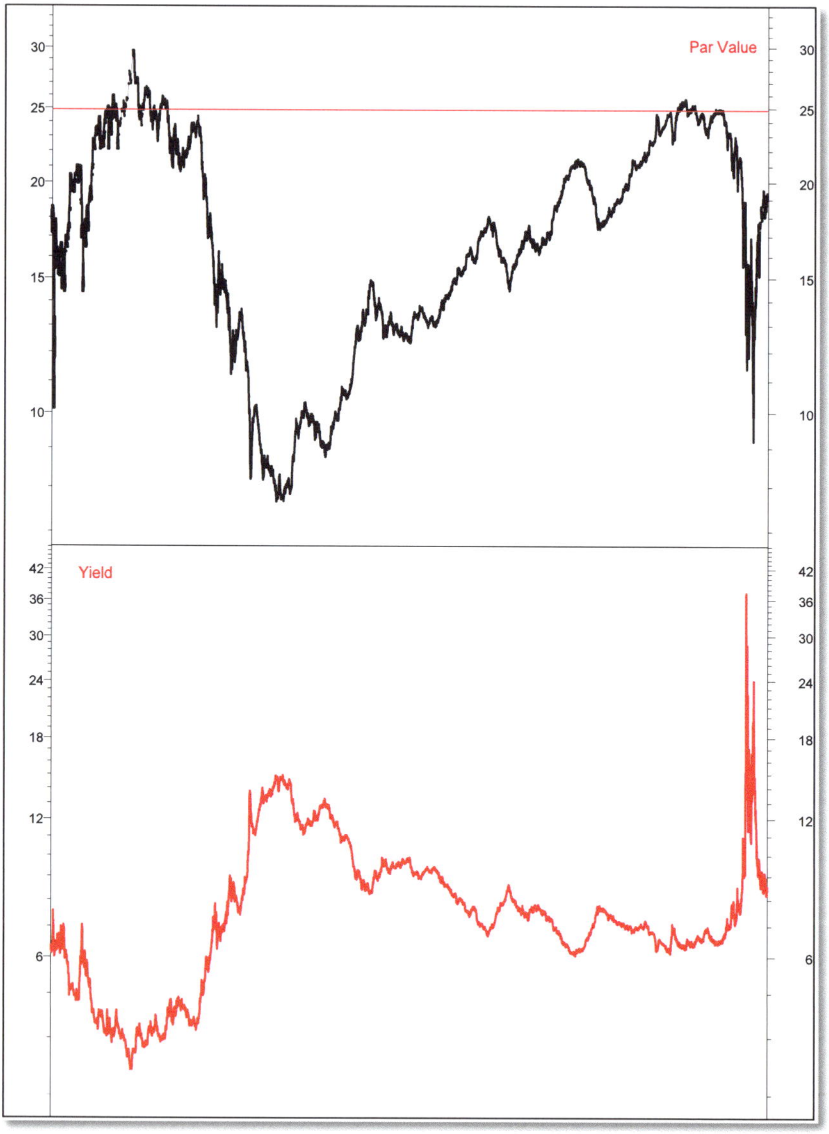

Created in MetaStock from Equis International

years, and the worst housing market since World War II, to force investors back to reality. It is safe to stay that people finally realize that mega bull markets in stocks and real estate are not returning anytime soon and their individual investment strategy must change with the times.

While equity "buy and hold" strategies worked well in the 1980s and '90s, many stock investors have learned WHEN to buy and sell is as important as WHAT to buy and sell during "sideways" market conditions such as 2000-2010 or 1965-1981. Since 1900, common stocks have posted negative returns 29% of the time and preferred stocks decline 25% of the time during the same time frame. This historical fact means that a successful investment strategy must incorporate a policy for reducing investment risks during bear markets. In sporting events and military operations, overall victory comes only from executing a good offense AND an effective defense. The same is true of investing.

Also, with the "baby boomers" aging and their tolerance for volatility diminishing rapidly, this period in history should prove to be a permanent, accelerating shift away from the common equities toward income investments such as corporate bonds and preferred stocks. Simply put, today's investors are willing to trade higher overall returns for more predictable, less volatile performance.

In this chapter, we focused on "what not to do." In the next chapter, the emphasis will shift toward "what to do now" with my rules of successful income investing that I have learned as a money manager, investment analyst, and individual investor over the past 28 years.

Chapter 2

Basic Rules for Income Investing

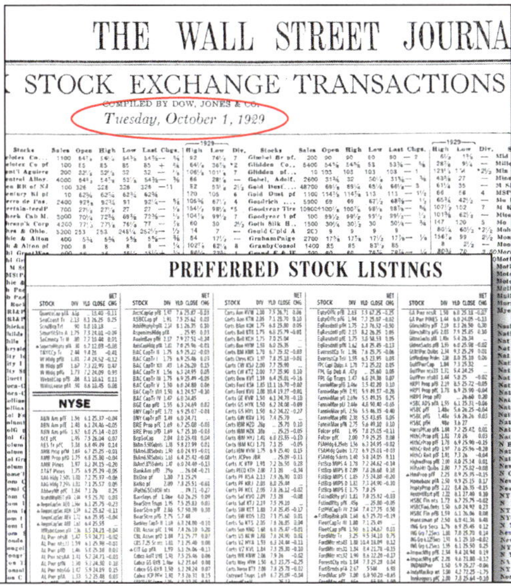
THE WALL STREET JOURNA

STOCK EXCHANGE TRANSACTIONS

COMPILED BY DOW, JONES & CO.

Tuesday, October 1, 1929

PREFERRED STOCK LISTINGS

NYSE

Some Things Never Change!

Preferred stocks listed in The Wall Street Journal 1929 and Today

"A great many investors find the highest grade preferred stocks, like the top grade bonds, at prices so high and yields so low to meet reasonable objectives for income. Nevertheless, close study will reveal that some opportunities still exist."
THE MAGAZINE OF WALL STREET (2/5/1944)

"Baby Boomers appear to be swapping growth stocks for equity income vehicles. Thus, investment managers, investment banks and corporations will have to rethink their current investment offerings."
BARRON'S (4/14/2005)

"You may decide to buy an individual preferred stock. The level of due diligence is tremendous. You'll need not only to study the stocks as a bond investor, but also a common stock investor."
USA TODAY (2/9/2009)

As discussed in the last section, many investors poorly handled their assets before, during, and after 2008's financial hurricane. History has once again shown us how easy it is to fall prey to financial bubbles where well-known economic pitfalls can be stumbled into, even by experienced investors, with devastating results. Remember, only through continuous education and discipline, independent from the masses, can you successfully invest over the long haul.

Before we focus on preferred stocks, let's review some basic rules of investing in income investments that I have learned during nearly three decades of work in the financial "trenches."

NOTHING IS REALLY NEW

It is helpful to remember that there is very little that is truly "new" in the world of investing. Stocks, bonds, and real estate are continuously being repackaged and renamed by Wall Street, but the basic investments in the money game stay the same, even though the "it's something new" crowd seems to take center stage most of the time.

Look at preferred stocks and bonds. Both types of investments have been in existence for a long time. Yet many of the most technologically advanced and best-educated investors in history still don't understand the basic tenets and techniques of income investing.

OWNING AND LOANING—THE CORE OF INVESTING

I taught MBA investment courses for many years. The first thing I told my students was that all investing comes down to owning and loaning, where a solid financial offense and defense require knowing the pros and cons of the investments used.

"Owning" refers to investments, such as common stocks or real estate, where the main objective is to have the assets appreciate over the long term even though there will be setbacks caused by bear markets.

"Loaning" is lending money to a government or company in the form of bonds, notes, or bills, where the focus is on having consistent, secure income and the certainty of knowing the exact date of the repayment of principal.

Sounds easy enough, right?

Sadly, many bond mutual funds consistently show high-trading turnover (i.e., no stable income), and many of the largest stock mutual funds simply "buy and hold" (i.e., no profit taking) and offer no defensive action to protect financial gains during bear markets. It seems that the mutual fund industry has done it completely backward, and investors have suffered for it.

FINANCIAL HISTORY AS A TEACHER

Though personal experience is an important teacher, learning to correctly interpret and apply history's lessons is a more important factor in successful investing. Only investors knowledgeable of history's trends can successfully navigate the investment world over time. Remember, most people really don't change over time, and "those who don't study history are bound to repeat it."

Just like learning multiplication tables for fast recall, there are key long-term statistics that all investors should memorize before they risk hard-earned capital in the fast-moving ebbs and flows of market volatility. A good place to start is knowing the investment landscape since 1900, because it captures how the markets reacted to every type of extreme situation, good and bad, over a long period of time.

TABLE 3: Historical Performance
1900-2009

	Cumulative	Annual	Interest / Dividend	Best (yr)	Worst (yr)
Common Stocks	18,267%	11.7%	4.4%	88% 1915	(42%) 1931
Preferred Stocks	1,337%	7.4%	6.5%	41% 1986	(23%) 1907
Corporate Bonds	695%	6.5%	6.3%	36% 1982	(11%) 1931
T-bills (90 days)	52%	3.8%	n/a	15% 1981	0% 1940
Inflation		3.1%			

Percentage of time:	Up Yrs	Down Yrs	Back-to-Back Down	Last Occurred Yrs
Common Stocks	71%	29%	9%	2001-02
Preferred Stocks	75%	25%	7%	2007-08
Corporate Bonds	84%	16%	3%	1979-80

CHART 23: Dow Jones Bond Average $ and Yield 1900-2009

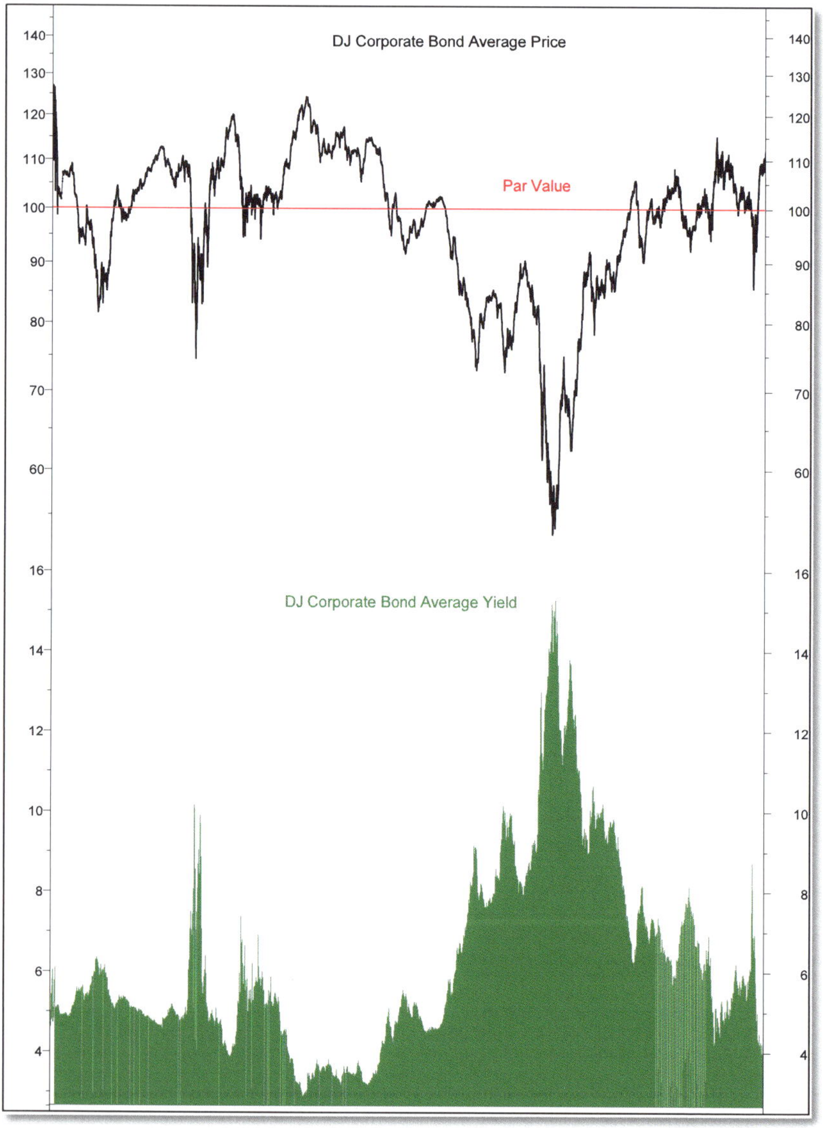

Created in MetaStock from Equis International

The table on page 43 (Table 3) answers important questions about the overall characteristics of four important types of investments:

- How well have the investments performed (cumulatively and annually)?
- How much annual income do they pay?
- What have been their best and worst years?
- What percentage of the time do they annually advance and decline?
- What percentage of the time have these investments had back-to-back negative years and when did this last happen?

Here are some time-tested facts to remember:

Common Stocks

Without a doubt, this investment class is the best overall performer, with an 18,267% return! And with the lowest income yield and higher volatility than other corporate investment mediums, they are not particularly good income investments for the investors who need high levels of regular income.

Preferred Stocks

Although they are, from an accounting standpoint, equity, "preferreds" are income investments because most of their historical return is provided by dividend income. They have outperformed corporate bonds (1,337% versus 695%) but have historically produced significantly higher levels of volatility. With no maturity date, "when to buy" can be as important as "what to buy" to avoid poor overall performance.

Corporate Bonds

As can be seen in (Chart 23), bond results are not "exciting," yet they have produced positive results 84% of the time and are significantly less volatile than either common or preferred stock. These securities lend themselves well to a buy and hold-to-maturity strategy. It is also important to note that contrary to popular belief, this investment medium has historically outperformed inflation by a significant margin (6.5% versus 3.1%).

TABLE 4: Five-Year Portfolio Performance Projections
1994-2009

15-Year Historical Performance (Average Annual Returns)	Initial Value	Capital Appreciation	Income	Total Return	Success Probabilities	Discounted Return
S&P 500 Index		8.4%	1.8%	10.2%	71%	7.3%
Dow Jones Corporate Bond Index		1.4%	6.0%	7.4%	84%	6.2%
Five-Year Projections						
	Initial Value	**Capital Appreciation**	**Income**	**Total Return**	**Success Probabilities**	**Discounted Return**
100% Stock Portfolio	500,000	210,500	42,250	255,750	71%	181,583
100% Bond Portfolio	500,000	35,000	150,000	185,000	84%	155,400

It cannot be stressed enough that this information is necessary for setting realistic investment goals and expectations, and thus not succumbing to the misuse of statistics often committed by the press and financial service industry to sell products and services.

Now with a general understanding of what to expect from different types of investments, let's practically apply this knowledge to a common investment scenario.

TABLE 4 is helpful in setting realistic performance goals over the next five years. It is based on 15-year historical returns of the stock and bond markets, and clearly demonstrates how different stocks and bonds perform.

Compare the projected returns of two different types of $500,000 portfolios. The first is fully invested in stocks and the second is in corporate bonds held to maturity.

Notice that the stock portfolio has a 71% chance (based on % of negative years since 1900) of producing an average annual profit of 7.3% ($181,583 over the next five years), and the bond portfolio has 84% odds of making an average annual profit of 6.2% ($155,400 over the next five years).

To the novice investor, who focuses solely on gain, the choice is simple—invest 100% common stocks. Yet other factors need to be considered to meet all of an investor's goals and expectations:

A need for greater certainty of return

While it is common for the investment community to set an investor's asset allocation based mainly on his/her age, I have found that an investor's personality and temperament have more to do with the investment mix of a portfolio than a given point in time in his/her life.

In essence, many people, regardless of age, can't handle high investment uncertainty and will panic and abandon a time-tested investment strategy at the first signs of trouble.

Remember, U.S. common stocks have been in negative territory 29% of the time, and corporate bond losses are, not only less extreme, but are less frequent. History reminds us that income investments are a more attractive choice for low-risk investors.

CHART 24: Income and Capital Gains Taxes
1915-2009

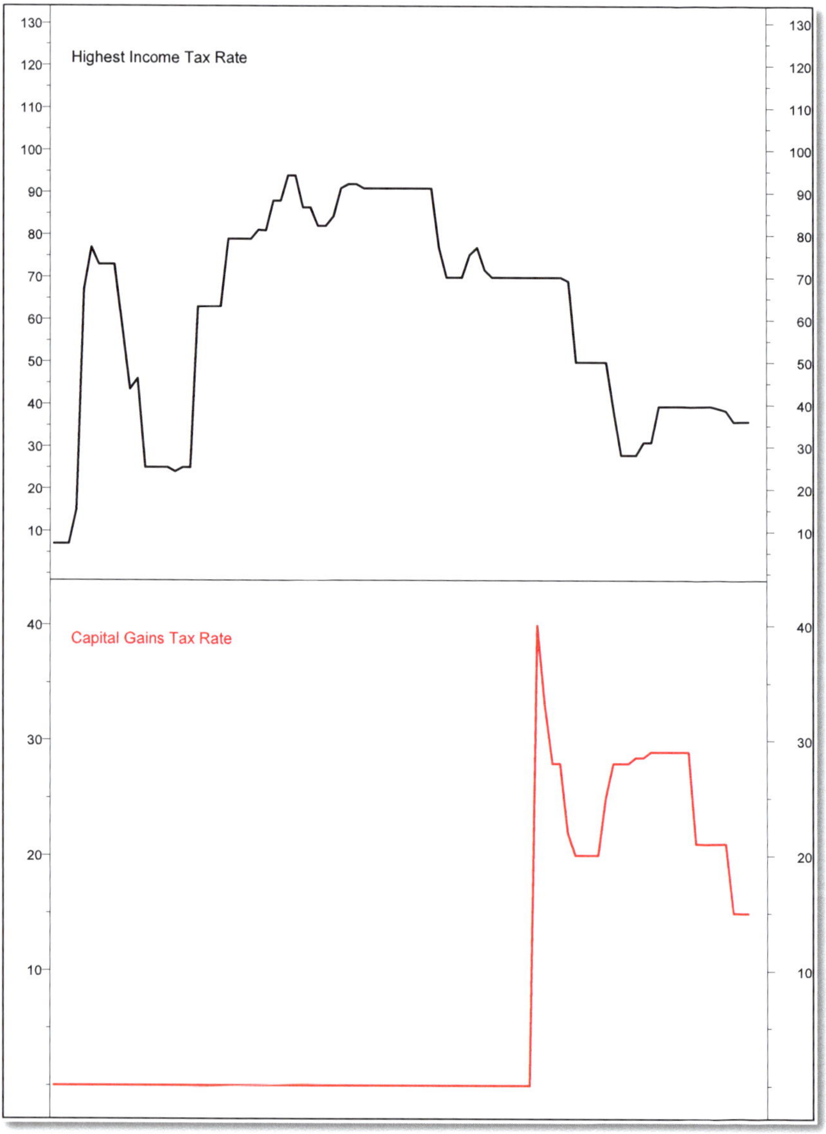

Created in MetaStock from Equis International

What type of portfolio profit is needed

For investors who need to regularly withdraw funds from a portfolio, the type of investment profit is an important consideration?

In a common stock portfolio, most of the expected profits are in the form of capital gains ($42,100 annually in the previous example) that would require selling an investment or borrowing on margin for an investor to access the needed funds. Furthermore, since stocks historically have negative years 29% of the time, there would probably be instances when stock investors would need to withdraw funds when their portfolio is at a low point, thereby selling investments at less than opportune times.

On the other hand, most of a bond portfolio's profits are in the form of income that arrives at regular, predictable intervals and can be accessed without changing the investor's holdings.

Taxes

Historically, the government has treated profits generated by investments differently, with interest income typically taxed at a higher level than gains realized by selling an investment (Chart 24). There are many time-tested techniques that can minimize taxes in an income portfolio, such as using municipal bonds, tax loss selling, bond swaps, amortizing premiums, and using tax-deferred investment accounts. Investment strategy and tax planning need to go hand in hand for the best investment results.

There is no such thing as a "single best" investment! While there's no doubt that stocks can generate more wealth than bonds over time, their profitability can't be guaranteed. Many income investments can provide a projected return due to the regular payment of income and set dates for the repayment of principal.

Many Bond Markets = Shop for Yield

I can't count the number of times I've seen this statement in the financial press: "Stocks and bonds were up today!" While the commentary might seem accurate, often the types of bonds aren't disclosed. Are they U.S. Treasury, municipal, or corporate bonds?

While it is true that all bonds are generally affected by the level and direction of interest rates, each type is greatly influenced by different,

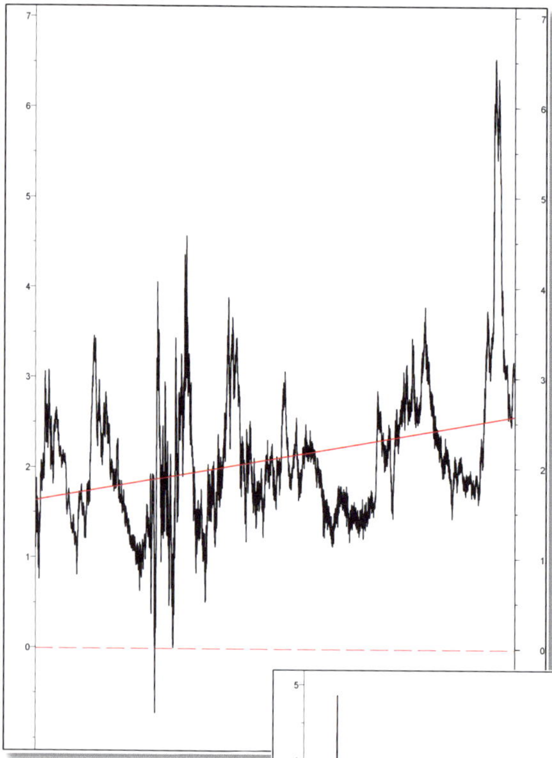

Chart 25:
Yield Spread Chart
Corporate Minus T-Bond
1970-2009

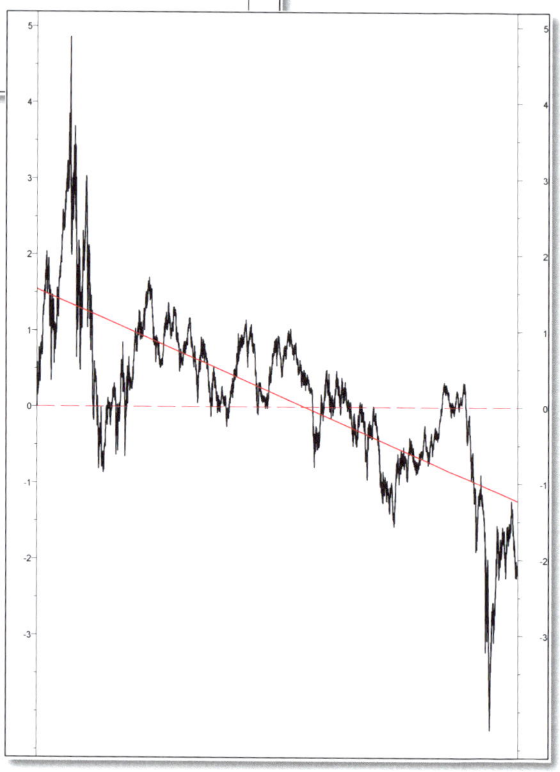

Chart 26:
Yield Spread Chart
T-Bond Minus Municipal
1970-2009

Charts created in MetaStock from Equis International

independent factors. For instance, Treasury bonds are more affected by the buying and selling of U.S. government bonds by central banks in other countries. Tax-exempt municipal bonds are more influenced than other bonds by changes in federal and state tax laws. Corporate earnings projections can affect common stocks, preferred stocks, and corporate bonds alike.

As a portfolio's current income holdings mature, investors should be comparing the yields of different types of income vehicles to find the best price for the replacement investments. A common, easy-to-use tool that helps make these evaluations is a yield spread chart.

Page 50 shows 40-year yield spread charts that display the differences between the yields of corporate, municipal, and treasury bonds (CHARTS 25 AND 26). Notice that the relationship between these three types of bonds is constantly changing.

For example, BAA rated corporate bonds have an average yield 2.6% higher than 10-year Treasury bond yields, and there have been several times when the spread was higher than 4%. During these periods of time, corporate bonds were a better deal to buy than Treasury bonds because the yield is relatively higher.

On the other hand, notice that the relationship between Treasury and municipal bonds is very different. The 10-year Treasury bonds typically have yields 1.2% below comparable municipal bonds but have ranged between 4.77% in the 1970s and as low as (4.29%) in 2008. During this year the fear of widespread municipal default caused by the severe recession forced many investors into the safety of treasuries, thus pushing its yield to record low levels relative to municipal bonds.

Remember, not all income investments are the same, and there are times in which an investment in one type of bond would provide a better buying opportunity than another.

INCOME INVESTMENT COSTS

There are two types of costs associated with income investing: transaction fees and management fees.

Transaction Fees

Everything bought or sold in the investment world has costs associated with the services provided by the brokerage houses. And yet there are common instances where investors are not aware of or are confused about what income investments actually cost to trade. It is not unusual for an investor to be told that investments bought from the brokerage house's own bond inventory "have no commission costs," and thus the client thinks the trade was done for "free." The truth is that the investments' prices were probably "marked up," and the same investments may have been bought cheaper at another brokerage house.

Keep in mind that income investments can be easier to buy than to sell, so make sure the brokerage house holding your investments can buy and sell your holdings for a reasonable price. As with any other large purchase, it is wise to shop around for the best deal.

Management Fees

Generally speaking, most professional money managers have different levels of fees based on the types of investments. It is standard practice for income portfolios to be charged at a lower rate than portfolios of common stocks. It is also important to remember that management fees charged for managing municipal bonds are usually not tax deductible.

DIVERSIFICATION

Over the past 60 years, there has been very little debate between investment professionals and academia on the need for investment diversification within a portfolio. Diversification, among other things, reduces the negative impact of a single investment on the entire asset base. Yet disagreements on how to diversify are common. Sadly, diversification is often misused for marketing purposes by unethical members of the investment community to sell unneeded investments.

Diversification within a portfolio of income investments is much more complicated than for other types of investments. In addition to diversifying by issuer, capitalization, and industry, the income investor also needs to consider maturity (i.e., duration), investment type (government debt, corporate bond, preferred stock, etc.), and credit quality. In my experience, improper diversification or no diversification at all in income investing is common and can lead to unknown risk and lost opportunities. This is especially true when it comes to the sole use of agency ratings as a means of building an income portfolio.

INVESTING'S TWO BIGGEST DANGERS

History has shown that any investor can "blow up" a portfolio with any type of investment if he/she leverages it high enough or uses too many illiquid investments. Such a situation will be exacerbated when a normal-to-severe bear market occurs. And they do happen in all markets!

Leverage

Many investors have successfully used margin loans and mortgages to enhance returns and withdrawal equity from fully invested portfolios. And yet they can be the seeds of destruction for those who don't pay attention to the saying that "too much of a good thing can be bad." Repayment guarantees won't protect you if you suffer a loss in market value from highly leveraged income investments and your broker or banker forces the sale of your leveraged holdings at the worst of times.

Illiquidity

Liquidity is the ability to buy and sell an investment quickly at a reasonable price. In the universe of income investments, liquidity spans from excellent to nonexistent, with illiquid investments generally offering much higher yields than liquid investments.

As a general rule, investors should limit their exposure to non-liquid investments while planning to keep all of their income investments to maturity. It is also important to avoid the temptation to trade for short-term gains or cut short-term losses based on prices posted on a brokerage statement or a website. There is a good chance the numbers are not accurate due to low trading activity (i.e., illiquidity) or due to regular dividend payments (Chart 27). Finally, do not normally use stop-loss orders with income investments. Because of poor order executions, due to frequent, sudden gaps in prices, it's a sure way to lose money.

If the greatest advantage of owning income investments is providing a projected and guaranteed return through its payment of income, then reducing the risks discussed above through proper diversification should be followed at all times.

Remember, income investments should be boring and not be used for trading. If you feel the need to gamble, then go to Las Vegas—don't use your investment portfolio!

CHART 27: "Price Gaps" BSC.X
2005

Created in MetaStock from Equis International

INFLATION, TAXES, AND THE U.S. DOLLAR

Although investors often happily focus on the price movements of profitable investments, most give only passing thoughts to the influence of inflation, taxes, and the value of the U.S. dollar on long-term performance. This is particularly true of income investments!

Inflation

Since the prices of income investments are not expected to appreciate in the long term, income investors will have to do one of two things to combat inflations effect on the overall portfolio's value (CHART 28):

- Own growth-oriented investments that have historically performed well above the expected inflation rate.
- Plan on reinvesting some of the annual income into more income investments and thus increase the size of the portfolio.

A dollar today and a dollar tomorrow are not the same value. In fact, every 10 years the value of money historically loses 20% to 30% of its real value. If steps are not taken to minimize the effects of long-term inflation, an income investor will receive significantly less real income in the future.

Taxes and Account Placement

As discussed earlier, the government has typically treated profits generated by investments differently, with investment income typically taxed at a higher level than gains realized by selling an investment (CHART 24). Since investors can't control when they are paid interest or dividends, tax-deferred accounts (such as retirement accounts or annuities) are ideal for holding taxable income investments, because the investor isn't taxed until the money is withdrawn from the accounts. One of the best examples of blindly using income investments without understanding the basic differences between the various types may occur when an investor places municipal bonds or municipal bond mutual funds into a tax-deferred account. Because the investment account type matters, tax-free yields may lose their benefits, depending on the type of account selected.

Remember, investment placement can have important implications for after-tax returns!

Chart 28: U.S. Annual Inflation Rate %
1900-2009

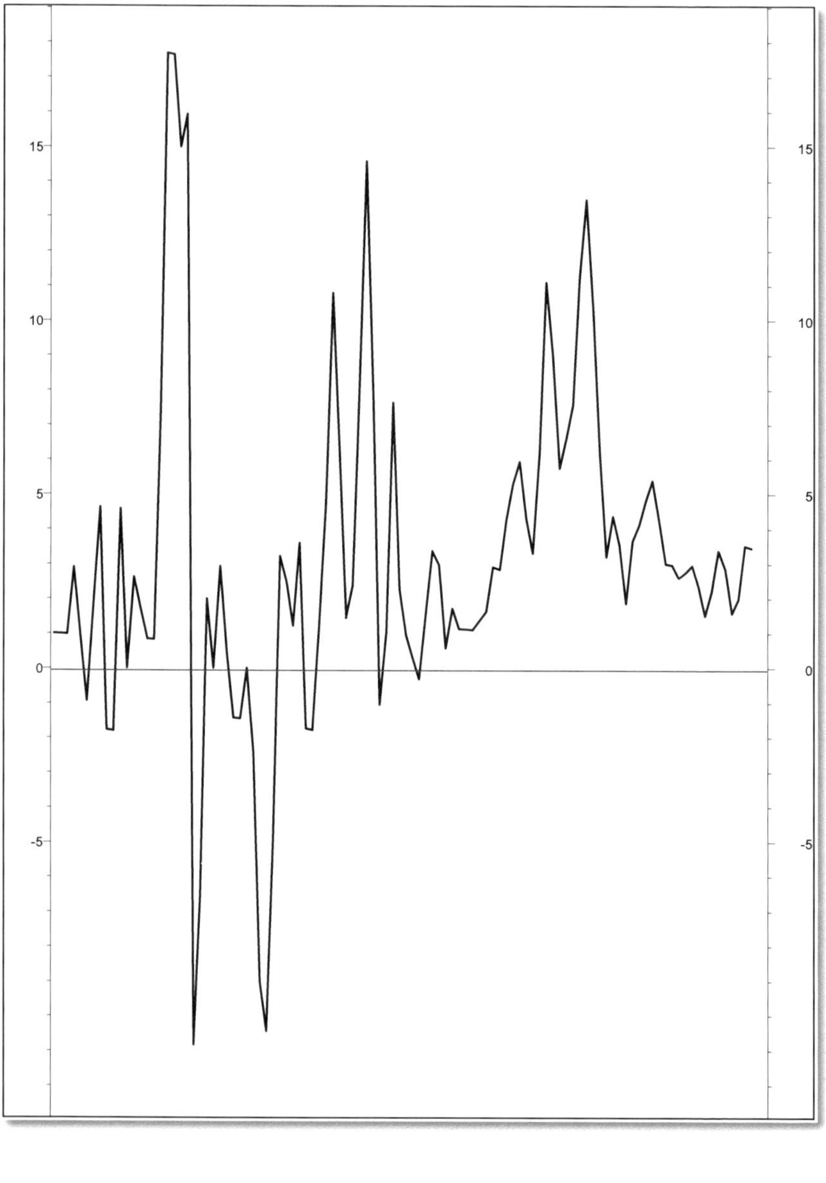

Charts created in MetaStock from Equis International

U.S. Dollar

More and more Americans have been investing outside of the U.S., and many investors have been adding foreign income investments to their portfolios. Sometimes, investors chase after foreign bonds because they have higher nominal yields than similar U.S. bonds. But what some investors forget is that the interest payments made on most of those bonds are in the currency of the issuer's country. A dramatic change in the value of that currency can cause a loss of true income after the interest is converted back into U.S. dollars (CHART 29).

CHART 29: U.S. Dollar Exchange Rate
1900-2009

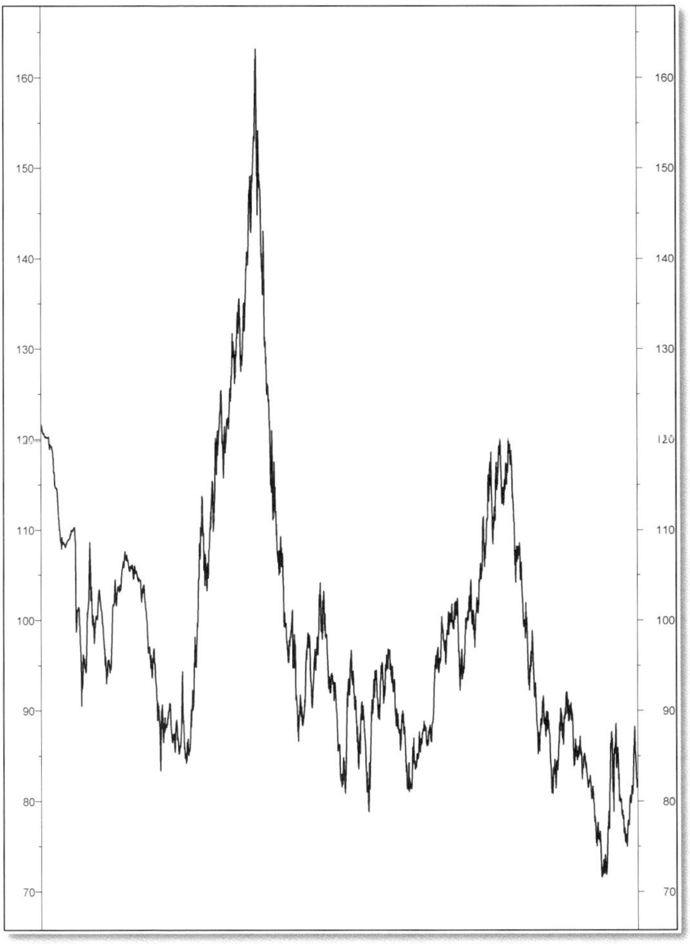

CHART 30: T-Bill 90-Day Yield
1970-2009

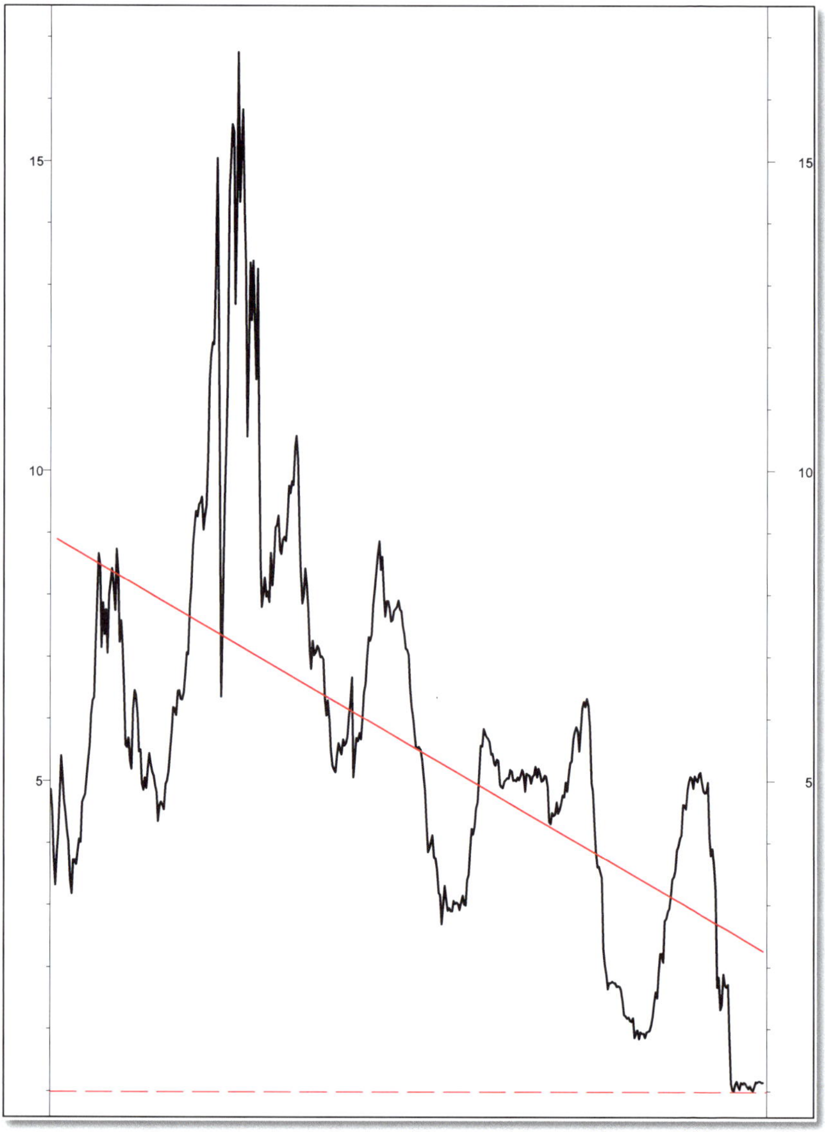

Created in MetaStock from Equis International

INTEREST RATES AND INVESTMENT RETURNS

Interest Rates

As can be seen on the chart of interest rates on 90-day T-bills over the past 40 years (Chart 30), it can easily be said that they are not stable. In fact, in the past 10 years we have seen short-term (Fed funds) rates swing 12% due to the Federal Reserve's attempt to influence investment valuations in a relatively inflation-benign environment.

Note that the market value of income investments is more directly affected by changes in overall interest rates than all other investment mediums.

The relationship is very simple: When the Federal Reserve raises interest rates, the current price of an income investment usually goes down. And yet when the Fed lowers interest rates, the current price of an income investment typically rises.

Unfortunately, this situation sometimes clouds the true long-term performance of income investments.

By the way, in an environment where there is an inverted yield curve between short- and long-term interest rates (i.e., short-term rates are higher than long-term interest rates), an income investor should be more cautious and stick to new investments with shorter maturities.

Investment Returns

If the original purpose of "loaning" is to provide an investor with a projected return due to its regular payment of income and set date of the repayment of principal (i.e., near certainty of return), then one must ask why the current price of an income investment is of any importance unless an investor wants to acquire more of, or wishes to sell, the investment.

Furthermore, is it of any value to review an income portfolio or an index of income investments quarterly because much of the portfolio's projected income isn't paid until the last quarter of the year?

Ultimately, it is a question of which is more important: annual returns or the cumulative returns since the investment was first made.

On the next page are reports I use to measure the performance of income investments. The top section is for bonds (Exhibit 4) and the bottom is for income stocks (such as preferred stocks, real estate investment trusts, energy partnerships, etc.) (Exhibit 5).

See Disclaimer

EXHIBIT 4: Sample Performance Report (Corporate Bonds)

Description	Market Value	Par Value	Annual Yield %	Year to Date Change %	Cumulative Change $	Cumulative Income
Corporate Bonds						
CORPORATE BOND 7.5% 02/15/11	$25,470	$25,000	7.5%	-0.2%	$465	$1,808
CORPORATE BOND 7.2% 07/15/08	$15,559	$25,000	7.1%	-1.9%	$60	$7,042
CORPORATE BOND 7.75% 03/01/07	$6,053	$6,000	7.5%	-1.9%	($113)	$2,744
CORPORATE BOND 9.05% 11/15/11	$26,013	$24,000	8.1%	-2.1%	($843)	$4,630
CORPORATE BOND 7.875% 07/15/13	$11,220	$12,000	7.9%	-9.2%	($766)	$7,826
CORPORATE BOND 7.625% 5/15/0	$25,563	$25,000	7.3%	-2.0%	($723)	$7,458
CORPORATE BOND 7.75% 02/1/10	$15,000	$15,000	7.7%	-4.3%	($103)	$4,255
CORPORATE BOND 9.375% 06/01/11	$15,675	$15,000	9.1%	-0.2%	$259	$4,369
CORPORATE BOND 8.75% 07/15/07	$21,394	$21,000	8.2%	-2.0%	($927)	$15,593
CORPORATE BOND 8.25% 12/15/11	$24,750	$25,000	8.3%	2.1%	($5)	$1,712
CORPORATE BOND 10.75% 10/15/06	$8,150	$10,000	10.5%	-19.3%	($2,136)	$1,496
CORPORATE BOND 6.5% 08/15/10	$23,500	$25,000	6.7%	-1.8%	($755)	$1,345
CORPORATE BOND 7.75% 03/15/13	$45,360	$48,000	7.4%	-3.4%	($4,975)	$5,668
CORPORATE BOND 7% 05/01/12	$15,525	$15,000	6.9%	-1.4%	$380	$3,153
CORPORATE BOND 6.85% 06/01/08	$9,135	$9,000	7.1%	-1.5%	$494	$2,809
CORPORATE BOND 6.0% 01/04/14	$28,050	$30,000	6.9%	-6.5%	$1,940	$5,701
Corporate Bonds Subtotal	**$326,416**	**$330,000**	**7.8%**	**-2.9%**	**($7,747)**	**$74,608**

See Disclaimer

EXHIBIT 5: Sample Performance Report (Income Stocks)

Description	Shares	Market Value	Average Div. Yield %	Year to Date Change %	Cumulative Change $	Cumulative Income $
Equity Income						
COMMON STOCK	865	$26,132	7.9%	2.9%	$1,094	$1,603
PREFERRED STOCK 8.7%	887	$24,295	7.1%	0.3%	($2,907)	$3,647
PREFERRED STOCK 8.00%	949	$24,627	7.5%	-0.9%	($579)	$3,588
PREFERRED STOCK 8.6%	956	$24,311	8.2%	-3.6%	$897	$1,064
COMMON STOCK	221	$9,724	8.0%	14.3%	$2,143	$1,700
PREFERRED STOCK 8.765%	838	$21,646	7.9%	0.4%	($1,754)	$3,485
PREFERRED STOCK 8.3%	848	$22,345	7.3%	-30.5%	($2,994)	$2,934
PREFERRED STOCK 8.125%	919	$23,591	7.4%	-1.9%	($1,710)	$4,953
PREFERRED STOCK 7.25%	284	$7,214	6.7%	-0.5%	($414)	$1,738
COMMON STOCK	276	$9,748	5.2%	-19.0%	($2,896)	$535
PREFERRED STOCK 8%	282	$26,085	10.1%	4.3%	$1,066	$56
PREFERRED STOCK 9%	950	$24,064	8.4%	0.3%	($1,425)	$5,675
COMMON STOCK	1,335	$21,654	8.4%	0.2%	($2,255)	$1,618
Equity Income Subtotal		**$265,433**	**7.7%**	**-3.8%**	**($13,526)**	**$32,596**

This format is very useful and provides information usually not available on brokerage statements. When looking at the report, there are several ways to review the overall performance of this income portfolio:

Market (Liquidation) Value and Par (Maturity) Value

In comparing the market value with the par value, you will notice that the bond holdings are currently worth more at maturity than if they were to be liquidated today. Remember that par value is a legal obligation that the issuer owes the holder of these bonds at maturity, so liquidation value is of less use than for a common stock owner.

Annual Yield and Year-to-Date Price Change

The "Annual Yield" (projected income for the year/cost basis) shows the percentage earned from interest paid this year. Note that this is different from the YTM calculation that assumes the reinvestment of all income.

The "Year to Date Price Change" measures the change in the price of the investment for the current year. For example, the report shows the market value of the investments has dropped since the beginning of the year. And if the prices do not decline any further, the total return (Annual Yield +/- YTD price change) of the portfolio will be positive after all income is collected by the end of the year. A common mistake is to compare a bond's annual price change to a market benchmark without including the estimated income.

Cumulative Change in Price vs. Cumulative Income Received

Since the bond investments in this portfolio have been purchased, they have declined $7,747 in value. And yet they have also produced $74,608 in interest payments over the same time frame. The investments have indeed been profitable to own!

Notice that the information is nearly identical for equity income investments, except I don't include par value because they don't have meaningful maturity dates. Some equity income investments have dividend yields that can fluctuate over time, so the "Dividend Yield %" is an estimate based on the average of the past two years of dividend payments. As was seen with the bonds, the values of the investments have dropped since being purchased ($13,526), yet the dividends collected over the same period were a higher amount: $32,596.

There are many ways to evaluate the performance of an income portfolio. Each should be reviewed. All investments are distinctly different. There is no single, uniform way to analyze every investment. Ultimately, successful investment performance should be based on meeting a realistic expectation, not in comparing what your friends and neighbors are doing with their money. It is a journey, not a horse race!

BOND MUTUAL FUNDS

For the past 50 years, mutual funds have been a popular way to invest in stocks and bonds. In income investing, municipal bond funds are the most popular, with more than 702 open-end and 287 closed-end funds to choose from.

Just because something's popular doesn't mean it's the best way to invest. If a projected return through a regular payment of income and set date of the repayment of principal are the greatest "pluses" of owning fixed-income investments, then many mutual funds miss the mark.

Here are some things to consider before investing in bond mutual funds:

Asset Turnover

Bond funds have been known for having the highest amount of annual turnover (i.e., trading) of any type of mutual fund. In 2009, Morningstar data show that corporate bond funds with more than $50 million in assets had an average portfolio turnover of 148%. A bond portfolio of non-callable issues evenly laddered over 10 years would imply that only 10% of the portfolio would come due every year, so the high turnover ratio suggests that the funds are actively trading bonds (i.e., not holding investments to maturity), which means they could be giving up one of income investing's best advantages.

Bond Mutual Funds Performance

The trading activity described above can be justified only if it produces better returns than directly buying and holding income investments to maturity. In the following exhibit, a comparison of the average 15-, 10-, and 5-year returns of corporate bond funds with more than $50 million in assets was made and compared to the Dow Jones Corporate Bond Average during the same period of time. Since the bond yields were noticeably higher than the mutual fund group's average return overall, an investor should consider that buying and holding a portfolio of bonds directly could produce better overall returns than those found in investing in most corporate bond funds.

TABLE 5: Mutual Funds Annual Performance Versus Corporate Bond Market 1994-2009

	Total Returns			Asset	Expense
	15 yr	10 yr	5 yr	Turnover	Ratio
U.S. Corporate Bond Funds	6.8%	6.1%	7.7%	148.0%	.69%
Dow Jones Corporate Bond	7.4%	6.9%	5.9%		
Index Difference	(.6%)	(.8%)	1.8%		

It is not uncommon for mutual fund investors who own an assortment of funds to think they are properly diversified. Remember that many funds own bonds from the same issuers.

Open-End Versus Closed-End Funds and ETFs

Although they are all considered mutual funds, they are structured and managed differently. In general, closed-end funds, and their close cousin exchange-traded funds, typically have lower turnover ratios and management fees than open-end funds.

Management Fees

The average corporate bond fund fee in 2009 was .69%. This needs to be incorporated into any comparison with the low cost of buying and holding income investments directly. Remember that these fund management fees do not include sales loads, 12b-1 fees, and transaction expenses resulting from asset turnover.

Monthly Income Offered

The greatest advantage of bond funds is that they offer investors the ability to receive a monthly income instead of having to wait for income investments to pay dividends quarterly or interest payments semiannually.

Small Investors: A Good Place to Start

With discount brokerage houses offering more income investments, an investor with as little as $75,000 can invest directly in a well-balanced income portfolio of approximately 15 bonds or equity income securities. Also, it is not uncommon for investors to start with bond funds and convert their portfolio to direct investments after their portfolio reaches a larger size.

Bonds Are Better Than Mutual Funds for Income Investors

Many investors have mistakenly embraced income investment products, including mutual funds, as equal substitutes for buying and holding conventional bonds. In reality, a large number of these investments don't mature and do not provide a projected rate of return. In the next major market correction in income investments, a painful truth will emerge—these investments have more in common with dividend-paying stocks than bonds held to maturity. Simply put, investors are getting income but not a certainty of return.

In the next section we focus on how, why, and when preferreds can be a useful addition to most income portfolios.

Chapter 3

Preferreds: An Investing Enigma

Preferred Stock Issued to Thomas A. Edison
The Edison Portland Cement Company, 1906

"It is sometimes said that preferred stocks provides more liberal yields than bonds and a greater certainty of income than common stocks. From another viewpoint, the preferred stock possesses some of the disadvantages of both bonds and common stocks without all the advantages of either. At least the advantage of each of the two classes is not possessed by preferred stock unrestrictedly."
Investment Fundamentals, Roger Babson, 1935

"While preferred shares are listed on major stock exchanges, they aren't widely followed or understood– so there's a chance to unlock hidden value."
The Wall Street Journal (8/6/2006)

"Investors who never heard of preferred stock just a few years ago are trying to get up to speed quickly."
USA Today (8/11/2010)

In Chapter 1, we discussed how an obscure security known as preferred stocks (or commonly called "preferreds") was one of the key tools used by the U.S. government in its intervention efforts to stabilize the world economy during the fall of 2008. Since then, "preferreds" have rapidly grown in popularity with investors and have been one of the best-performing investments since the financial hurricane ended. A good example of this is how the iShare S&P U.S. Preferred Stock Index ETF (symbol: PFF) has rapidly attracted net assets of $3.9 billion since its inception in 2007, while many stock mutual funds have lost assets during this same time.

It was very different in 2007. When I wrote *Preferreds: Wall Street's Best-Kept Income Secret,* it was the first book since the 1930s devoted to preferred stocks, and the media scarcely covered the security at all.

It is still a mystery to me why preferred stocks, one of the oldest exchange listed securities in existence, had "fallen between the cracks" with a global investment industry overly fixated on constructing market benchmarks and offering the public as many investment products as possible. Even more interesting is the extreme range of opinions expressed by the media. For instance, *Forbes Magazine* in recent years had an article titled "The Case For Preferred Stocks," and yet one of its senior columnists wrote in the book *The Wall Street Waltz*, "Common stocks offer appreciation, while preferreds offer nothing at all."

Needless to say, there is a lot of confusion about preferred stocks that this chapter will help to explain:

WHAT ARE PREFERRED STOCKS ANYWAY?

The definition can be complicated, but preferred stocks are considered equities. This means that they represent ownership in a corporation. And that is where the similarities with common stocks end and the problems begin. Historically, they have more in common with bonds, because they are income investments that have historically generated most of their return through dividend income. Since 1900, preferred stocks have generated an average annual return of 7.4%. Some 88% of the profit came from dividends (versus 38% for common stocks). In some respects, it is easier to view them as a third type of security that, from an asset allocation standpoint, fit between common stocks and corporate bonds. If you have trouble picturing this, then take the word "stocks" out and just call them "preferreds."

Below are nine key factors that need to be understood before investing in preferred stocks:

Fixed-Rate Dividends Paid Indefinitely: Fixed-rate (traditional) preferred stocks must pay a specified stream of income at predetermined dates. Unless there is a call provision, which will force the investor to give up a security, preferred stocks will pay the established dividend in perpetuity. Most preferred dividends are paid quarterly and are subject to the same rules about ex-dividend dates as common stocks.

Call Provisions: Many preferred stocks have call or sinking fund provisions in which the issuer can buy back the security from you at a predetermined price and date.

Unpaid Dividends Usually Accumulate: Unlike bonds, the failure to pay the promised dividend does not result in a bond-like default. Instead, the owed dividends of traditional preferreds accumulate (i.e., build up), and the common stockholders will not receive any future dividends until owed preferred stock dividends have been paid in full. Preferred stocks rarely give their holders full voting rights, but if the dividend is missed, the preferred shareholders will be provided with some voting power.

Share Price: At issuance, most preferred stocks start trading at $25, $50, or $100 per share (i.e., par value). The share price rarely splits, and par value is the price normally used if the security is called.

Exchange Listed: Most preferreds are listed on major stock exchanges around the world and can be bought and sold similarly to any other stocks. Commission costs are usually similar to common equities. They normally qualify as a security covered by SIPC insurance. This protects investments held by a brokerage house in bankruptcy.

Corporate Issuers: Utilities, financial companies, real estate investment trusts, railroads, manufacturers, and companies with a large number of subsidiaries primarily issue preferred stocks as a source of long-term financing. In fact, many foreign-based companies issue preferred stocks on U.S. stock exchanges.

Multiple Series from Same Issuer: Many corporations issue multiple types of preferreds (known as "series") with different dividend rates, call provisions, credit ratings, and issuance size. In other words, it is not uncommon to find a company having numerous preferred stocks listed at the same time, and each with a different symbol and CUSIP number. For instance, Bank of America currently has 14 different types of preferreds listed with the NYSE.

Dividend Tax Treatment: Under current tax law, certain types of preferred stocks can qualify for a significantly lower tax rate (15% vs. 35%) called Qualified Dividend Income (QDI). Corporations that buy preferreds in other companies can get special tax deductions called intercorporate Dividends Received Deduction (DRD).

Many Different Types of Preferred Stocks: Although the focus of this book is on traditional (fixed-rate) preferreds, there are several different types that investors can choose from:

> **Convertible**: These preferreds allow investors the option to exchange their preferred stocks for the issuer's common stocks (at a preset price and share swap formula) in exchange for a lower dividend payout than offered on the fixed-rate preferred-stock issues.
>
> **Floating Rate**: The dividend rate will vary according to percentage changes in an interest rate benchmark such as LIBOR, Bank Prime Rate, etc.

Noncumulative: Often issued by big banks, these preferreds don't accrue overdue dividends but pay a higher dividend than fixed-rate preferreds.

U.S. Paid: Some foreign preferreds are issued and pay dividends in U.S. dollars to reduce currency risk for American investors.

Trust and 3rd Party Trust: A company can place its bonds into a trust structure, and the trust can then issue preferred stocks. These popular hybrid securities are offered by major investment firms and go by abbreviations such as: PINES, SATURNS, QUIBS, QUICS, QUIDS, QUIPS, TRUPS, TOPRS, etc. In reaction to concerns that banks may have used these trusts to mask the high levels of leverage prior to 2008's market meltdown, new financial legislation might put restrictions on banks issuing these securities for their Tier 1 regulatory capital requirements.

Analogies can be useful in describing preferred stocks. Many years ago, one of my clients, who grew up on a farm, told me that he viewed all investments as cows. Some were owned for their meat (appreciation), and others were used to produce milk (income). While they are both important to a farm or ranch, they serve very different purposes. This is a great analogy of common and preferred stocks in the same company—both equities, different uses!

WHAT ARE THE PROS AND CONS OF PREFERREDS?

Preferred stocks have several advantages that make could them an important part of a portfolio:

Margin Use: Many preferreds are marginable securities that can be used as collateral for brokerage house loans. This can provide an experienced investor with the flexibility to take advantage of new investment opportunities without committing new capital. If margin rates are low, then small amounts of margin can be used to buy new bond or preferred-stock investments at opportune prices, which might not be around when cash is available in the future.

In a properly laddered portfolio, some investments are maturing or being called annually. The recently borrowed funds used to buy new investments will be paid back when older bond investments mature and are cashed in. Using margin in this manner is not commonly done, yet is a cost-effective means to take advantage of income investment opportunities when cash is not in hand.

Bond Substitutes: They are a great substitute for fixed-income securities with medium- to long-term maturities. Since preferred stocks are exchange-listed, they can be easily purchased, during times when new bond investments are scarce, or when they are overpriced relative to comparable preferred stocks.

No Accrued Interest: In addition to investment and transaction costs, new bond purchasers also have to pay the previous holder's interest owed up to the point of sale. The purchaser of preferred stocks doesn't owe accrued payments of any type and is subject to the same rules about ex-dividend dates as the holders of common stocks.

Another Way to Own Real Estate: Real estate investment trusts (REITs) regularly issue preferred stocks that pay yields comparable to illiquid trust deeds or rents collected from income properties.

Global Opportunities: Many foreign companies also issue preferreds that trade in the U.S. and abroad.

Fortunately, there are only a few major disadvantages that can hinder preferred-stock investors.

Limited Mutual Fund Availability: Currently, there are very few sound choices in preferred-stock mutual funds, so mutual fund investors might have to consider directly investing in preferred securities themselves.

Few Preferred-Stock Indices: Before 2005, there were no active benchmarks to track the preferred-stock market. Since then, the Winans International Preferred Stock Index (WIPSI) and the S&P Preferred Stock Index have been developed. Sadly, neither is commonly offered through free media outlets, as is typically done with common stock indices such as the S&P 500 Index.

No Listed Stock Options: No listed stock options are currently available on preferred stocks, which can limit hedging capabilities for sophisticated investors.

Preferreds have always been a relatively small player in global finance, when compared to the massive capitalization of the bond or common stock markets. This causes liquidity and availability problems for many large institutional investors, and therefore limits their involvement in the security over the long term. This has created one of those rare occurrences where the individual investor has an edge over big-money managers.

PREFERRED PRACTICAL TRADING TIPS

There are practical issues surrounding all investments that only experience teaches most investors. Listed below are things investors will need to know to avoid making a rookie mistake and to maximize the benefit of using preferred stocks in their portfolios:

Patience Is Required: Many of these stocks don't trade every day, so you must be patient to buy or sell them at reasonable prices.

Order Types: Preferred stocks can be bought or sold using various types of orders, yet caution is required due to their liquidity. Limit orders can be useful to purchase these stocks at reasonable prices, but market and stop-loss orders can be a horrible way to buy or sell. You also need to confirm with the brokerage house that limit order prices are automatically adjusted for recent dividend payments. Bottom line—handle transactions with care!

Ex-Dividend Date: As with common stocks, the ex-dividend date is the date that the stocks must be owned to collect the upcoming quarterly dividend. You must own the stocks before that date to collect the dividend, and be careful not to cut it too close due to weekends and T3 settlement rules.

Brokerage House Information: Much of the information provided in brokerage house documents (monthly brokerage statements, trade confirmations, and 1099 forms) is inaccurate or useless. Remember that:

- On most monthly brokerage house statements, a current yield percentage is used that assumes the investor bought the investment at the end of the month. This is generally useless to the investor who has owned the investment prior to the end of the month or owns a floating-rate preferred.

- The current prices of income investments posted on monthly brokerage statements or daily websites are commonly inaccurate and show "wild" swings in the investment's value that didn't happen in reality. This is especially true if posted prices were not adjusted for recently paid dividends.

The old saying "garbage in, garbage out" really applies here, and it is essential that income investors consider using information, from the independent sources listed below, to get the full picture on preferred stocks.

HOW TO FIND PREFERRED-STOCK OPPORTUNITIES

Investors need to come up with a list of potential investment candidates.

Preferreds are like common stocks in that they are listed on major exchanges and can be purchased and sold at most brokerage houses. A logical place to start is reviewing the services offered by your investment firm. Even though research is minuscule when compared to other investment types, brokerage houses are beginning to expand their coverage of preferred stocks.

The Wall Street Journal and *Barron's* have lists of actively traded preferred stocks in their newspapers and websites. Subscription-based websites (such as PreferredsOnline.com) post daily trading activity in preferred stocks. This website also provides critical information such as dividend rate, call provisions, and security structure (fixed-rate, dividend accrual, etc.).

If you are trying to find out if a company has preferred stocks currently issued, then try using Value Line's Investor Survey or its "Investment Analyzer" software (valueline.com). These services list the amount of total preferred stocks outstanding within a company's capital structure. In fact, Value Line's software has a screening criterion called "Preferred Equity" that allows you to quickly find the biggest issuers of preferreds out of the 6,834 corporations in its universe.

A good source for finding which mutual funds use preferreds is Morningstar's subscription-based "Principia" software (morningstar.com). It allows the user to screen for the funds that invest in preferred stocks by looking in the criteria field called "% Other Preferred."

Global Financial Data (globalfinancialdata.com) has the largest of databases of individual preferred-stock prices (active and de-listed), as well as the complete Winans International Preferred Stock Index data series. This includes price, yield, and total return data on preferred stocks since 1900. If you want to do long-term research on this security, this is the best place to go!

Equis International (equis.com) offers a technically based charting software program called "MetaStock." While it has access to Reuters' database of 30 years of historical price data on many of the larger issues of individual preferred stocks, it offers very limited data on preferred-stock indices themselves.

As you can see, there is no single source for finding all the data needed to succeed in investing in preferred stocks. I find that all the products and services listed above are reliable and cost-effective in helping find buying opportunities as well as monitoring the current portfolio holdings in an effective and efficient manner.

WHICH INDEX TO USE TO TRACK THE PREFERRED-STOCK MARKET?

Throughout this book, the Winans International Preferred Stock Index (WIPSI) is used to represent the preferred-stock universe. WIPSI was the first investment index created in recent history that is devoted to tracking the price and yield of traditional preferred stocks, and is available from numerous sources (winansinternational.com has details). A reporter recently referred to it as "The Dow of Preferreds," because WIPSI is the only benchmark that covers preferred-stock trading history back to 1900 (Charts 31 & 32).

One might ask, "Why is it important to have an index for preferred stocks?" The simple answer is that people are being exposed daily to individual preferred stocks and they need a benchmark to broadly monitor the overall activity in the preferred-stock market. After all, a common-stock

Chart 31: WIPSI Price
1900-2009

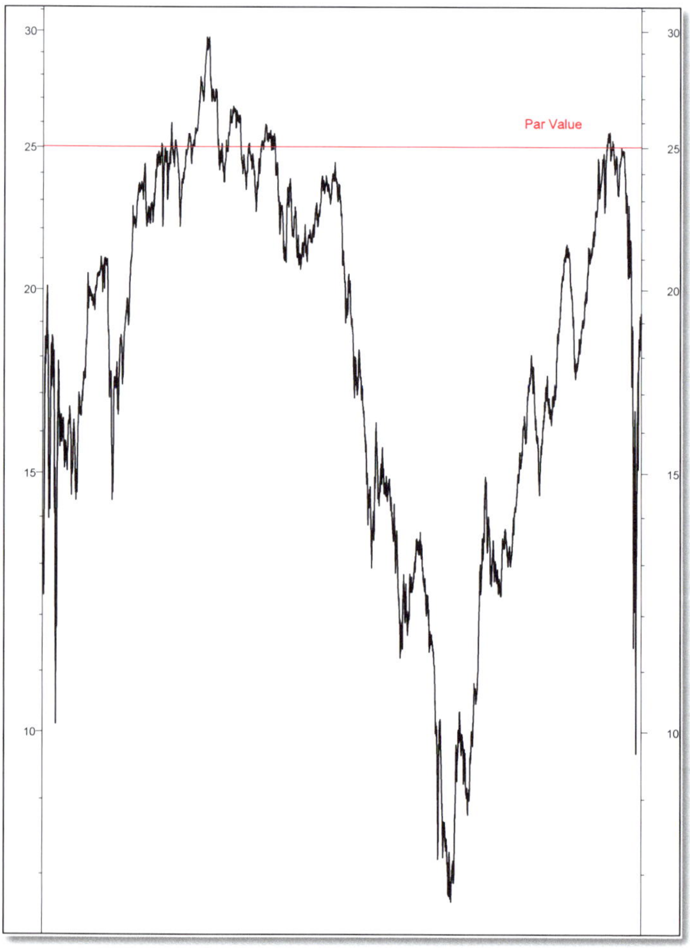

investor uses the S&P 500 Index or the Dow Jones Industrial Average to track the daily movements of common stocks.

Surprisingly, there was no preferred-stock benchmark prior to 2005. I initially realized there was a problem in 2003 as I began to add more preferred stocks to my client's portfolios due to the increasing shortage of exchange-listed corporate bonds. As with most investors, I had been tracking the various types of fixed-income investments (U.S. Treasury, municipal, corporate, etc.) and other equity-income investments (REITS, utilities, Master Limited Partnerships, etc.) through established indices,

CHART 32: WIPSI Yield
1900-2009

Charts created in MetaStock from Equis International

and yet when it came to preferred stocks, I was somewhat "flying blind" due to the lack of an index to help me gauge price trend and historical valuations versus other types of income investments.

All the known sources were contacted, but no one had a "pure" preferred-stock index to offer. In fact, the two associations that most investment analysts are members of, The Chartered Financial Analyst Institute and The Market Technicians Association, produce "think tank"-type publications devoted to market and investment analysis. Surprisingly, I found very little research on preferred stocks—past or present.

The problem became more evident when I assisted *Forbes Magazine* in compiling data for an article titled "Reaching for Yield" in the 2004 Special Summer Issue. The reporter became frustrated because there was no existing way to show the long-term performance of preferred stocks and to compare them with other investments.

In 2005, Winans International created WIPSI. It became the first modern-day index of preferred-stocks, and it is also the only index that accurately covers preferred stock price and yields since 1900. Since the introduction of WIPSI, Standard & Poor's had introduced an index to track the performance of preferreds. I noted in a 2007 *Technically Speaking* magazine article that the S&P index had problems. For starters, it covers data only from 2003 to present, and thus is useless for long-term analysis. It was also more volatile and performs worse than WIPSI due to differences in index construction. For example, in 2007, its Ford Motor Co. preferred component was weighted at 10% of the S&P Index, disproportionate to the actual capitalization and trading characteristics within the preferred universe valued at $200 billion. In other words, this index's component weightings were not representative of the preferred-stock universe and could misrepresent the true performance of the preferred-stock market.

For more details on the index's construction, data used, and weighting, please review "WIPSI Specifications" later in this book.

Preferred stocks have been a part of Wall Street since the 1830s. In fact, most undergraduate and graduate textbooks devote much time to the differences between common stocks, bonds, and preferred stocks, but prior to the invention of WIPSI, there was no effective way to evaluate the long-term investment performance of preferred stocks.

HOW HAVE PREFERRED STOCKS PERFORMED LONG TERM?

To properly review how preferred stocks have performed, and compare them to other investment mediums, an investor needs to study their historical performance throughout different periods of time. The Winans International Preferred Stock Index is the perfect tool to evaluate historical performance.

The first step in this evaluation process is to select periods of time that are relevant. The follow periods were selected for important reasons:

> **1900-2009** This captures the investment landscape over several generations. It shows how the investments reacted in many different types of extreme situations (such as both world wars and the Great Depression) over a long period of time.
>
> **1950-2009** This time frame allows for an investment analysis without the volatile economic effects of the Great Depression and both world wars.
>
> **1990-2009** A time frame commonly used by the financial community or historical evaluations, because it captures the post-Cold War boom and the "lost decade" that started in 2000.
>
> **2000-2009** This captures the investment history since the dot.com bubble popped. This era is commonly called the "lost decade," because common stocks as a whole haven't produced any capital appreciation.
>
> **1965-1981** Investments can be greatly affected by inflation. This time frame was the last high inflation era in U.S. history.

As with any historical evaluation of investment mediums, the objective is to identify a reasonable expectation of return and risk associated with that investment.

Table 6: Historical Performance Since 1900

	Annual	Inflation	Interest / Dividend	Best (yr)	Worst (yr)
Common Stocks	11.7%	8.6%	4.4%	88% 1915	(42%) 1931
Preferred Stocks	7.4%	4.3%	6.5%	41% 1986	(23%) 1907
Corporate Bonds	6.5%	3.4%	6.3%	36% 1982	(11%) 1931
T-bills (90 days)	3.8%	0.7%	n/a	15% 1981	0% 1940
Inflation		3.1%			

% of time (years)	Up	Down	Back-to-Back	Last Occurred
Common Stocks	71%	29%	9%	2001-02
Preferred Stocks	75%	25%	7%	2007-08
Corporate Bonds	84%	16%	3%	1979-80

Table 7: Historical Performance Since 1950

	Annual	Inflation	Interest / Dividend
Common Stocks	12.3%	8.6%	3.6%
Preferred Stocks	7.3%	3.6%	7.3%
Corporate Bonds	7.3%	3.5%	7.2%
T-bills (90 days)	4.9%	1.1%	n/a
Inflation	3.8%		

% of time (years):	Up	Down
Common Stocks	77%	23%
Preferred Stocks	72%	28%
Corporate Bonds	85%	15%

The facts listed in Tables 6-8 provide answers to the question: How did preferreds compare to other investments?

Very well!

In time frames reviewed (Tables 6-8), they produced nominal annual returns between 10.2% and 7.3%. When adjusted for inflation, the annual returns ranged between 7.4% and 3.4%. The best annual return was 41% in 1986 and the worst annual return was -23% in 1907. As with any income investment, most of the return was generated by dividends, and these yields ranged from 7.6% to 6.5%. It is also interesting to note that if $1 had been invested in WIPSI in 1900, it would have been worth $1,472 by 2009.

Preferreds are volatile investments and had negative years 25% of the time, and back-to-back negative years 7% over the past 109 years.

> **Common Stocks**: Without a doubt, common stocks were the best overall performers, with nominal annual returns that ranged between 12.3% and 9.9%. And yet their income yield ranged between 4.4% and 2.1% and was the lowest income yield of the investments reviewed. This clearly demonstrates that preferred stocks overall are better income investments for investors who need access to high levels of regular income. Common stocks were also the most volatile and had the highest percentage of negative years (between 29% and 23%). They have also had the worst performance of all investments studied since 2000.

> **Corporate Bonds**: While the results are lower than preferred stocks, with a nominal annual return between 6.5% and 3.9%, they have produced positive results between 90% and 84% of the time and thus are significantly less volatile than either common or preferred stocks. These securities lend themselves well to a buy and hold-to-maturity strategy. It is also important to note that contrary to popular belief, this investment medium has historically outperformed inflation by a significant margin.

Table 8: Historical Performance Since 1990

	Annual	Inflation	Interest / Dividend
Common Stocks	9.9%	7.1%	2.1%
Preferred Stocks	10.2%	7.4%	7.6%
Corporate Bonds	7.6%	4.9%	6.5%
T-bills (90 days)	3.9%	1.2%	n/a
Inflation		2.8%	
% of time (years)	**Up**	**Down**	
Common Stocks	75%	25%	
Preferred Stocks	80%	20%	
Corporate Bonds	90%	10%	

Table 9: Historical Performance Since 2000

	Annual	Inflation	Interest / Dividend
Common Stocks	1.2%	(1.2%)	1.8%
Preferred Stocks	9.1%	6.6%	7.4%
Corporate Bonds	6.9%	4.4%	5.6%
T-bills (90 days)	3.0%	0.4%	n/a
Inflation		2.6%	
% of time (years)	**Up**	**Down**	
Common Stocks	60%	40%	
Preferred Stocks	80%	20%	
Corporate Bonds	100%	0%	

Table 10: Historical Performance Since 1965-1982

	Annual	Inflation	Interest / Dividend
Common Stocks	8.0%	1.4%	4.4%
Preferred Stocks	1.4%	(5.2%)	7.5%
Corporate Bonds	5.5%	(1.1%)	8.8%
T-bills (90 days)	6.6%	0.0%	n/a
Inflation		6.6%	
% of time (years)	**Up**	**Down**	
Common Stocks	65%	35%	
Preferred Stocks	47%	53%	
Corporate Bonds	76%	24%	

UGLY TIMES: 1965-1981 AND 2000-2009

The media have recently called the period after the dot.com bubble to present "The Lost Decade," because the U.S. stock market has traded sideways with huge corrections in 2000-2002 and 2008 (TABLE 9). While they are quick to draw comparisons to the Great Depression, this time frame has much in common with 1965 to 1981 (TABLE 10) when the Dow Jones Industrial Average didn't make a meaningful new high for 16 years.

In real terms, common-stock returns ranged between 1.4% and (1.2%) with a high percentage of negative years (40% and 35%). They underperformed most investment classes, including T-bills. On the other hand, corporate bonds produced real returns that ranged between 4.4% and (1.1%) and had positive years between 100% and 76% of the time.

Preferreds had mixed results. They have been the best-performing investment class in the 2000-2009 period, with an amazing 6.6% real return. Yet in the 1965-1981 period they had the worst performance, with a (5.2%) real return. The key difference between the two periods in time was the inflation rate (6.6% vs. 2.6%). Clearly, preferred stocks performed terribly during the high inflation of the 1970s.

What the above studies have clearly shown is that preferred stocks are historically one of the best-performing income investments in existence. And yet they are volatile and should be avoided during inflationary periods.

An amazing fact that resembles the "tortoise and the hare" fable is that preferred stocks are in a 20-year statistical tie with fast-moving common stocks and had 20% fewer negative years (TABLE 8). So much for being a "boring stock!"

This chapter answered the questions "What is a preferred stock?" "Where to find them?" and "Have they performed well?" The following chapters will focus on answering the question "When to buy preferreds stocks?" This is an important question to answer because of the high level of volatility associated with this security.

The next section will cover the market analysis of preferred stocks to help investors identify bull and bear markets, as well as to compare relative valuations of preferred stocks to corporate, Treasury, and municipal bonds.

Chapter 4

Analysis of the Preferred-Stock Market

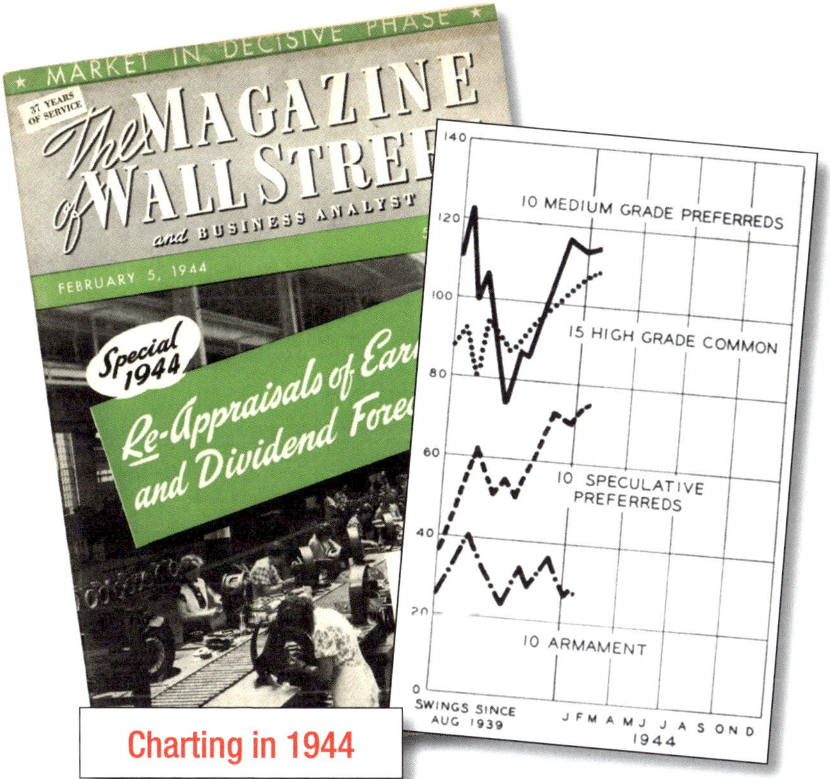

Charting in 1944

"Market analysis is based heavily on the movement of broad market averages."
Technical Analysis of the Financial Markets, John Murphy, 1999

"While preferred stocks rarely enjoy the same price gains as common stocks, these shares also are not as vulnerable to sharp declines. The average preferred stock fell only 3% in the past year versus a 21% drop in the S&P 500."
Forbes 11/18/2002)

Before investors start investing in preferred stocks, they need a disciplined approach to deal with the volatility of the entire preferred-stock market. In the last chapter, it was revealed that preferred stocks historically have negative years between 28% and 25% of the time, so when to invest in preferreds is as important as what preferred stocks to buy or sell.

Market analysis has two purposes:

- To identify the current trend of the preferred-stock market.
- How the current yields in preferreds historically compare with the rates of return in other income investments such as corporate, Treasury, and municipal bonds.

Investment research is done through two different methods: technical and fundamental analysis. Technical focuses on the direct relationship of past security price activity to current market conditions. Fundamental analysis primarily deals with the relationship of various industrial and economic figures to current investment prices to determine if the investment medium is overvalued or undervalued.

While both types of analysis come into play in evaluating individual corporate securities, technical analysis is a superior method for evaluating the overall market conditions of income investments because market activity leads financial and economic data. In addition, investors are also reviewing government and municipal issues, and the analysis needs to take into account more than just the finances of the private sector.

Ultimately, changes in interest rates relative to the supply and demand of an investment are of equal, if not more, importance than overall financial conditions in evaluating income investments.

USING INDEX CHARTS

It is often said that "a picture tells 1,000 words." The "pictures" in this book are primarily charts of past investment prices and yields. Coupled with indicators that identify overbought and oversold market conditions, charts are an effective way to analyze many different types of investment markets in different financial conditions.

Charts are easy to use. The vertical scale is the level of the index, and the horizontal scale displays time. Any point on the chart represents the price of the index at a given point in time and thus is a graphic history of the investment.

To prove this point, look at the following examples of the Winans International Preferred Stock Index (WIPSI). Which is more useful in identifying price trends, the chart or the same data listed as a column of numbers (Chart 33, Table 11)?

Chart 33: WIPSI $
1989-2009

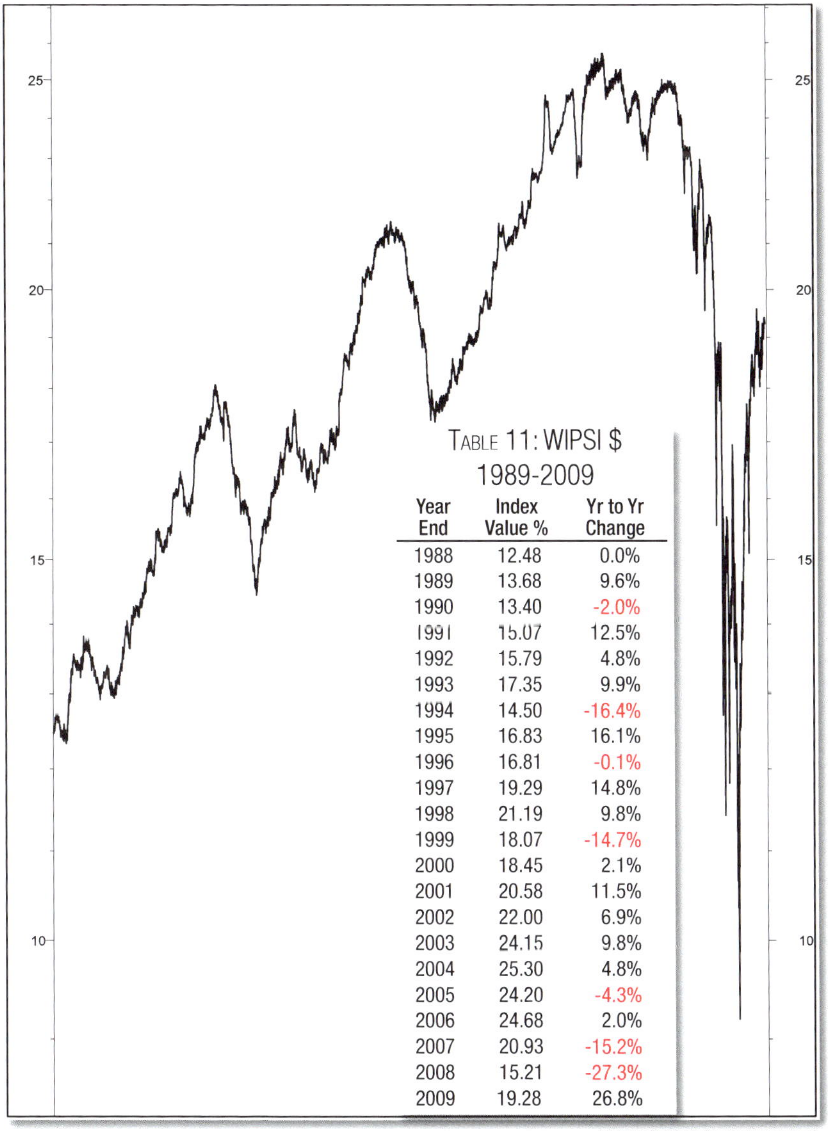

Table 11: WIPSI $
1989-2009

Year End	Index Value %	Yr to Yr Change
1988	12.48	0.0%
1989	13.68	9.6%
1990	13.40	-2.0%
1991	15.07	12.5%
1992	15.79	4.8%
1993	17.35	9.9%
1994	14.50	-16.4%
1995	16.83	16.1%
1996	16.81	-0.1%
1997	19.29	14.8%
1998	21.19	9.8%
1999	18.07	-14.7%
2000	18.45	2.1%
2001	20.58	11.5%
2002	22.00	6.9%
2003	24.15	9.8%
2004	25.30	4.8%
2005	24.20	-4.3%
2006	24.68	2.0%
2007	20.93	-15.2%
2008	15.21	-27.3%
2009	19.28	26.8%

Created in MetaStock from Equis International

Clearly, the chart is a more effective and efficient way to analyze WIPSI's price history!

Critics of technical analysis will tell you that investment prices don't trend but move randomly through time. Their unrealistic answer to investing is "buy all the time." As you study the charts in this book, it's obvious that investment prices do trend over long periods of time, and there are clearly times when investors, in any type of investment, should be on the defensive.

IS IT A BULL OR BEAR MARKET?

A key objective of market analysis (also referred to as top-down analysis) is to identify changes in an index's current price trend early enough to make timely changes to the asset allocation of an investment portfolio to enhance profitability or protect hard-won gains. *It is not to attempt to consistently pick the elusive bull market top or bear market bottom!*

Since accurate market analysis requires sufficient data (at least 20 years) to compare various periods in time to current economic conditions, the only index suitable for long-term market analysis of preferred stocks is the Winans International Preferred Stock Index (WIPSI). In fact, the S&P Preferred Stock Index covers data only from 2003 to present.

One of the most effective indicators to use on a chart for analyzing long-term trends is the 40-week simple moving average (SMA). This is also known as the 200-day simple moving average. On Chart 34, notice that, in addition to the WIPSI's line, there are two red lines. These represent the 40-week SMA of the weekly high and low prices of WIPSI. This band acts as a filter to help reduce false signals and thus improves the performance of the 40-week SMA.

The general interpretation of this indicator is:

- The preferred-stock market is in an uptrend (i.e., bull market) if the Friday price of the index is trading above the moving average band.
- The preferred-stock market is in a downtrend (i.e., bear market) if the Friday price of the index is trading below the moving average band.
- If the moving average is flat over an extended period, then the index is in a sideways trading range, going neither up nor down.

- A change of the index's trend is signaled by the Friday price of the index penetrating the moving average band. For example, if WIPSI drops below its moving average, then it has entered a new downtrend. The inverse situation signals a new uptrend.

Solid Results (Chart 34, Table 12)
Over the 20 years studied (1989-2009), six signals indicated the beginning of an uptrend and six indicated the beginning of a decline in the preferred-stock market. The 40-week simple moving average band was accurate 88% of the time in indicating a change in the trend of preferred stocks. The Winans International Preferred Stock Index (WIPSI) had an average advance of 22% on successful uptrend signals from the 40-week moving average band and an average decline of 16% from successful downtrend signals from the same indicator. There were usually long periods of time between signals. This ranged between 1,682 days (4.6 years) and 210 days (7 months).

My first book, *Preferreds* (written in 2006), introduced this indicator as "useful because it helps identify good times to be an investor in preferred stocks and periods when investors should be cautious." This tool was quickly put to the test. Soon after *Preferreds* was published, WIPSI crossed below its 40-week simple moving average and preferred stocks entered their worst bear market since 1907 (a high-to-low decline of 63%). It also successfully signaled the beginning of a new bull market for preferreds in May 2009 as the world economy stabilized.

Clearly, this information is useful to the investor because it helps identify opportunities to increase exposure in preferred stocks and periods of time to take defensive action. The 40-week simple moving average has been the "keel of the ship" of Winans International's investment strategy surrounding preferred stocks since we starting using these securities in our clients' portfolios. It played an important role in our decision to reduce exposure in preferred stocks before the financial meltdown in 2008.

Unfortunately, there are limited defensive options for preferred stockholders during bear markets. Short selling is problematic due to the high costs associated with the strategy (margin costs plus the large dividends owed on the borrowed preferred shares). Hedging strategies are limited do

CHART 34: WIPSI $ and 40-Week Moving Average Bands
1989-2009

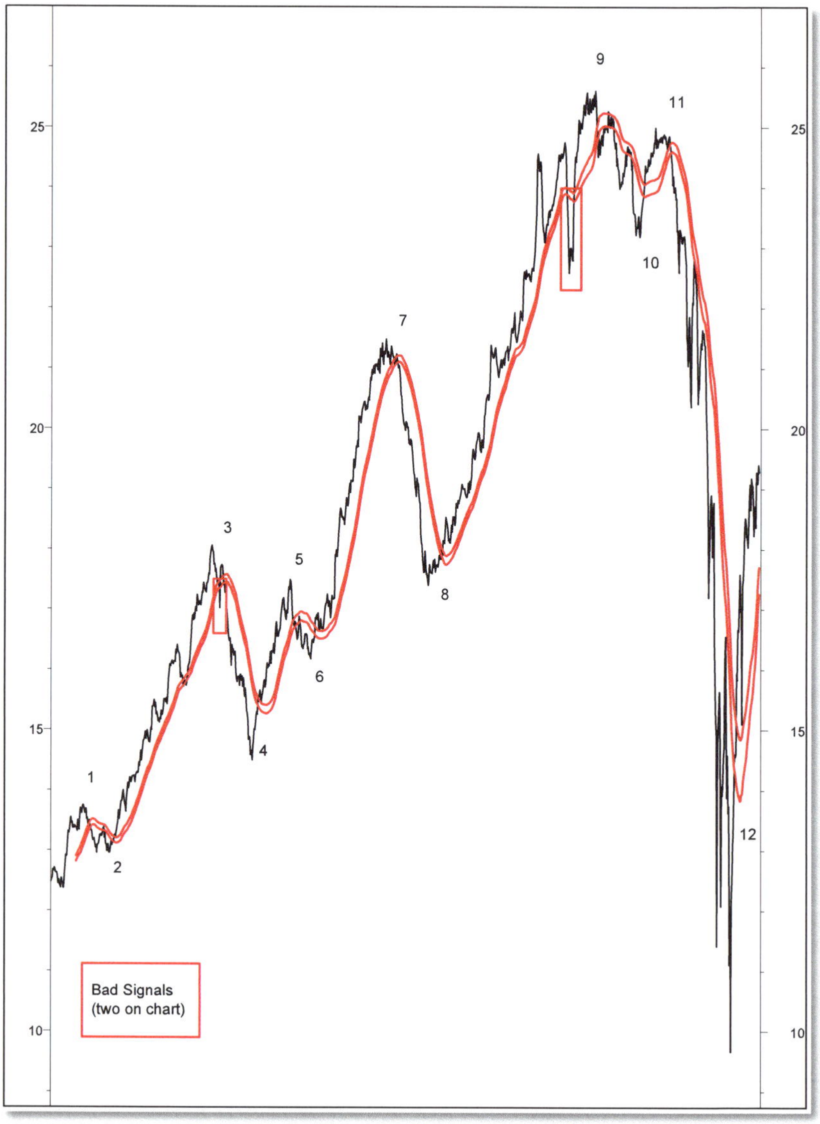

Created in MetaStock from Equis International

TABLE 12: WIPSI $ and 40-Week Moving Average
1989-2009

40-week SMA With High and Low Bands (False Signals Excluded)

	Downtrend					Uptrend			
Number		WIPSI	Low Point	%	Number		WIPSI	High Point	%
1	03/16/1990	13.33	13.27	-0.5%	2	11/30/1990	13.26	18.49	39.4%
3	02/18/1994	17.40	14.50	-16.7%	4	03/10/1995	15.54	17.86	14.9%
5	04/12/1996	16.66	16.48	-1.1%	6	11/08/1996	18.86	21.80	15.6%
7	04/16/1999	21.01	17.75	-15.5%	8	08/15/2000	18.15	24.97	37.6%
9	03/24/2005	24.52	24.03	-2.0%	10	08/11/2006	24.07	25.00	3.9%
11	05/25/2007	24.52	9.19	-62.5%	12	05/08/2009	15.94	?	
	Average			**-16.4%**		**Average**			**22.3%**
	Median			**-8.8%**		**Median**			**15.6%**

Chart 35: WIPSI Price and Yield
1989-2009

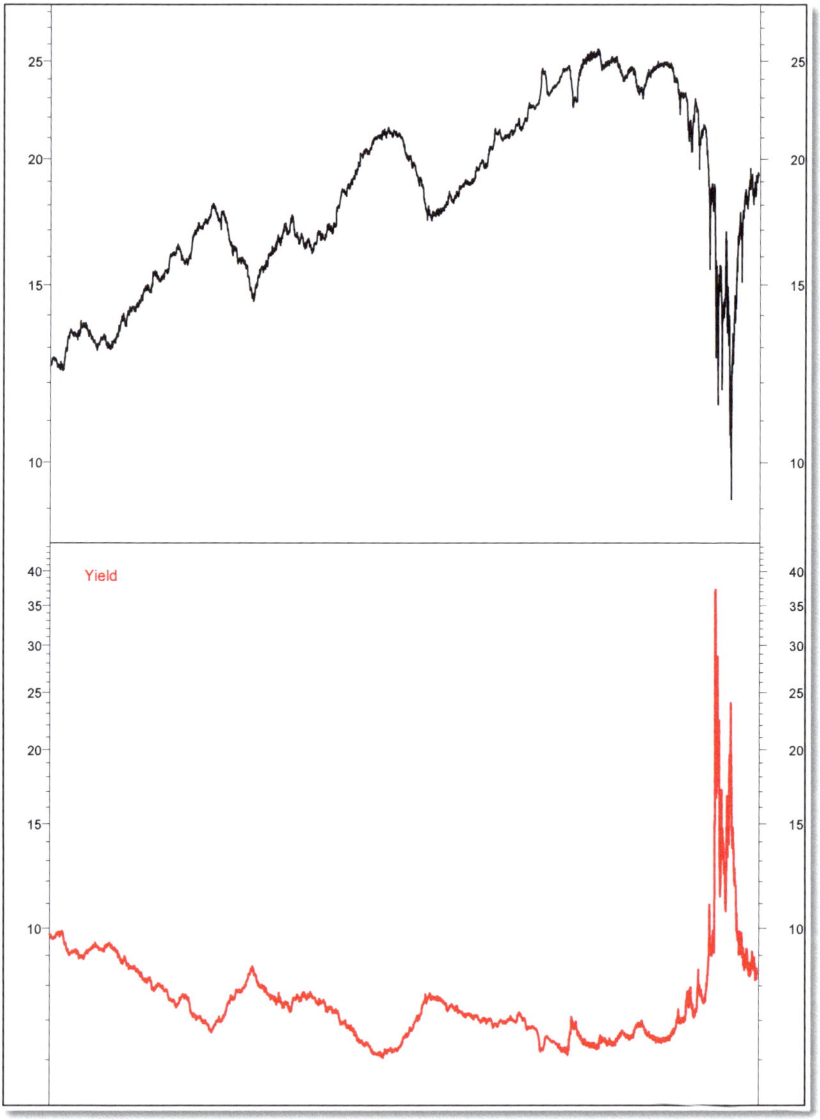

Created in MetaStock from Equis International

to the lack of preferred-stock derivatives. The best course of action during bear markets is to simply reduce exposure to preferred securities by cutting individual position sizes by 25% to 50% and reallocate to fixed-income holdings or cash.

Finally, remember that this indicator was wrong 17% of the time over the past 20 years, and other types of investment analysis can be useful in confirming a change in the trend of the preferred-stock market and thus to filter out failed 40-week simple moving average signals. Several other effective indicators are presented later in this chapter.

SHOPPING FOR THE BEST INVESTMENT YIELD

In Chapter 2, it was demonstrated why it is important for income investors not exclusively to invest in just one type of investment but rather to shop for the best rate of return throughout the investment universe during bullish times.

While it is true that all income investments are generally affected by the level and direction of interest rates, each type is greatly influenced by different, independent factors. For instance, Treasury bonds are more affected by the buying and selling of U.S. government debt by the central banks of other countries. Tax-exempt municipal bonds are heavily influenced by changes in federal and state tax laws. Corporate financial projections can generally affect the valuations of preferred stocks and corporate bonds.

As a portfolio's current income holdings mature or are called, investors should be comparing the yields of different types of income vehicles in hopes of finding the best price for the replacement investments. A common, easy-to-use tool that helps make these evaluations more effective is a yield spread chart.

YIELD SPREAD CHART

Interest rate and bond yield charts are typically found in financial publications and websites. They are similar to price charts except that investment yields have an inverse relationship to an index price (CHART 35). In other words, when the WIPSI price (black line) index goes down, the WIPSI yield (red line) component goes up and vice versa.

Many investors try to spot opportunities by simply comparing the yield charts of various income investments over a short period of time. While this

CHART 36: Yield Spread, WIPSI Minus DJCBA
1989-2009

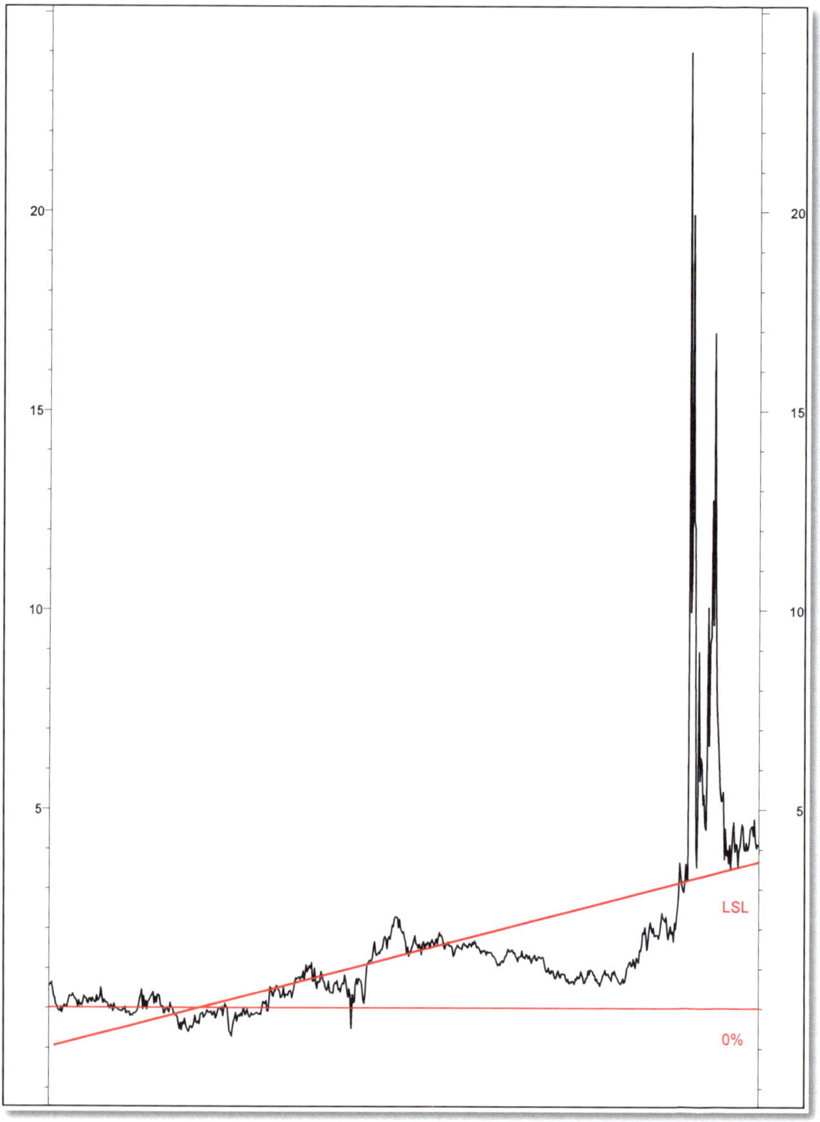

Created in MetaStock from Equis International

is a good preliminary step, seasoned investors also use yield spread charts for a more thorough analysis of the historical relationships between income investments, and to answer the question "Which investment medium will the best individual investment choices come from at this time?"

To construct a yield spread chart, simply subtract the yield of the index of interest from another benchmark. I also suggest using regression lines with the least square calculation (red line on chart) to pinpoint the mean yield and the high-to-low range (variance). For example, to show a preferred stock yield comparison to corporate bonds, subtract the Winans International Preferred Stock (WIPSI) dividend yield from the interest yield of the Dow Jones Corporate Bond Average (DJCBA) (CHART 36).

An analysis of yield charts revolves around the concept of relative change where both yields could be declining (or rising) at the same time but one yield is declining (or rising) farther and faster than the other. Simply put, investment opportunities will present themselves when the yield spread chart is at a high level.

The following pages show the 20-year yield spread charts and summary table of the preferred-stock market versus other income investment indices. Due to the extreme volatility of preferred stocks during 2008, the yield charts have been "cropped" to better magnify the current data.

TABLE 13: 20-Year Preferred Stock Yield Spreads
1989-2009

Chart Number/Name	Mean	High (year)	Low (year)
37. WIPSI Yield	7.6%	31% (2008)	6.0% (1998)
38. WIPSI–BAA Corporate Bonds	1.3%	30% (2008)	-2.1% (1991)
39. WIPSI–AA Corporate Bonds	2.4%	32% (2008)	-0.7% (1999)
40. WIPSI–Muni Bonds	3.1%	31% (2008)	0.8% (1992)
41. WIPSI–T-bonds (10yr)	4.4%	34% (2008)	0.1% (1994)
42. WIPSI–90-day T-bills	6.0%	30% (2008)	0.7% (1989)

CHART 37: WIPSI Yield
1989-2009

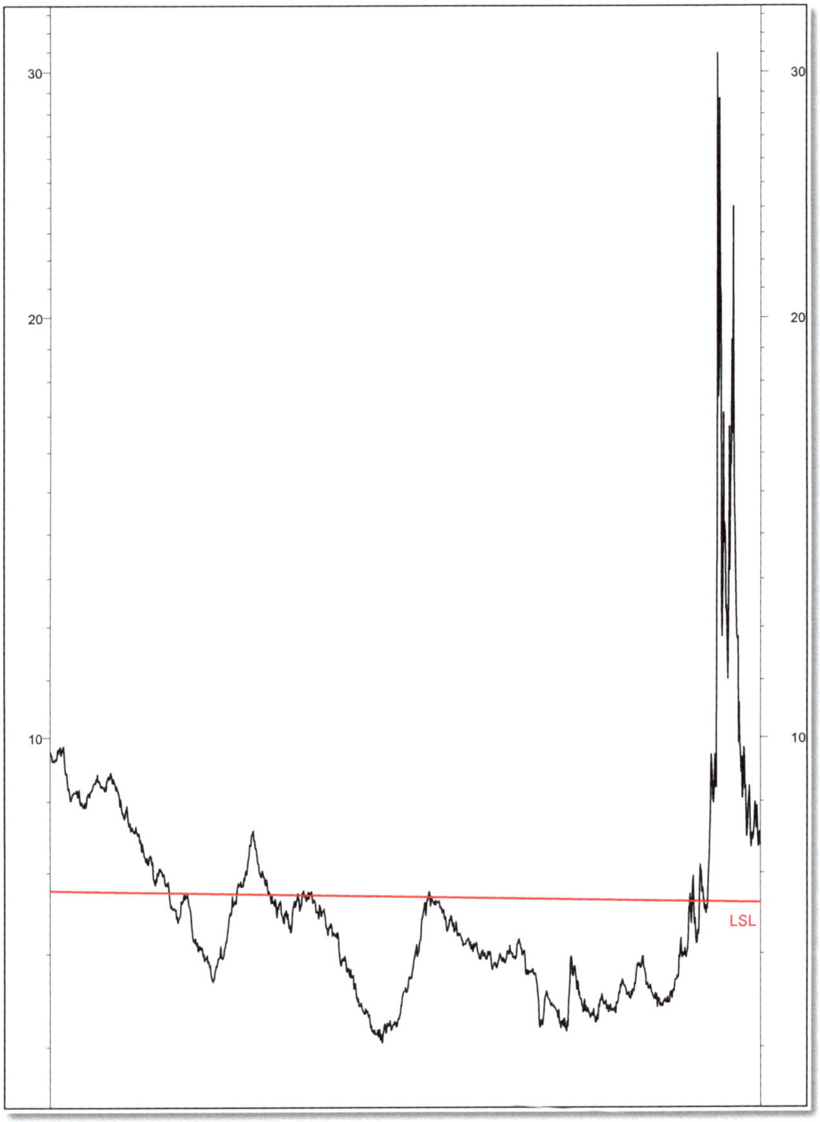

CHART 38: Yield Spread, WIPSI Minus Mid-Grade Bonds
1989-2009

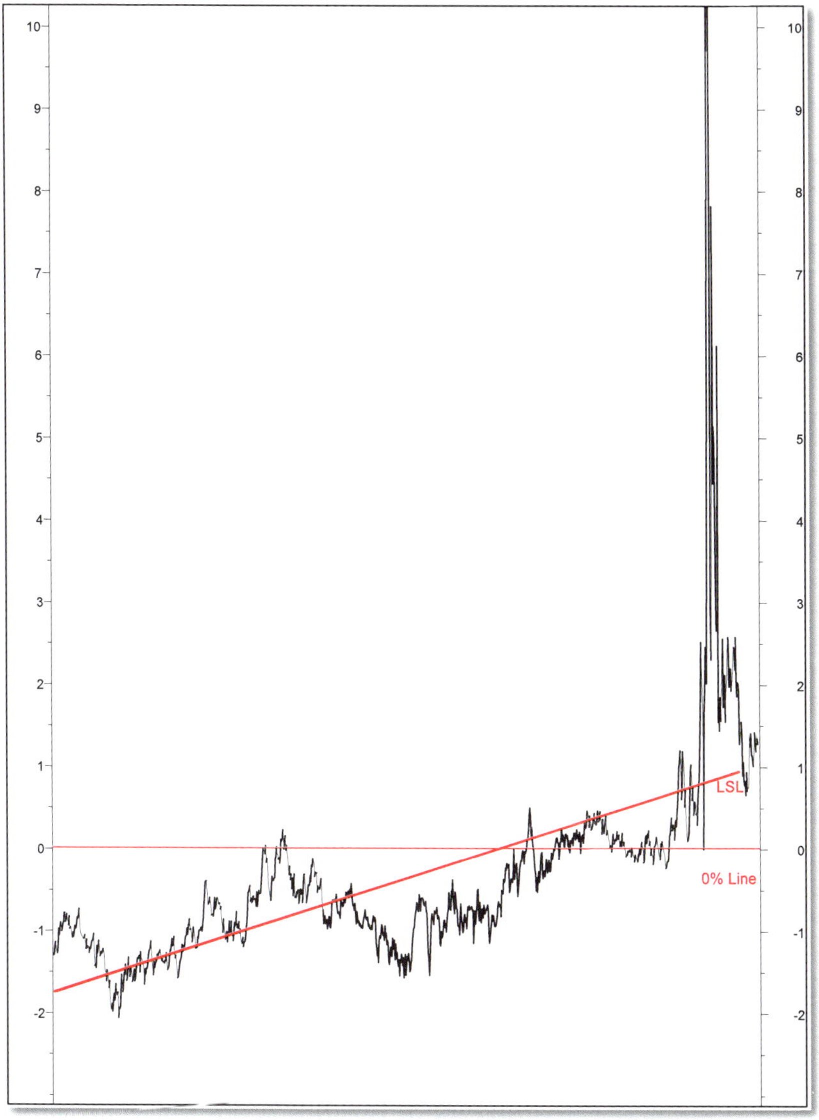

Created in MetaStock from Equis International

Chart 39: Yield Spread, WIPSI Minus High Grade Bonds
1989-2009

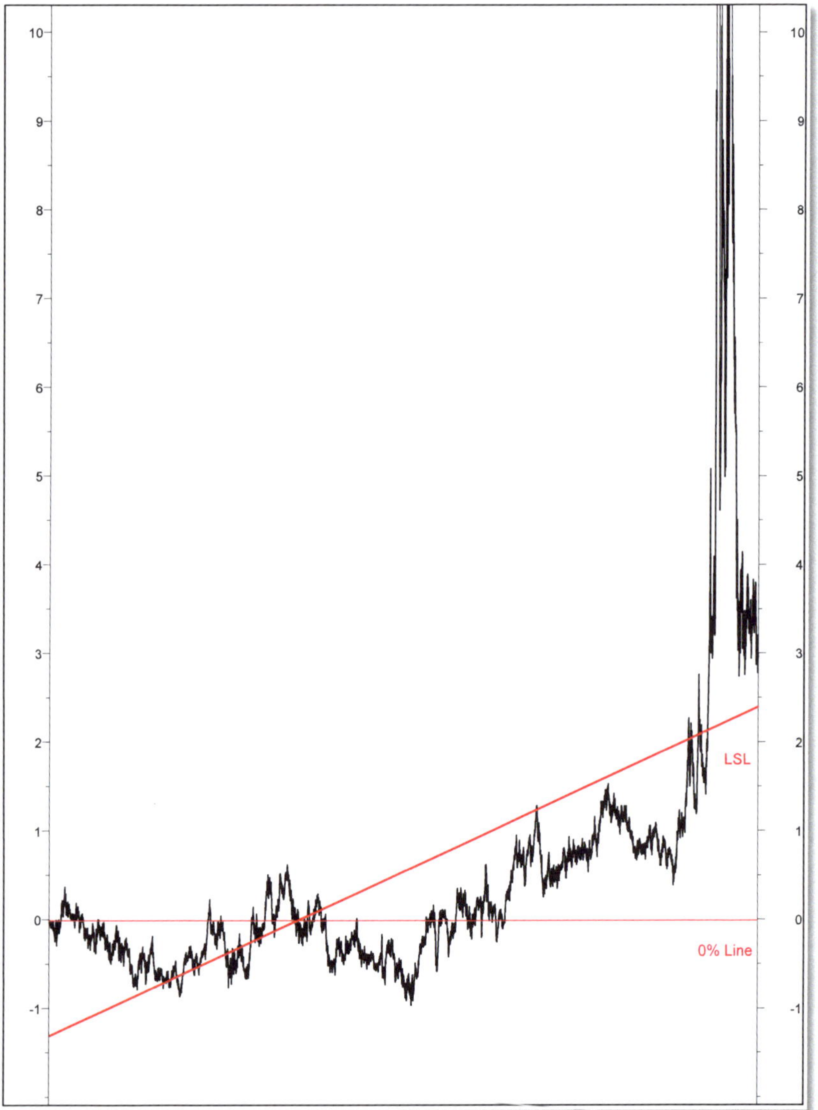

CHART 40: Yield Spread, WIPSI Minus U.S. Municipal Bonds
1989-2009

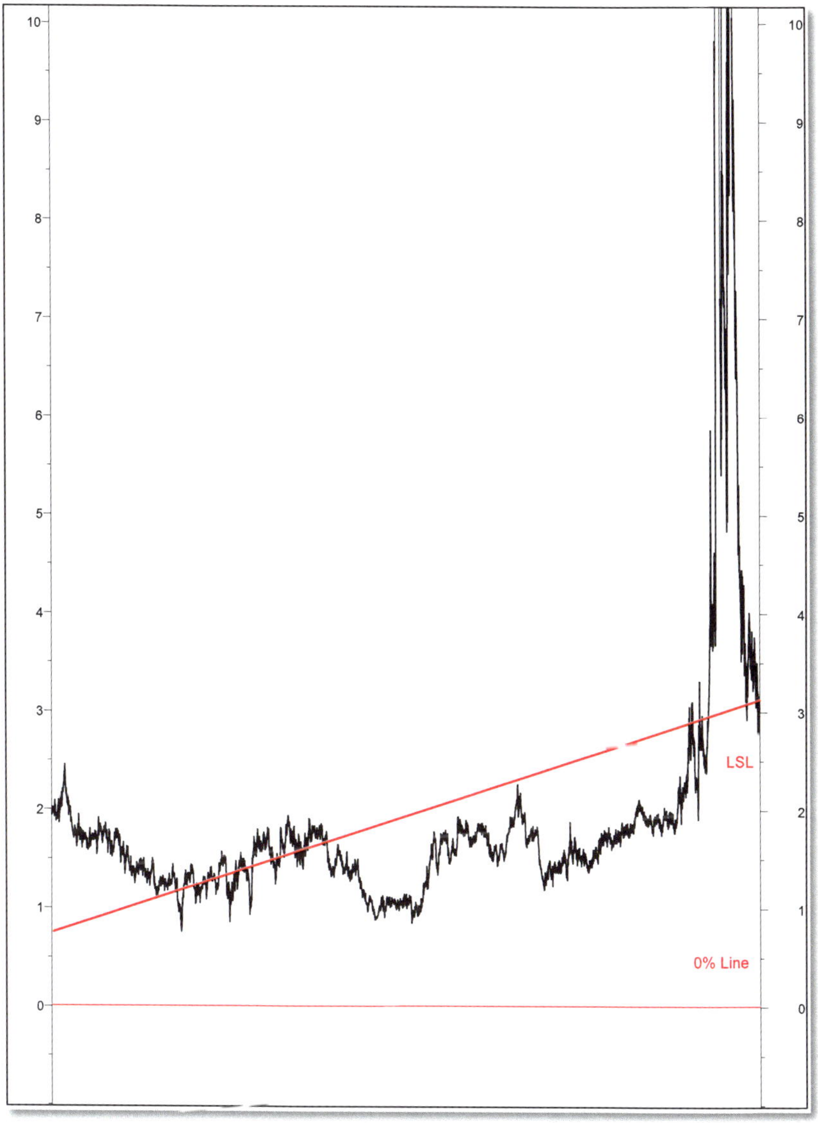

Created in MetaStock from Equis International

Chart 41: Yield Spread, WIPSI Minus T-Bonds (10-Year)
1989-2009

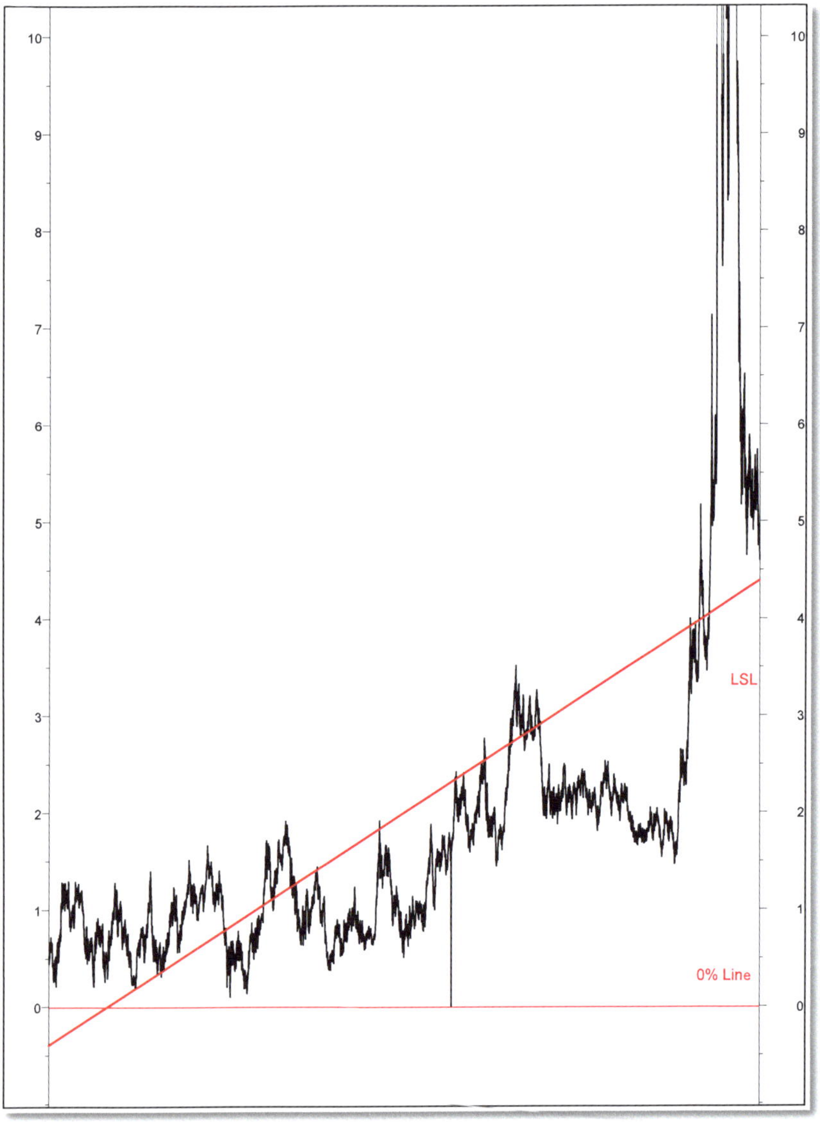

CHART 42: Yield Spread, WIPSI Minus T-Bills (3-Month)
1989-2009

Created in MetaStock from Equis International

While many of the charts look similar, the relationship between preferred stocks and these other types of income investments is not static and thus constantly changing.

For example, the WIPSI yield has averaged 7.6% and is higher than all the other investment yields reviewed by as much as 6% and as little as 1.3%.

The highest spread for all the securities versus preferred stocks was in 2008, when they had a more severe sell-off relative to other income investments, and it was a great time to buy preferred stock versus other income investments.

On the other hand, throughout the 1990s there were clearly times when the preferred yield spreads were very low and bonds offered better returns overall, such as in 1991 when the relative yield of WIPSI was (2.1%) versus mid-grade (BAA) grade corporate bonds.

Remember, not all income investments are the same, and sometimes an investment in one type of security would provide a better buying opportunity than another.

ADVANCED ANALYSIS OF THE PREFERRED-STOCK MARKET

There are literally hundreds of technical indicators. If you are new to technical analysis, please consider reading *Technical Analysis of the Financial Markets* by Murphy or *Technical Analysis Explained* by Pring to gain a better understanding of this type of analysis. Also, see the list of "Preferred Stock Information Sources" section in the back of this book (page 201).

The focus of this section is to find technical tools that aid in identifying changes in the long-term trend of the preferred-stock market (not timing signals for short-term trading). To lay the foundation for future research, this analysis focused on the common interpretation of signals (without filters), default settings on indicators were used, and overbought and oversold signals from the same indicator were analyzed independently from one another. Last, each indicator was studied individually without confirmation from the other indicators examined.

CHART TYPES

Before investors jump into charting, they need to determine which type of chart best serves their purposes. To minimize price gaps that can be caused when several components of WIPSI do not trade on a given day, weekly data are recommended for preferred-stock charting. In comparing bar and candlestick charts, it became evident that candlestick charts were more useful for both price and yield studies due to their ability to better display inter-week high and low points (CHARTS 43-44).

Since individual preferred-stock components of WIPSI pay dividends at different times, a year-end total return chart can be used for direct annual performance comparisons with other investment types (CHART 45).

WIPSI meets the requirements needed to conduct effective technical analysis, because long-term oversold (support) and overbought (resistance) points were easy to identify during the 20 years studied.

CHART 43: WIPSI $ Candlestick Chart
1989-2009

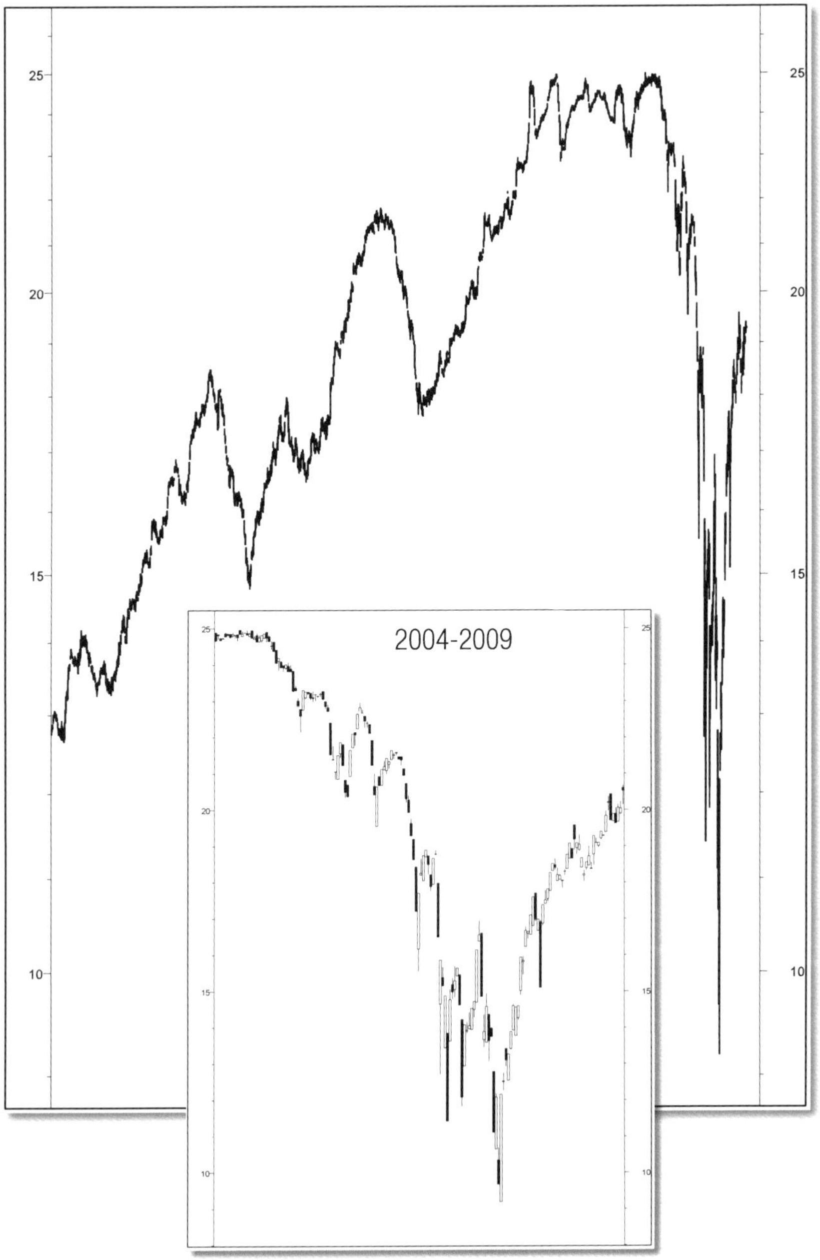

CHART 44: WIPSI % Candlestick Chart
1989-2009

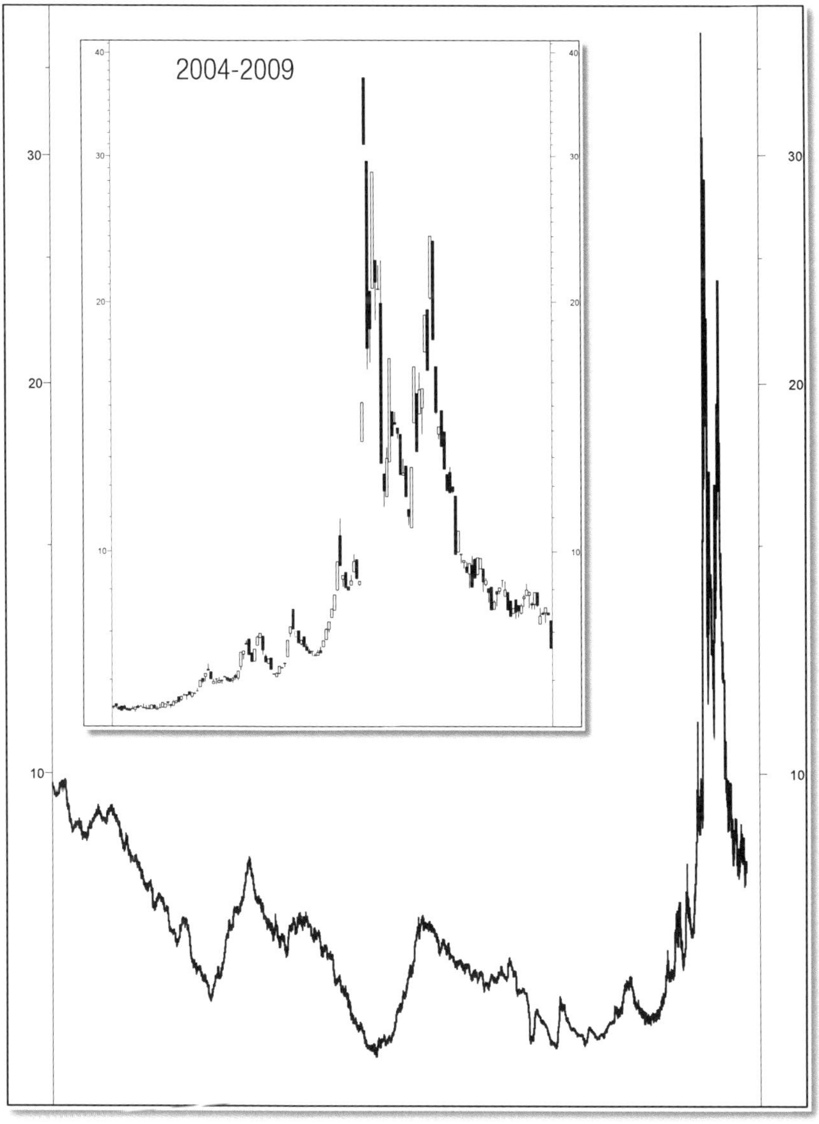

Created in MetaStock from Equis International

CHART 45: WIPSI Total Return
1989-2009

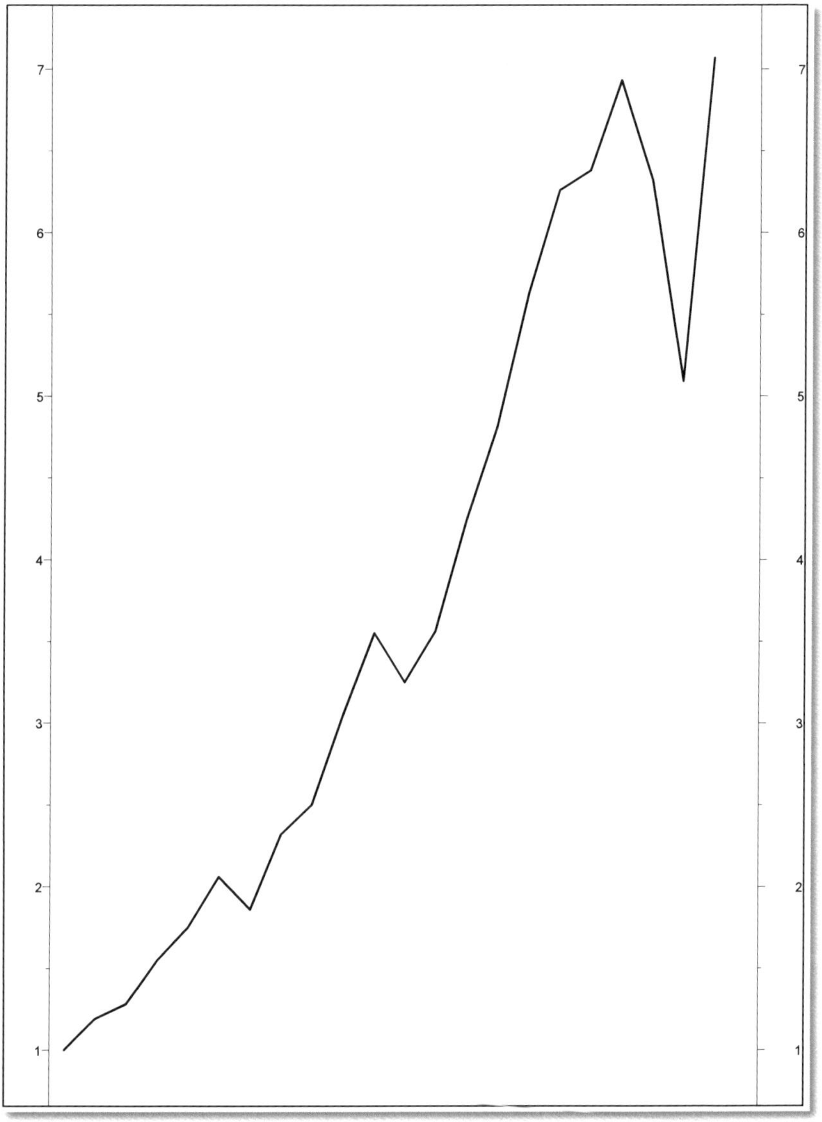

Created in MetaStock from Equis International

TRENDLINE ANALYSIS

The oldest and most commonly used type of technical analysis is charting. Due to the long time frame covered, both linear (red) and logarithmic (gray) trendlines were use to help identify long-term support and resistance points (Chart 46).

Signal Rules

- A signal occurred at the first closing price at the trend line.
- Both oversold and overbought signals were observed.
- Trendlines periodically crossed through candle shadows and bodies to have more contact points and best fit the trendline to the data.

Conclusions (Chart 46, Table 14)

There were three levels of support and four points of resistance or trend breakdown signals. WIPSI had an average advance of 42% over 207 weeks from previous support and an average decline of 26% over 58 weeks from resistance. The signals were accurate in indicating the future trend. Most of the total move was captured with the oversold signals occurring within 0.7% of the declining move's low and overbought signals occurring within –0.8% of the advancing move's high. Last, chart analysis was very effective in indicating trend change in 2008 and thus avoiding much of the bear market's decline.

Chart 46: WIPSI $ Trendlines
1989-2009

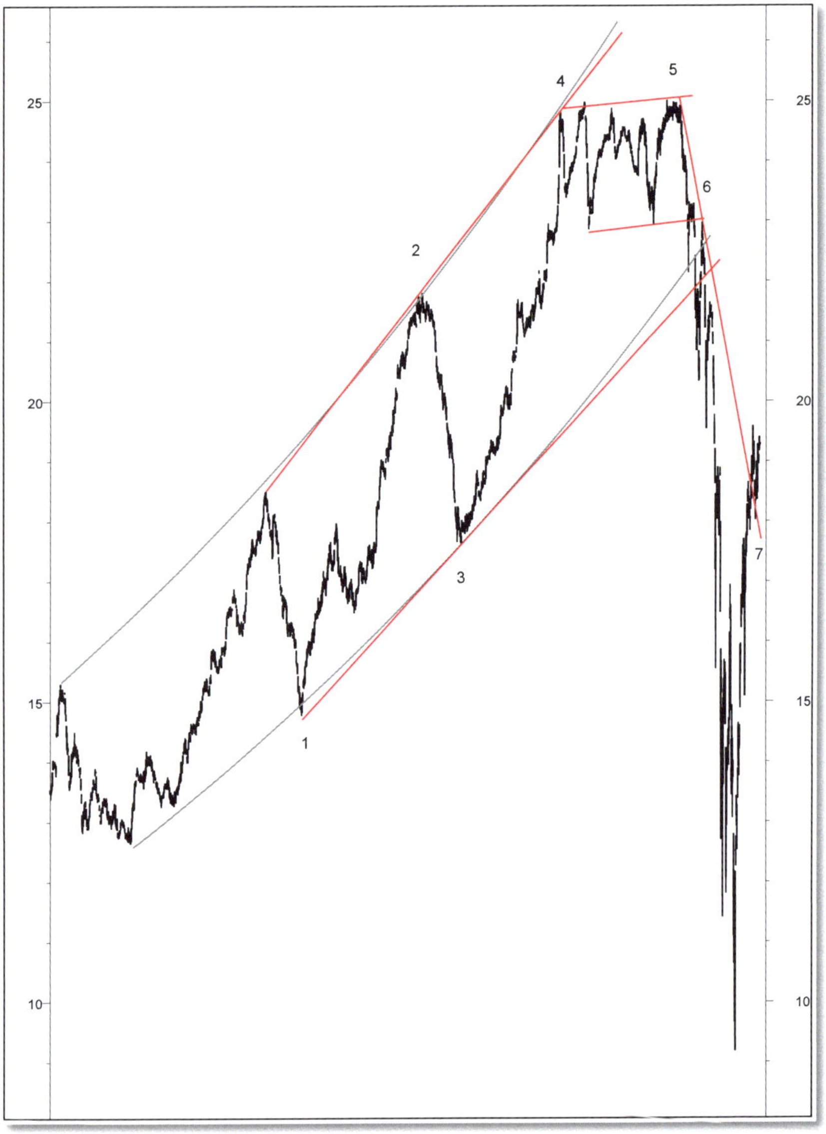

Created in MetaStock from Equis International

TABLE 14: Trendlines Analysis
1989-2009

Support / Breakout

Signal	Price	Signal Date	Total Advance	%	Date	Duration Weeks	Low	%	Date	Duration Weeks
1	14.93	02/09/1994	21.52	44.1%	10/16/1998	244	14.79	-0.9%	12/30/1994	-46
3	17.74	03/17/2000	24.65	39.0%	06/20/2003	170	17.64	-0.6%	03/17/2000	0
7	18.31	09/11/2009								
Average				41.5%		207		-0.8%		-23
Median				41.5%		207		-0.8%		-23

Resistance / Breakdown

Signal	Price	Signal Date	Total Decline	%	Date	Duration Weeks	High	%	Date	Duration Weeks
2	21.52	10/16/1998	17.34	-18.0%	03/17/2000	74	21.80	1.3%	12/04/1998	-7
4	24.64	06/20/2003	22.86	-7.2%	05/14/2004	47	24.97	1.3%	03/26/2004	-40
5	25.00	12/08/2006	20.33	-18.7%	12/21/2007	54	25.00	0.0%	12/08/2006	0
6	22.97	02/01/2008	9.19	-60.0%	03/13/2009	58	22.97	0.0%	02/01/2008	0
Average				-26.0%		58		0.7%		-12
Median				13.4%		56		0.7%		-4

CHART 47: WIPSI $ Regression Lines
1989-2009

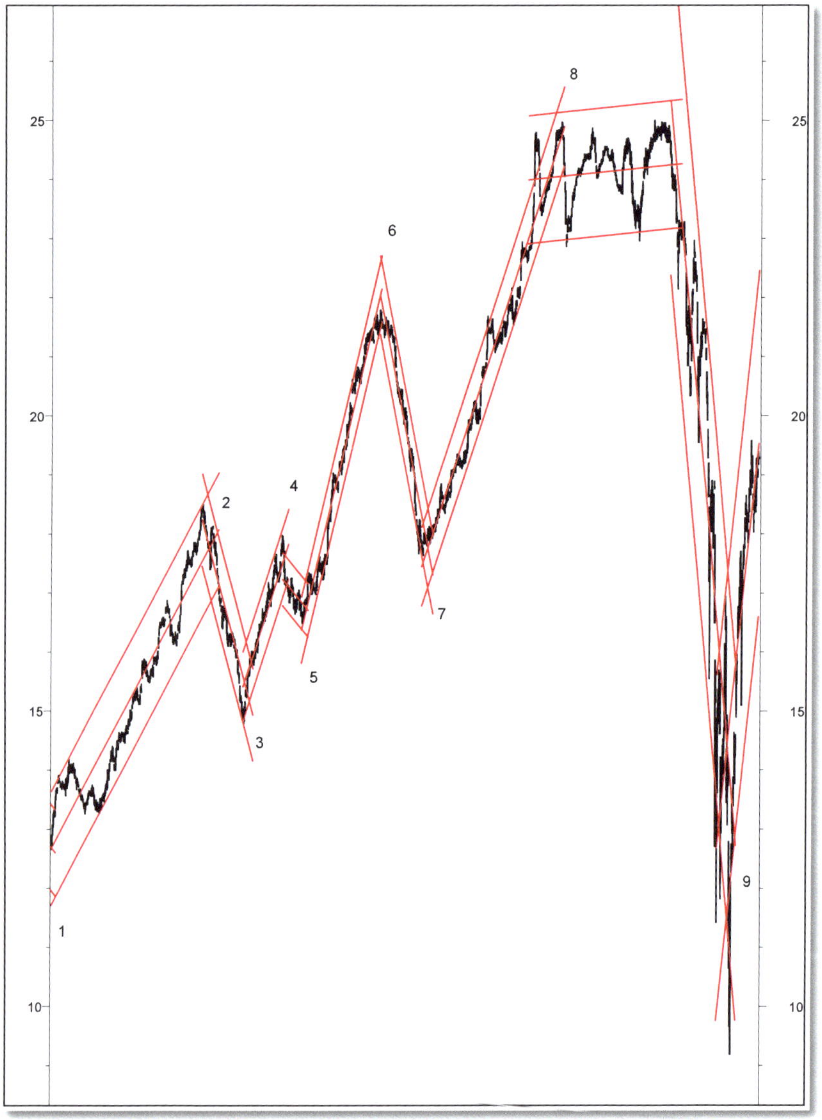

Created in MetaStock from Equis International

REGRESSION LINES AND STANDARD ERROR CHANNELS

Since chart analysis can be very subjective, a statistical way to draw trendlines was used for identifying intermediate trends. Least squares linear regression analysis is a statistical tool that plots a line through prices so as to minimize the distance between the prices and the resulting trendlines. Standard error analysis is helpful in determining where the "extremes" lie and thus help identify trends and changes in trends.

Signal Rules

- A signal occurred at the first crossing of the standard error channel by the full body of a candlestick.
- Channels had to be at least one year in length.
- Repeat signals were ignored.
- The high or low of the previous move was used as the start point of the next channel.
- Both oversold and overbought signals were observed.

Conclusions (Chart 47, Table 15)

There were five oversold and four overbought signals. The index had an average advance of 27% over 135 weeks from an oversold signal and an average decline of 24% over 94 weeks from an overbought signal. Although most of the signals were accurate in indicating a future change in WIPSI's direction, the overbought signals had a tendency to give up too much "ground." Excluding 2008, the overbought signals gave up –5% from the move's high (approximately 33% of the entire decline). This indicator was effective in maneuvering through the four-year trading range of 2003 to 2007 and the bear market of 2008.

TABLE 15: WIPSI Regression and Standard Error Analysis 1989-2009

Oversold (OS)

Signal	Price	Signal Date	Total Advance	%	Date	Duration Weeks	Low	%	Date	Duration Weeks
1	13.65	07/07/1989	18.50	35.5%	10/15/1993	223	12.66	-7.3%	05/19/1989	7
3	15.91	04/14/1995	17.98	13.0%	02/09/1996	43	14.79	-7.0%	12/30/1994	15
5	18.09	06/13/1997	21.80	20.5%	12/04/1998	77	16.49	-8.8%	09/13/1996	39
7	18.05	06/30/2000	24.97	38.3%	03/26/2004	195	17.64	-2.3%	03/17/2000	15
9	15.84	05/15/2009								
Average				26.8%		135		-6.4%		19
Median				28.0%		136		-7.1%		15

Overbought (OB)

Signal	Price	Signal Date	Total Decline	%	Date	Duration Weeks	High	%	Date	Duration Weeks
2	16.99	04/08/1994	14.79	-12.9%	12/30/1994	38	18.50	8.9%	10/15/1993	25
4	16.95	04/19/1996	16.49	-2.7%	09/13/1996	21	17.98	6.1%	02/09/1996	10
6	21.53	12/24/1998	17.64	-18.1%	03/17/2000	64	21.80	1.3%	12/04/1998	3
8	23.79	04/30/2004	9.19	-61.4%	03/13/2009	254	24.97	5.0%	03/26/2004	5
Average				-23.8%		94		5.3%		11
Median				-15.5%		51		5.5%		8

MOVING AVERAGES

Earlier in this chapter, the 40-week simple moving average (with the high-low band as a filter) was shown as an effective tool in market analysis of preferred stocks. This moving average wasn't randomly selected. An extensive study was conducted to find the best moving average for intermediate and long-term studies. In analyzing the simple, weighted, and exponential moving averages for 10-, 20-, and 40-weeks, the first objective was to identify the moving averages that had the fewest false signals without the need for filters that could delay the effectiveness of a signal for long-term trend change. As can be seen on CHARTS 48-49, the 10- and 20-week moving averages would require significant filters such as the two-week or 3% penetration rule to be a useful long-term indicator. In reviewing the various types of 40-week moving averages on CHARTS 50-51, the simple moving average had 46% fewer false signals than either the weighted or exponential moving averages and thus was the focus of this chapter.

Signal Rules

- A crossing of the Friday closing price above or below the simple moving average.
- Both oversold and overbought signals were observed.

CHART 48: WIPSI $ 10-Week Moving Average
1989-2009

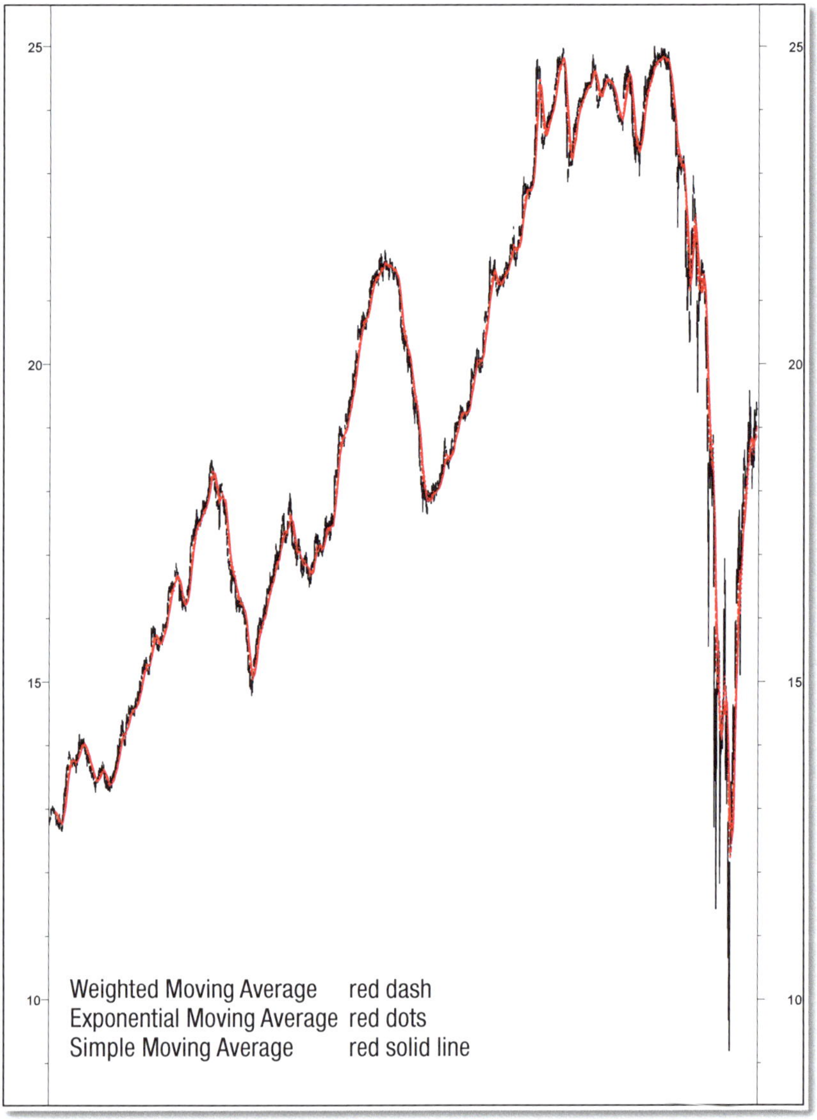

CHART 49: WIPSI $ 20-Week Moving Average
1989-2009

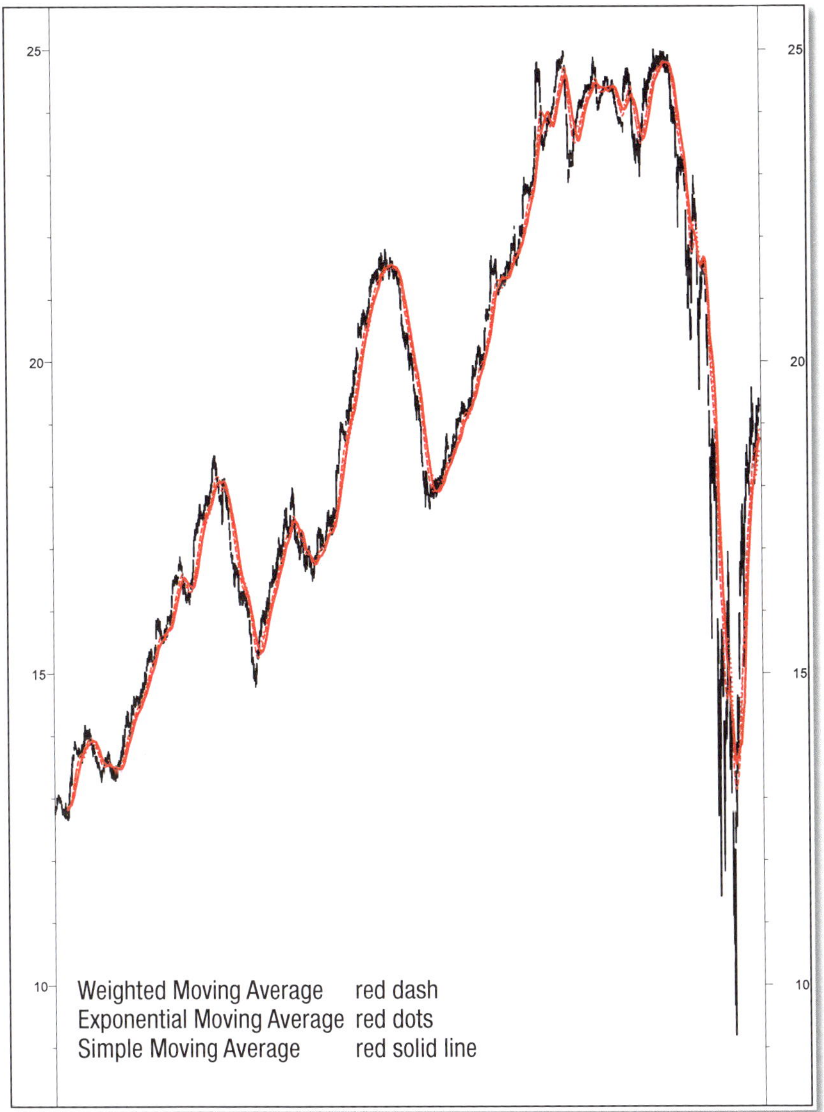

Created in MetaStock from Equis International

CHART 50: WIPSI $ 40-Week Moving Average
1989-2009

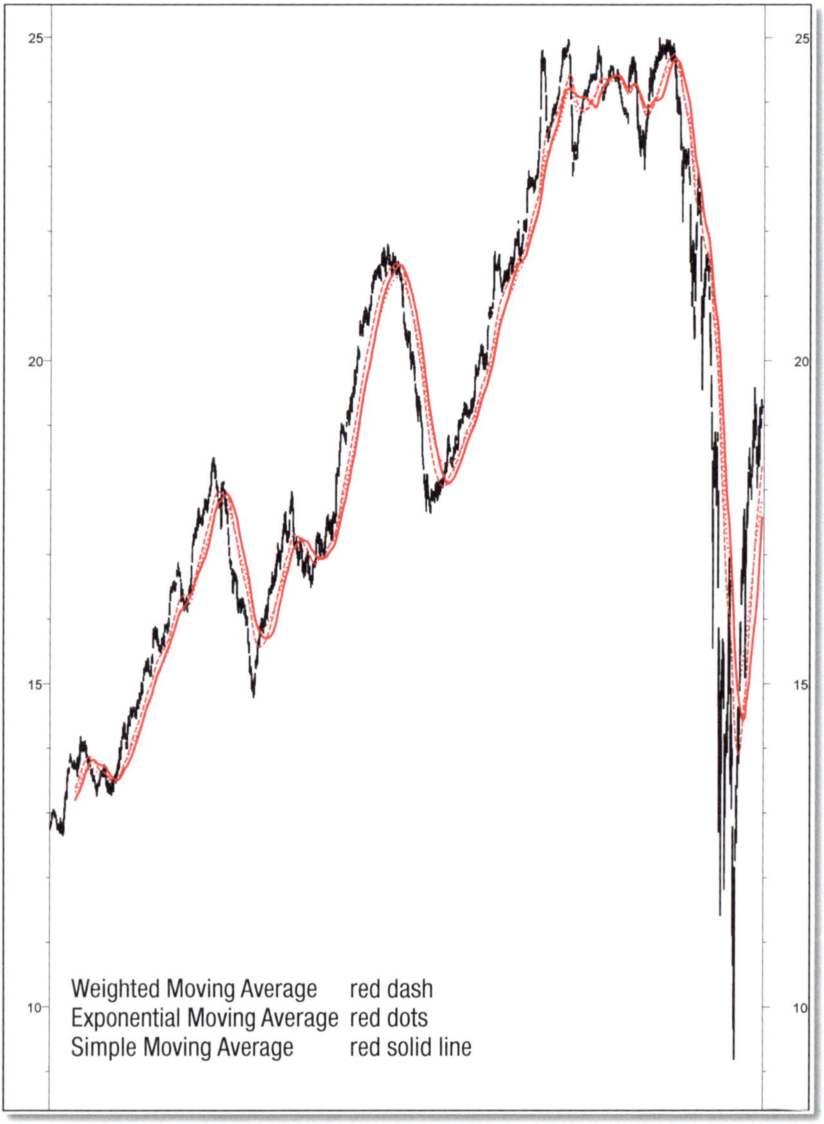

CHART 51: WIPSI $ 40-Week Moving Average Analysis
1989-2009

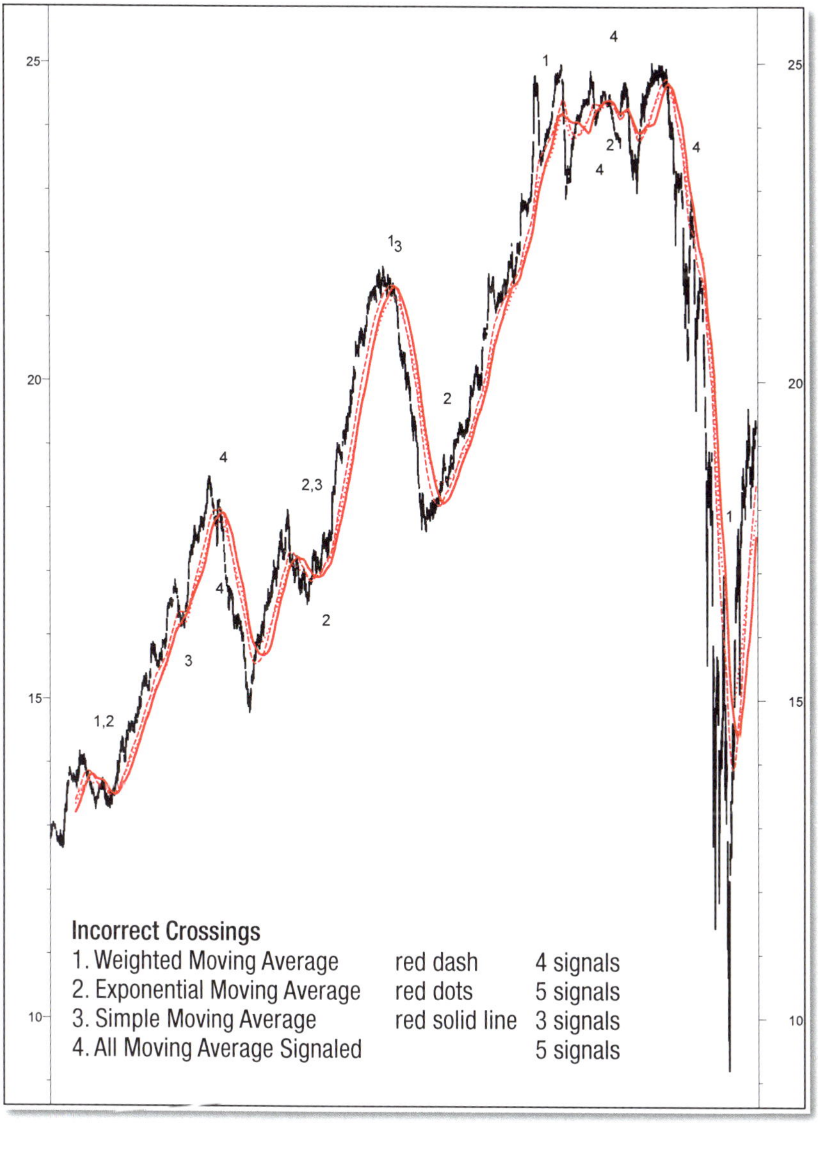

Created in MetaStock from Equis International

TABLE 16: $ 40-Week Simple Moving Average Without Filter
1989-2009

Oversold (OS)										
Signal	Price	Signal Date	Total Advance	%	Date	Duration Weeks	Low	%	Date	Duration Weeks
1	13.08	06/02/1989	14.18	8.4%	11/24/1989	25	12.66	-3.3%	05/19/1989	2
3	13.55	11/23/1990	18.49	36.5%	10/23/1993	152	13.27	-2.1%	10/19/1990	5
5	15.89	03/10/1995	17.86	12.4%	02/09/1996	48	14.76	-7.7%	12/30/1994	10
7	17.23	11/08/1996	21.80	26.5%	12/04/1998	108	16.48	-4.6%	09/13/1996	8
9	18.19	08/04/2000	24.97	37.3%	03/26/2004	190	17.75	-2.5%	03/17/2000	20
11	24.11	10/01/2004	24.87	3.2%	02/11/2005	19	22.93	-5.1%	05/14/2004	20
13	24.35	05/20/2005	24.56	0.9%	07/15/2005	8	24.02	-1.4%	04/01/2005	7
15	24.28	01/06/2006	24.70	1.7%	02/24/2006	7	23.67	-2.5%	12/30/2005	1
17	24.07	08/11/2006	25.00	3.9%	12/08/2006	17	22.96	-4.6%	06/30/2006	6
19	15.94	05/08/2009								
Average				**14.5%**		**64**		**-3.8%**		**9**
Median				**8.4%**		**25**		**-3.3%**		**7**

Overbought (OB)										
Signal	Price	Signal Date	Total Decline	%	Date	Duration Weeks	Low	%	Date	Duration Weeks
2	13.75	03/02/1990	13.27	-3.5%	10/19/1990	33	14.18	3.0%	11/24/1989	14
4	17.75	12/31/1993	14.76	-16.8%	12/30/1994	52	18.49	4.0%	10/23/1993	10
6	17.02	04/12/1996	16.48	-3.2%	09/13/1996	22	17.86	4.7%	02/09/1996	9
8	21.35	03/05/1999	17.75	-16.9%	03/17/2000	54	21.80	2.1%	12/04/1998	13
10	24.05	04/23/2004	22.93	-4.7%	05/14/2004	3	24.97	3.7%	03/26/2004	4
12	24.14	03/25/2005	24.03	-0.5%	04/01/2005	1	24.87	3.0%	02/11/2005	6
14	24.40	08/05/2005	23.67	-3.0%	12/30/2005	21	24.56	0.7%	06/24/2005	6
16	23.79	03/31/2006	22.96	-3.5%	06/30/2006	13	24.70	3.8%	02/24/2006	5
18	24.65	05/18/2007	9.19	-62.7%	03/13/2009	95	25.00	1.4%	12/08/2006	23
Average				**-11.5%**		**29**		**2.6%**		**9**
Median				**-3.5%**		**22**		**3.0%**		**8**

Conclusions (Chart 52, Table 16)

There were nine oversold and nine overbought completed signals. The indicator had an average advance of 15% over 64 weeks from an oversold signal and an average decline of 12% over 29 weeks from an overbought signal. Although most of the signals were accurate in indicating the future trend, sideways-moving markets proved problematic for moving averages and caused most of the false signals. The 40-week simple moving average was the most effective indicator studied in dealing with the bear market of 2008.

Chart 52: WIPSI $ 40-Week Simple Moving Average Signals 1989-2009

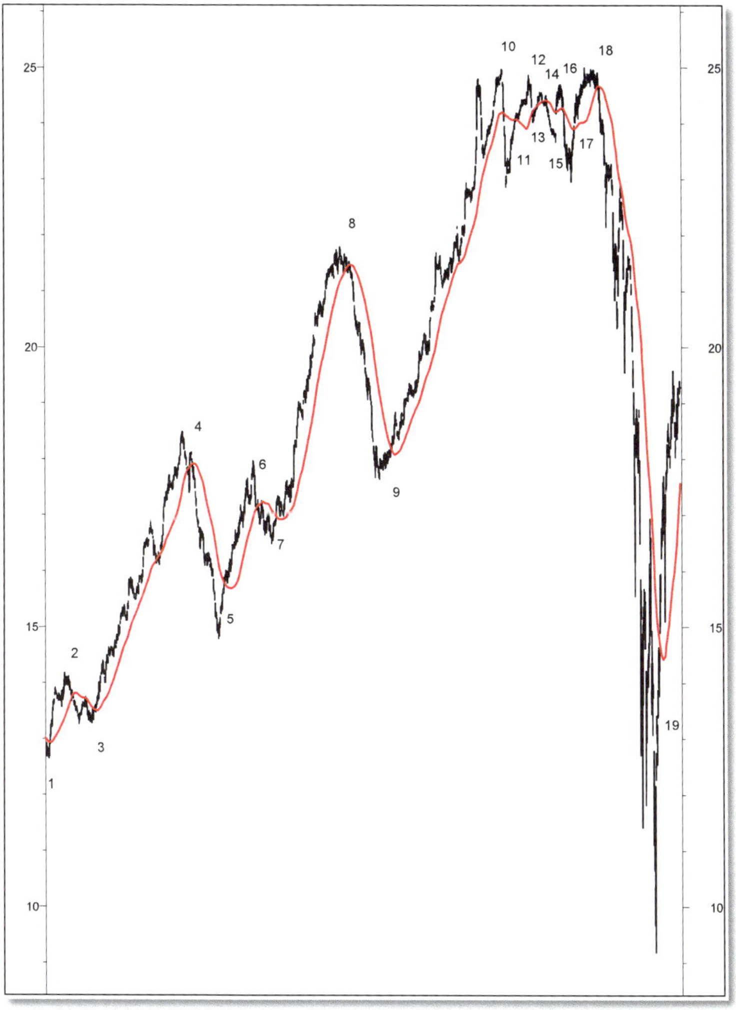

Created in MetaStock from Equis International

CHART 53: WIPSI $ Wilder RSI Oscillator
1989-2009

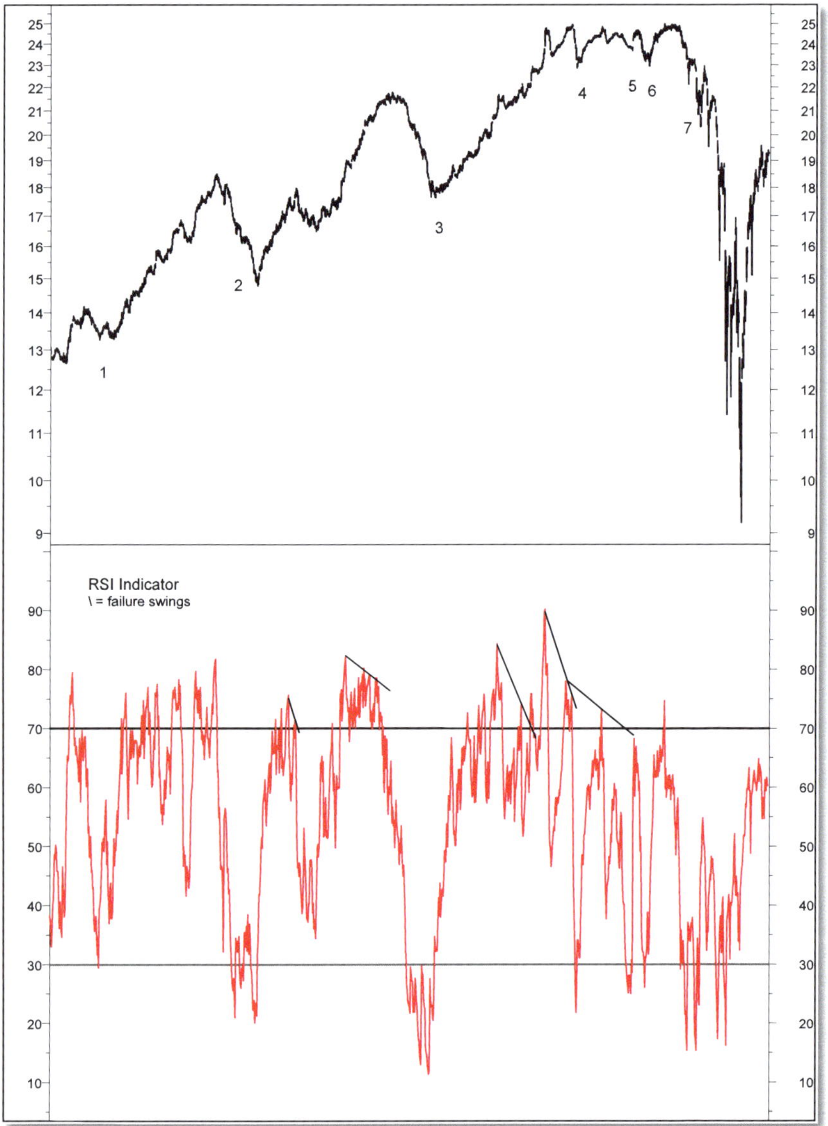

Created in MetaStock from Equis International

WILDER RELATIVE STRENGTH (RSI)

Oscillators are primarily used in "sideways" markets (i.e., trading ranges) when moving averages are flat and can cause many false signals. For the purposes of this preferred-stock study, the primary focus was on whether this indicator would prove useful for providing oversold signals in all market conditions.

Signal Rules

- The 14-periods calculation was used.
- The focus was placed on 70 and 30 crossover points.
- First signal was used with secondary signals only for confirmation.
- Only oversold signals were observed.

Conclusions (Chart 53, Table 17)

There were seven oversold signals that were followed by an average advance of 18% over 100 weeks. While most signals were accurate in indicating the future market uptrends, it performed terribly during the 2008 bear market due to its premature oversold signal in August 2008. It should be noted that if median calculations are used to reduce the effect of the two bad signals, the signal was only 2% from the market's low. Although not the focus of this study, there were five overbought failure swings identified, with four occurring at or near significant tops.

TABLE 17: WIPSI $ Wilder RSI Analysis 1989-2009

Oversold (OS)										
Signal	Price	Signal Date	Total Advance	%	Date	Duration Weeks	Low	%	Date	Duration Weeks
1	13.43	05/25/1990	18.51	37.8%	10/15/1993	177	13.26	-1.3%	05/18/1990	1
2	16.77	05/20/1994	21.80	30.0%	12/04/1998	237	14.78	-11.9%	12/30/1994	-32
3	18.01	03/24/2000	24.97	38.6%	03/26/2004	209	17.64	-2.1%	03/17/2000	1
4	23.33	05/28/2004	24.87	6.6%	02/11/2005	37	22.86	-2.0%	05/14/2004	2
5	23.78	12/30/2005	24.70	3.9%	02/24/2006	8	23.68	-0.4%	12/30/2005	0
6	23.35	05/19/2006	25.00	7.1%	12/08/2006	29	22.96	-1.7%	06/30/2006	-6
7	23.31	08/24/2007	23.31	0.0%	08/24/2007	0	9.19	-60.6%	03/13/2009	-81
Average				**17.7%**		**100**		**-11.4%**		**-16**
Median				**7.1%**		**37**		**-2.0%**		**0**

STOCHASTIC INDICATOR

Stochastic Indicator is a popular oscillator used by active traders, and is much more sensitive than Wilder's RSI to short-term market volatility.

Signal Rules

- The 14-period k% calculation with the three-period average of d% was used.
- The focus was placed on 80 and 20 values with a crossing of the %k line below and above the %d line.

Conclusions (Chart 54)

The Stochastic Indicator was much more active than the Wilder RSI Indicator, with approximately 81 individual signals. With such a large number of signals and no filtering, the number of false signals made this an unreliable long-term indicator for WIPSI. For example, while it did provide a buy signal near the bottom of the recent bear market, it also gave three false oversold signals from December 2007 through March 2009.

Chart 54: WIPSI $ Stochastic Indicator 1989-2009

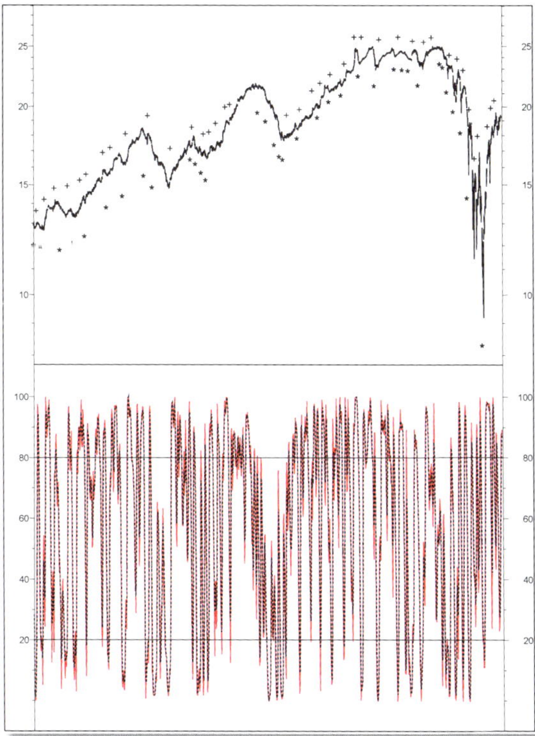

Created in MetaStock from Equis International

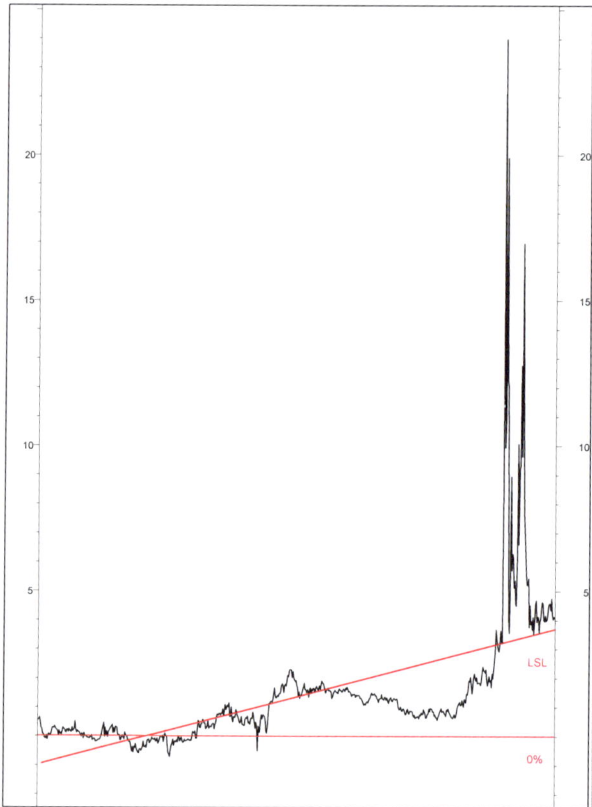

CHART 55:
Yield Spread,
WIPSI % Minus
DJ Corporate Bond
Average %
1989-2009

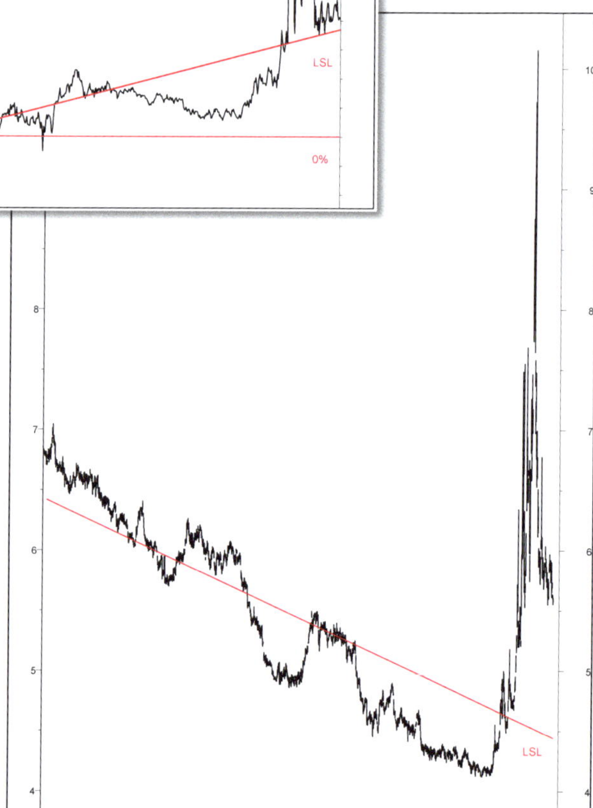

CHART 56:
Price Ratio,
WIPSI $ Minus
DJ Corporate Bond
Average $
1989-2009

Charts created in
MetaStock from
Equis International

RATIO CHARTS

Ratio charts are a means to measure the relative strength between two indices, similar to the yield spread charts discussed earlier in this chapter, except price is measured (not yield). The analysis revolves around the concept of relative change where both indices could be declining (or rising) at the same time, and yet one index is declining (or rising) farther and faster than the other. Simply put, investment opportunities present themselves when a ratio chart is at extreme levels.

The two charts on the opposite page show the 20-year relationship between the Winans International Preferred Stock Index and the Dow Jones Corporate Bond Average. The first chart is the yield spread chart and the second is ratio (price) chart (Charts 55-56). Notice how both confirmed the tremendous buying opportunity preferred stocks were in 2008 and early 2009. Simply put, ratio charts can be an excellent confirming indicator to yield spread signals.

In a final comment about market analysis, while it is important to use various indicators for conformation of trend changes, remember the K.I.S.S. (Keep It Simple, Stupid) principle. In the era of information overload, there is a tendency for investors to have their computer screen look like the instrument panel of a modern-day fighter jet. Remember, the key objective of market analysis is to identify changes in the current long-term trend of an index early enough to make timely changes to an investment portfolio. Select enough indicators to be effective, efficient, and profitable in your market analysis and STOP!

In the next chapter, the focus shifts to investment analysis and how to select individual preferred stocks and thus answering the questions "What preferreds should be bought or sold?" and "When should they be bought or sold?"

Chapter 5

Investment Analysis of Preferred Stocks

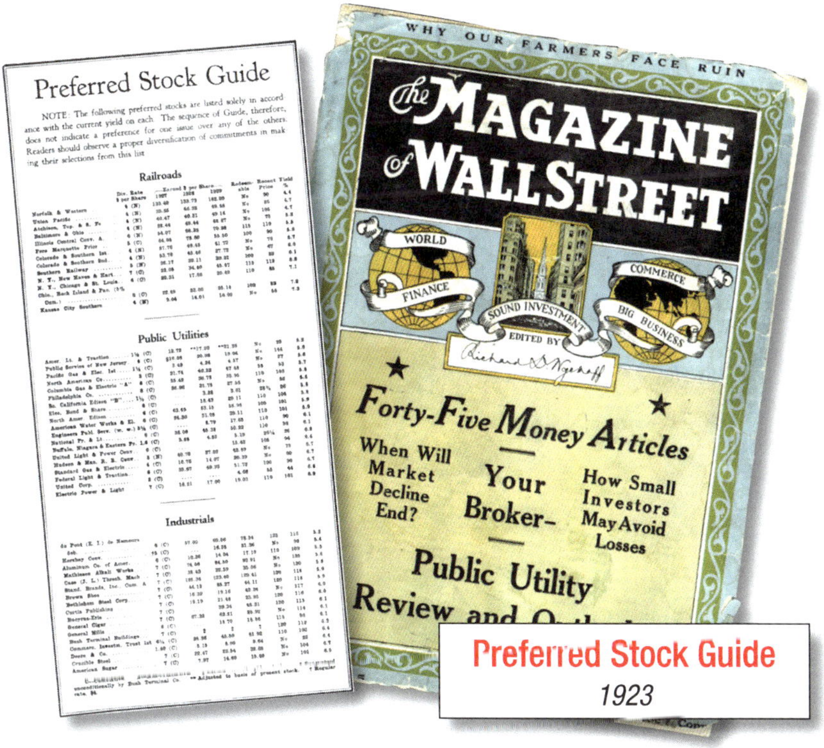

Preferred Stock Guide
1923

"There's a unique security that's kind of like Dr. Jekyll and Mr. Hyde of Wall Street: preferred stock."
Investing Online For Dummies, Krantz, 2008

"Preferred stocks have been around since the 1800s and have been a key holding for many old-money families."
USA Today (5/13/2008)

"Investors disappointed with low yields on bonds and savings accounts, but too scared to jump into common stocks, are taking a close look at preferred stock."
USA Today (2/24/2009)

Chapter 4 provided the tools to answer the strategic question "When is the investment climate right to invest in preferreds?" This chapter focuses on the tactical issues surrounding which individual preferred stocks to buy, and when they should be bought or sold.

During the numerous book lectures I've done since *Preferreds* was first published in January 2007, many experienced investors have tole me that they are confused about how they should analyze preferred stocks. My response is always the same. View them as a third type of security that, from an asset allocation standpoint, fits between common stocks and corporate bonds. If they have trouble picturing this, then they should take the word "stocks" out and just call them "preferreds."

Preferreds investment selecting is made harder by the fact that there are very few choices in preferred-stock mutual funds. In fact, Morningstar's Principia software shows only seven mutual funds (or exchange-traded funds) that have at least 75% of their holdings in preferred stocks. Worst yet, most of those funds concentrate their investments in financial preferreds, which led to disastrous results during the bear market of 2008 as many of their holdings filed bankruptcy and the underlying preferred stocks were deemed worthless.

Preferred-stock research uses both technical and fundamental analysis. Technical focuses on the price trend of the preferred security and whether it's overbought or oversold. Fundamental analysis deals with the preferred issuer's overall financial condition and risks that could affect the company's ability to pay dividends in the future.

Both types of analysis come into play in evaluating individual corporate securities and coming up with an investment candidate list.

ISSUER SCREENING PROCESS

As seen in Chapter 3, there are many ways to locate investment opportunities.

One time-tested method to find companies that have preferred stocks currently issued is through Value Line's "Investment Analyzer" software. This company was founded in 1931 and provides cost-effective, reliable financial data on 6,834 corporations.

This software has a screening criterion called "Preferred Equity" that allows you to quickly identify companies with preferred-stock issues.

Presently, there are 727 issuers of preferred stocks in Value Line's database (Table 18).

Since preferred stocks are a medium to long-term investment, with most of their total return generated from dividend income, the initial financial research focus is on the safety of future dividend payments. This type of research is ideally suited for fundamental analysis in that it focuses on finding companies that have a high probability of honoring their financial commitments to their stakeholders now and in the future. This is done by evaluating a series of financial statistics on the preferred issuer such as: revenue and earnings growth (past and projected), common dividend growth (past and projected), balance sheet strength, etc., to weigh the strengths and weaknesses of the company when compared to other candidates.

Similar to bond analysis, you're primarily looking for negative factors, so don't make the initial screening criteria too restrictive. It should be a "pass or fail" type of evaluation based on your investment risk tolerance. Remember, the focus of this financial analysis should be on issues that could affect the company's ability to pay dividends in the future.

In the example below, a simple Value Line screen that focused on larger companies with any sales and earnings growth narrowed the investment candidates from 727 to 54.

Table 18: Value Line Preferred Stock Screen

	Field Name	Logic	Value	Number
				6834
If	Preferred Equity	>=	1	727
And	Market Cap $ (mil)	>=	1000	153
And	Proj Sales Growth Rate	>=	1	63
And	Proj EPS Growth Rate	>=	1	54

A common mistake made by investors is to assume that a good common-stock investment must be a good preferred-stock choice as well. Many of the popular websites and investment newsletters are designed for common-stock evaluation to find the financially strongest, fastest-growing companies yet are useless for preferred-stock selection. Remember what

Table 19: Fundamental Analysis Checklist

Corporate Bond and Preferred-Stock Negative Factors

MAJOR	
Private Company	(no financial information)
Common-Stock Price	Within 10% of 52-week low
Common-Stock Price	Below $3.00 per share
Earnings	Three years of losses out of the past five years
Cash Flow	Three years of losses out of the past five years
Earnings	Big losses in the past two years
Cash Flow	Big losses in the past two years
Earnings	Losses expected this year
Cash Flow	Losses expected this year
Debt to Capital Ratio	More than 75%
Shares Outstanding	High levels of dilution
Value Line Safety Rating	4 or 5
Value Line Financial Strength	Less than B
Negative Accounting Notes and Other Concerns	
MINOR	
Revenue	Reduction expected this year
Earnings	Reduction expected this year
Cash Flow	Reduction expected this year
Common Dividends	Reduction expected this year
Operating Margin	Less than 7%
Long-term Debt vs. Equity	10% increase in debt and reduction in equity
Common Dividend Payout Ratio	Greater than 100%
Revenue	Less than $500 million
Value Line Earnings Predictability	Less than 60
S&P Rating	Lowered

legendary investor Warren Buffett said about choosing investments, "The business world is divided into a tiny number of wonderful businesses well worth investing in at any price, and a huge number of mediocre businesses where bonds (or preferreds) are often better investments than common stocks."

Notice that ratings were not used in the above screen. I feel that most agency ratings are useless as criteria in selecting investments. Experienced investors build their own rating system. On the opposite page is an example of what Winans International uses to financially evaluate and monitor the issuers of preferreds and fixed income (TABLE 19).

Regular Financial Monitoring

Reviewing the issuer's fundamentals with pre-established financial standards (similar to TABLE 19) needs to be done quarterly, or if there are unusual corporate developments that could affect an individual preferred stock. This process allows investors to keep apprised as to the financial strength of the preferred-stock issuers, and it can be useful in confirming a technically based decision to sell an existing investment.

SECURITY SCREENING PROCESS

Similar to fixed-income analysis, there is an additional step in the screening process of the investments themselves, because many companies have more than just a single preferred issue trading at a time. (By the way, PreferredsOnline.com is a great source for information on individual preferred-stock specifics.) The following items need to be reviewed before selecting investment candidates:

Preferred Type

Issuers use many different types of preferred stocks (convertible, floating rate, noncumulative, hybrids, etc.), and you need to know what you are investing in.

Longevity of the Security

Preferreds are issued at different times. Remember that preferred stocks with less than two years of trading history are difficult to technically analyze.

Call Conditions

Generally speaking, preferred stocks that are priced above par value and can be called within one year should be avoided. There are preferred issues whose call dates are continuous and in perpetuity. Since many of these securities had been trading for a long time (and there have been no corporate announcements to the contrary), they will probably not be called in the foreseeable future.

Trading Activity and Volume

It is safe to assume that preferred stocks do not trade as frequently as the common shares of the same issuer. Similar to the issues surrounding thinly traded fixed-income investments or micro cap stocks, there can be days in which there is no trading activity at all in preferreds. For technical indicators and trading rules to be reliable, a minimum level of daily volume needs to be established for selected preferred investments. As a general rule, avoid preferred stocks that often have reoccurring days of little or no trading activity.

Data Integrity

In a perfect world, all web-based financial information is useful and correct. Unfortunately, the quantity and speed of information produced by today's impatient world has often sacrificed quality and accuracy. Leading data vendors regularly produce incorrect data on preferred stocks, so price and volume figures need to be screened by the investor for inaccuracies. It is recommended that an investor use several different data vendors for preferred-stock information. Simply put, don't use raw price and volume data in technical analysis. Remember, GIGO—garbage in, garbage out!

Many investors skip the security screening process and end up with unexpected investment losses. Remember that not all preferred issues are the same, and the security screening process is as important as reviewing the financial strength of the issuing company when selecting investment candidates.

INVESTMENT CANDIDATE SELECTION

Three traditional preferred stocks were selected for continued analysis:

DTE Energy	Series A, 7.80% dividend, symbol: DTE.A	(CHART 57)
JP Morgan Chase	Series J, 7.00% dividend, symbol: JPM.J	(CHART 58)
Public Storage	Series Z, 6.25% dividend, symbol: PSA.Z	(CHART 59)

They were selected for the following reasons:

- They passed the previously mentioned issuer and security selection process.
- They are from industries that have historically issued preferred stocks (i.e., DTE Energy—utility, JP Morgan Chase—finance, Public Storage—real estate).
- They have continuously traded since 2005 and display typical trading characteristics found in most preferred stocks.
- They are issuers used in the Winans International Preferred Stock Index (WIPSI).

TECHNICAL ANALYSIS OF PREFERRED STOCKS

Technical analysis is a superior method for establishing actionable buy and sell points. Why? Investment prices generally move in long trends and price leads most economic and financial data.

Before an investor starts investing in preferred stocks, a disciplined approach to deal with their inherent volatility is needed. In Chapter 3, it was revealed that the overall preferred-stock market has negative years between 28% and 25% of the time, so when to invest preferreds is as important as what preferred stocks to buy or sell.

Technical analysis has two purposes:

- To identify the current price trend of the preferred stock candidates.
- How the current values in the preferred candidates compare with the overall preferred-stock market.
- Identify points where the securities would be-oversold and overbought.

CHART 57: DTE Energy Series A (DTE.A)
2005-2009

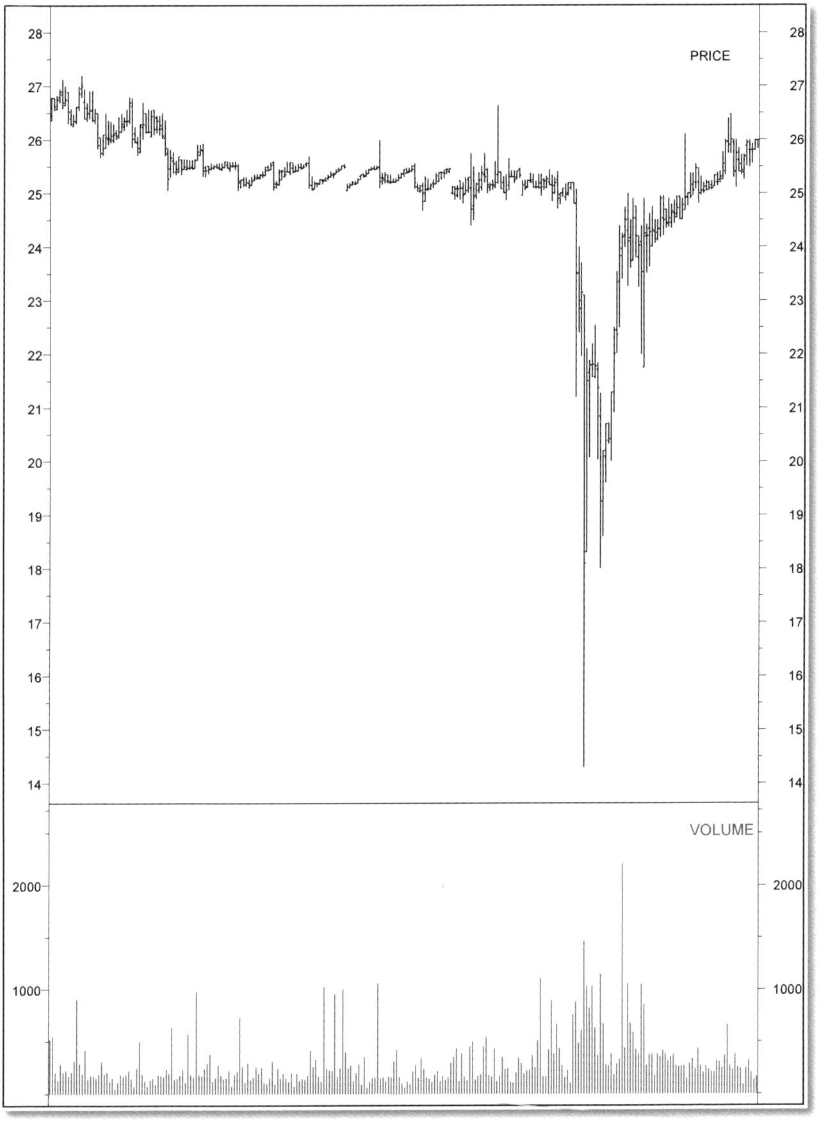

CHART 58: JP Morgan Chase Series J (JPM.J)
2005-2009

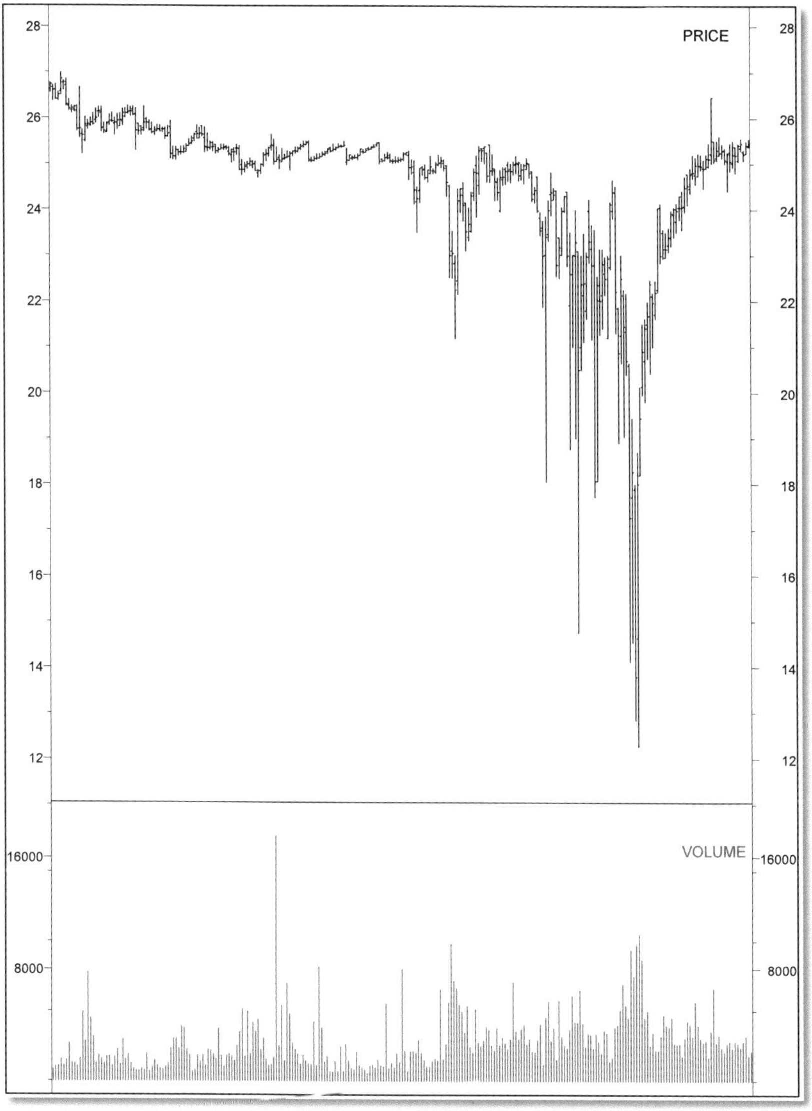

Charts created in MetaStock from Equis International

CHART 59: Public Storage Series Z (PSA.Z)
2005-2009

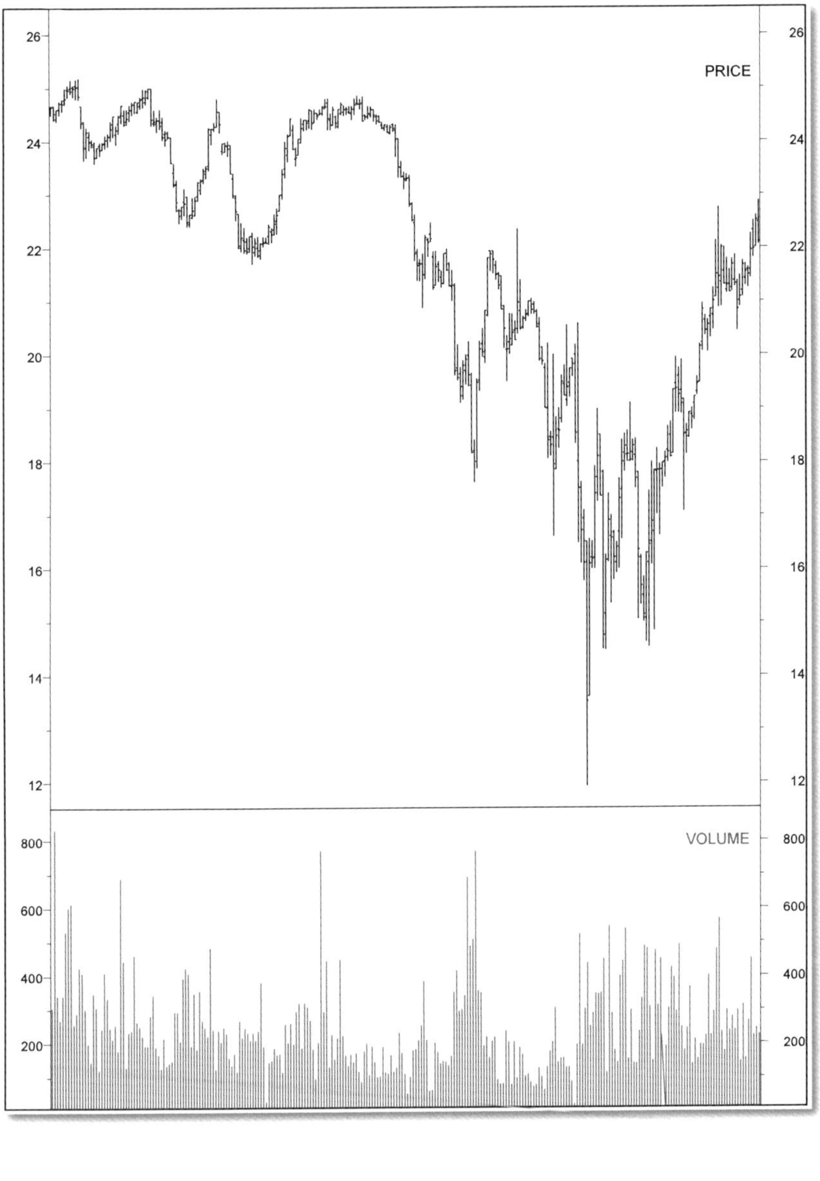

There are literally hundreds of technical indicators and methodologies. If you are new to technical analysis, please consider reading *Technical Analysis of the Financial Markets* by Murphy or *Technical Analysis Explained* by Pring to gain a better understanding of this type of analysis. Also, see the "Preferred Stock Information Sources" section in the back of this book (page 201).

Using Stock Charts

As discussed in the market analysis section, charts of past investment prices and yields are an effective and efficient way to evaluate the price history of an investment. Coupled with indicators that identify overbought and oversold conditions, charts are a timely way to analyze many different types of investments in many different financial conditions.

Charts are also easy to use. The vertical scale is the price (upper graph) and volume (lower graph) of the stock, and the horizontal scale displays time. Any point on the chart represents the price and volume level of the stock at a given point in time and thus represents a graphic history of the investment.

Candlestick charts are more useful due to their ability to better display inter-day high and low points. As with common stocks, trading volume can be used to help confirm price movement. Special attention was placed at resistance (overbought), support (oversold) where volume was expected to decline at low levels, as selling pressure subsides, and at high points that could not advance any further.

It should be finally noted that preferred stocks have a high frequency of price gaps caused by their large quarterly dividend payments.

Winans Preferred Stock Chart

The standard candlestick was modified for preferred stocks to be more effective in the following ways (Chart 60):

- To reduce price gapping and V price patterns caused by illiquidity or dividends, the charts are set in a logarithmic format for a weekly period and cover a five-year period. The candlestick format is perfect for this security because it identifies areas of support and resistance better than bar charts.

Chart 60: Winans Chart of DTE.A
2005-2009

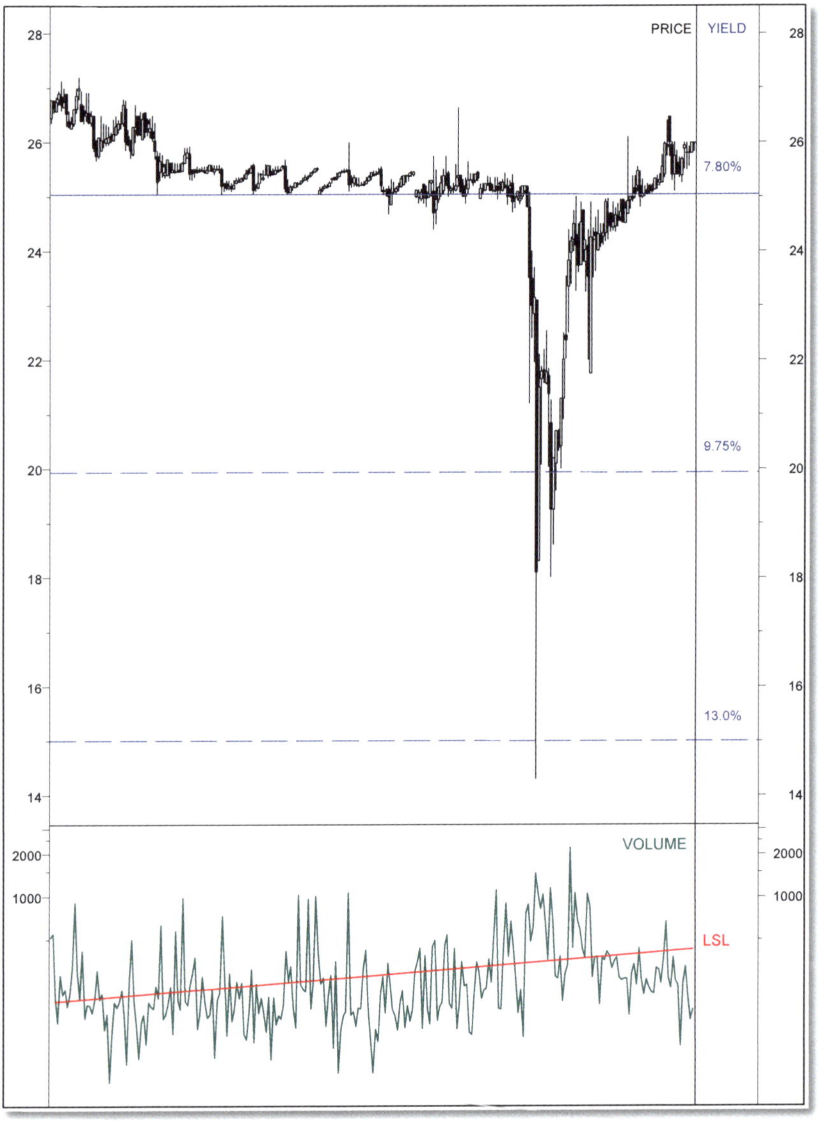

Created in MetaStock from Equis International

- Price and dividend yield scales are combined into one chart. Notice that the security's yield is stated for each $5 level on the right-hand side of the chart. Because it is important to look at the stock price and the level of dividend yield for each stock, this eliminates the need for constructing separate yield charts for each preferred stock.
- Volume on the bottom of the chart is also set in the logarithmic format and uses a least squares regression line (LSL red line) to better display high levels of volume.

Integrating Market Analysis

It is important to integrate market analysis into the investment evaluation process. As discussed in Chapter 4, market analysis will identify the preferred-stock market's current trend. If it is positive, this represents a good time to be looking for new investments. And if the trend is negative, caution is in order and investors might want to protect hard-won gains by taking profits.

One of the most effective trend indicators in preferred-stock market analysis is the 40-week simple moving average filtered with high and low price bands of the Winans International Preferred Stock Index (WIPSI) (Chart 61).

The general interpretation of this indicator is:

- The preferred-stock market is in an uptrend (i.e., bull market) if the Friday price of the index is trading above the moving average band.
- The preferred stock market is in a downtrend (i.e., bear market) if the Friday price of the index is trading below the moving average band.
- If the moving average is flat over an extended period, then the index is in a sideways trading range, going neither up nor down.
- A change of the index's trend is signaled by the Friday price of the index penetrating the moving average band. For example, if WIPSI drops below its moving average, then it has entered a new downtrend. The inverse situation signals a new uptrend.

CHART 61: WIPSI $ 40-Week Simple Moving Average Bands 2005-2009

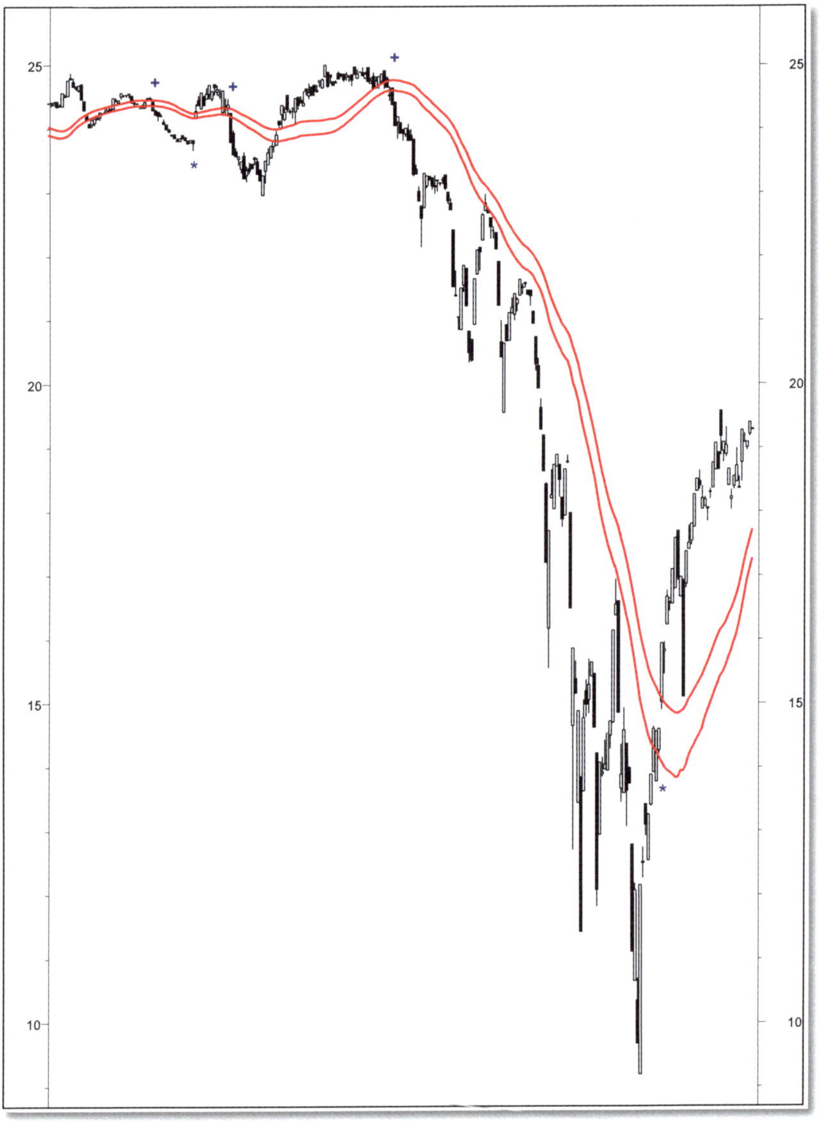

Created in MetaStock from Equis International

The periods in time when WIPSI was in a downtrend are marked as a red box on the individual preferred-stock charts to get a better feel of market conditions in relation to each security (CHARTS 62, 63, and 64).

It can be easily seen that negative market conditions put downward price pressure on all three stocks, yet not to the same extent. While the JPM.J and PSA.Z both had corrections of approximately (51%) during the preferred-stock bear market in 2007-2008, DTE.A's loss was less (43%), and it made the bear market losses back faster than the other two stocks.

Clearly, an overall defensive strategy is needed when the preferred-stock market is in a downtrend. Unfortunately, there are limited defensive options for preferred stockholders during bear markets. Short selling is problematic due to the high costs associated with the strategy (margin costs plus the large dividends owed on the borrowed preferred shares). Hedging strategies are limited due to the lack of preferred-stock derivatives.

The best course of action during bear markets is to simply reduce exposure to preferred securities by cutting individual position sizes by 25% to 50% and reallocate to fixed-income holdings or cash.

The Ratio Chart

Ratio charts are a means to measure the relative strength between a preferred stock and the preferred-stock market (or another preferred stock).

This is similar to the yield spread charts discussed in the last chapter, except price is measured instead of yield. The analysis revolves around the concept of relative change where both prices could be declining (or rising) at the same time, but one price is declining (or rising) farther and faster than the other. Simply put, investment opportunities present themselves when a ratio chart is at extreme levels.

To construct a ratio chart, simply subtract the price of the target preferred stock from WIPSI (or different preferred stock). I also suggest using regression lines with the least square calculation (red line on chart) to pinpoint the mean price and the high-to-low range (variance). For example, to show a preferred-stock comparison to WIPSI, subtract the preferred-stock price from the price of the Winans International Preferred Stock Index.

Chart 62: DTE.A with Market Analysis
2005-2009

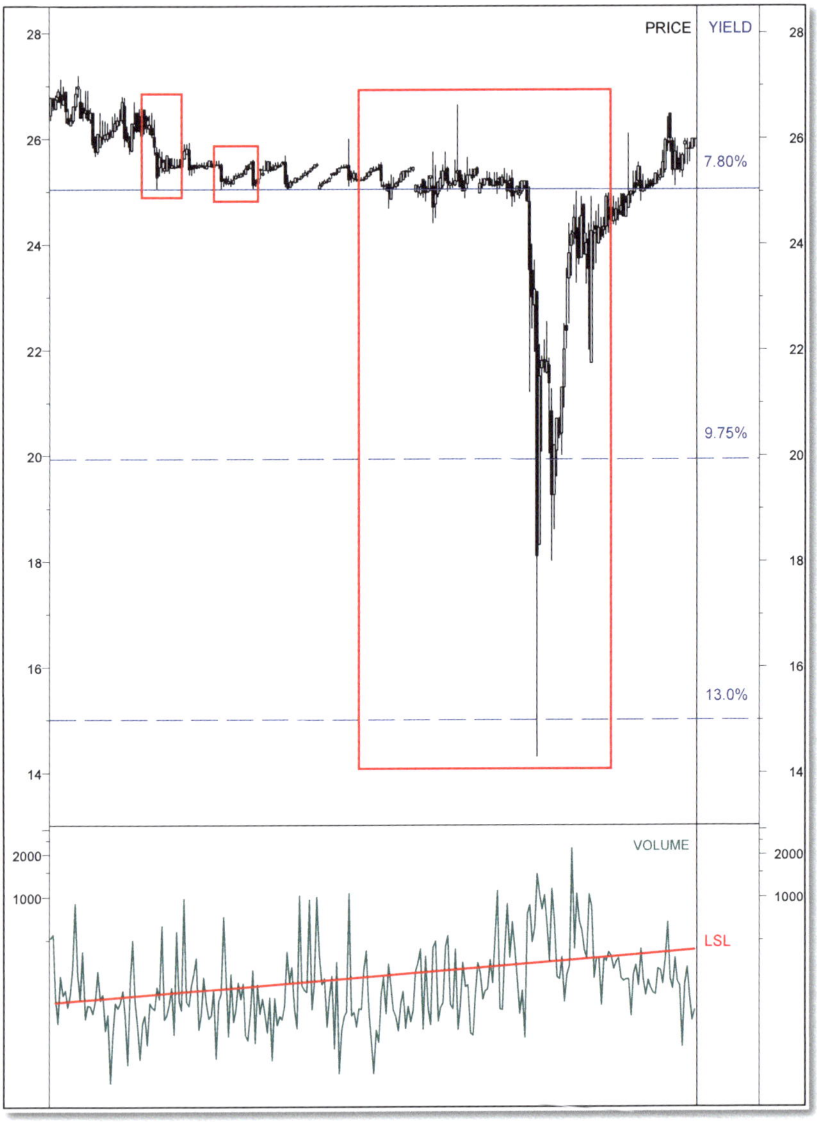

Chart 63: JPM.J with Market Analysis
2005-2009

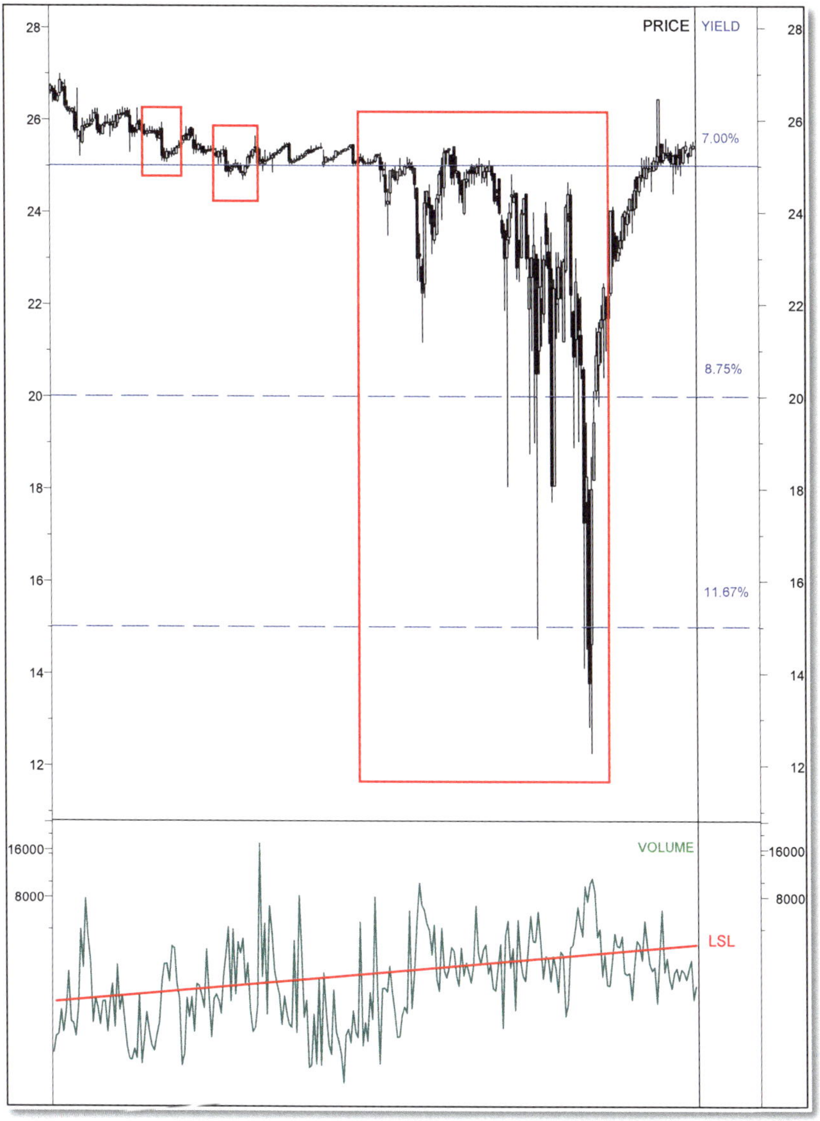

Charts created in MetaStock from Equis International

Chart 64: PSA.Z with Market Analysis
2005-2009

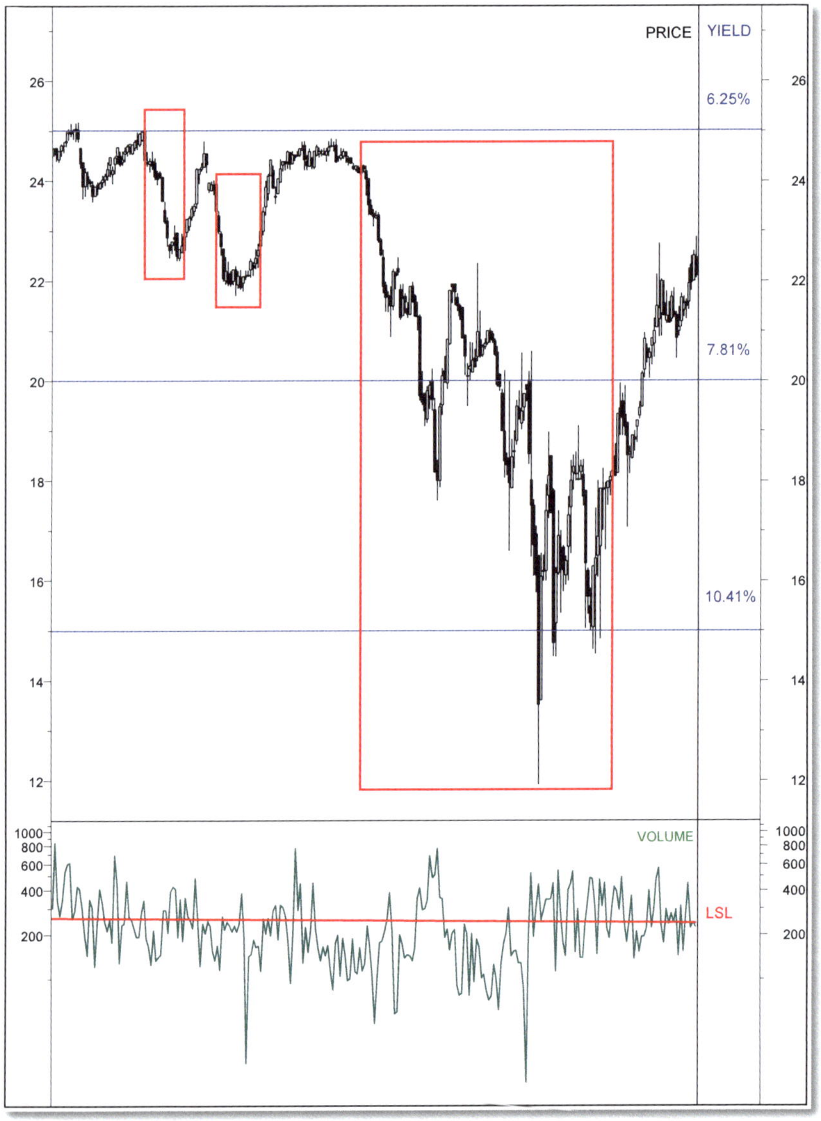

Created in MetaStock from Equis International

Target Preferred Stocks vs. WIPSI Ratio Chart

One of the advantages of WIPSI's par value-based pricing and even-weighted calculations are to make direct comparisons with individual stocks easy to perform.

The following table and accompanying charts show the five-year ratio spread of each preferred stock versus WIPSI.

TABLE 20: Five-Year Preferred Stock Ratio Spreads versus WIPSI

	Current	Mean	High (year)	Low (year)	(chart number)
DTE.A	6.7	7.9	14.3 (Mar 09)	0.2 (Jan 07)	CHART 65
JPM.J	6.1	6.8	9.3 (Oct 08)	0.3 (Feb 07)	CHART 66
PSA.Z	2.8	2.1	5.9 (Sep 08)	(3.0) (Jan 08)	CHART 67

While the charts look similar, with high angle regression lines, the relationship between these preferred stocks and the preferred-stock market is not static and thus constantly changing. In fact, all stocks have had periods where they relatively outperformed and underperformed versus the market.

For example, the ratio charts of all three stocks are currently near their five-year regression mean. But each stock had extreme levels of relative strength and weakness in different degrees.

Chart 65: DTE.A Minus WIPSI $ Ratio Chart
2005-2009

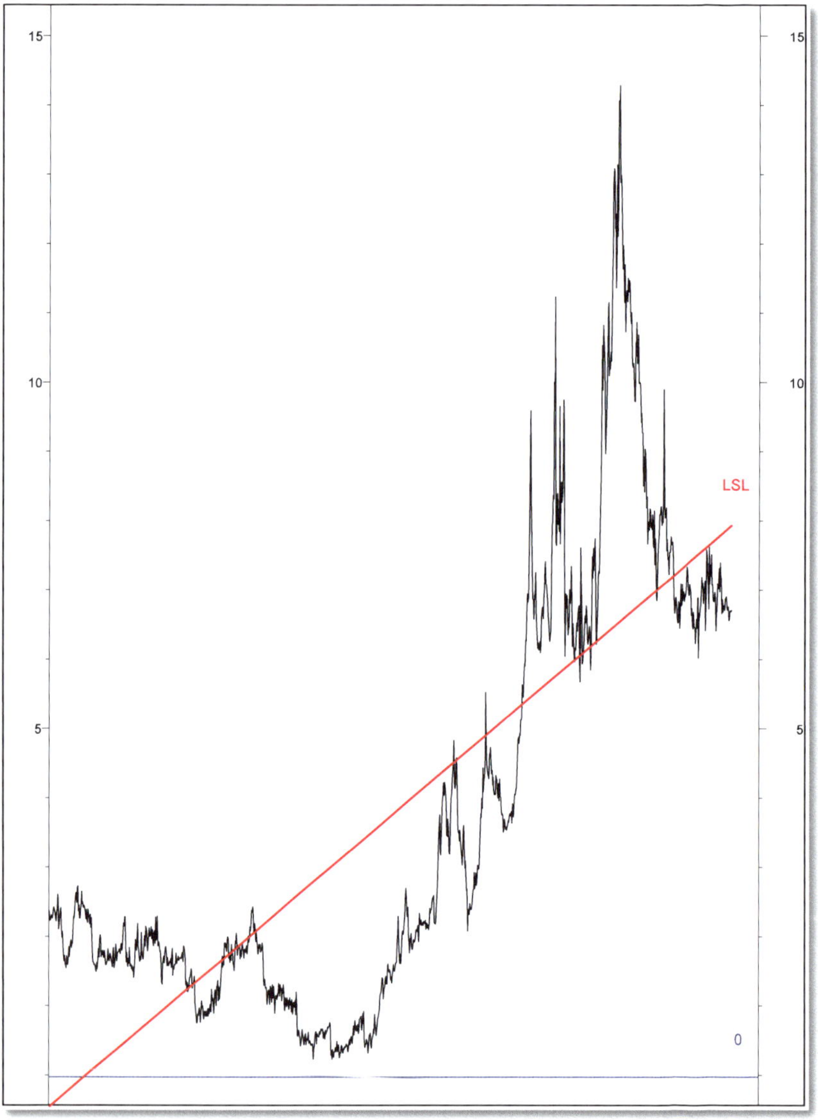

Chart 66: JPM.J Minus WIPSI $ Ratio Chart
2005-2009

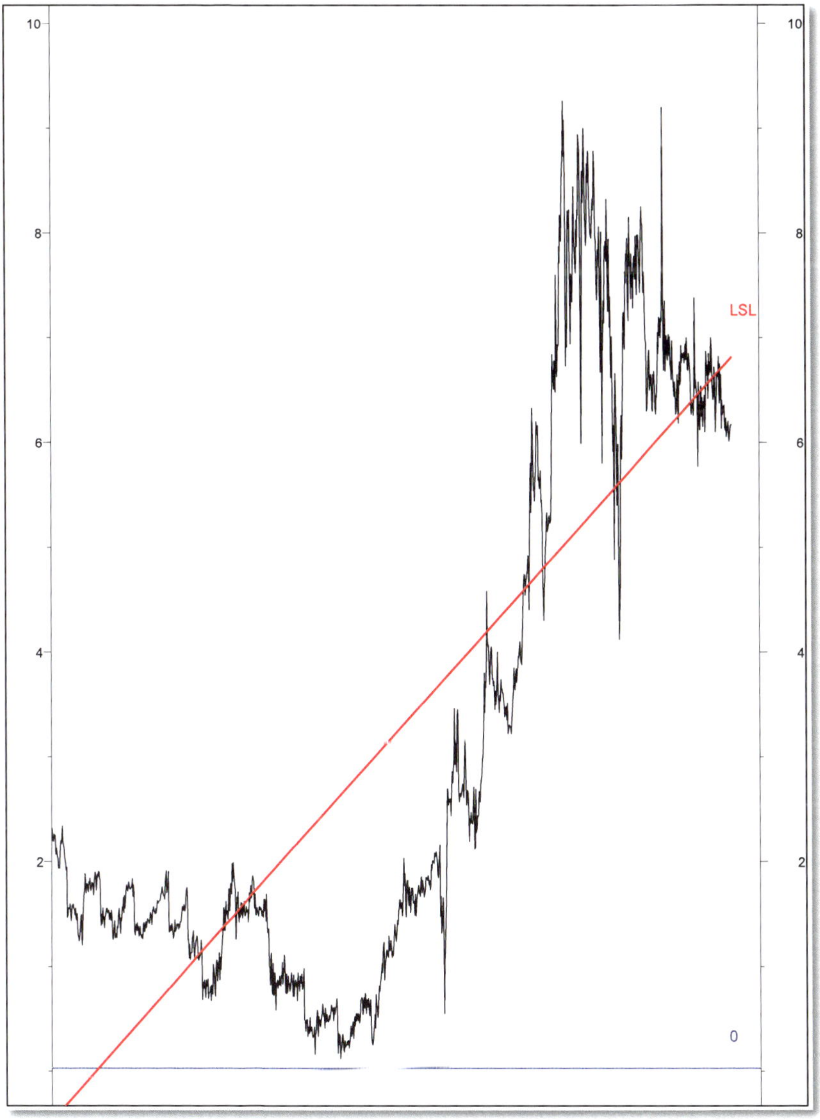

Charts created in MetaStock from Equis International

Chart 67: PSA.Z Minus WIPSI $ Ratio Chart
2005-2009

Created in MetaStock from Equis International

Target Preferred Stocks vs. Other Preferred Stocks

Ratio charts are useful, because most preferred-stock investors track more than one issue from the same company to find the best-priced preferreds at a given period of time. They also make comparisons between different types of preferreds (convertible, floating rate, etc.).

Below is a comparison of different preferred issues from our selected companies: DTE.A versus DTE.C, JPM.J versus JPM.K, and PSA.Z versus PSA.X. While theses securities can have different characteristics (dividend yield, call dates, etc.), their pricing relationship is worth tracking, because one might be more attractively priced than the other security at a given point in time.

The following table and accompanying charts show the five-year ratio spread of each of our target preferred stocks versus the other issues.

Table 21: Five-Year Preferred-Stock Ratio Spreads versus Other Preferreds

	Current	Mean	High (year)	Low (year)	(chart number)
DTE.A	0.4	0.3	3.7 (Mar 09)	(2.6) (Nov 08)	Chart 68
JPM.J	3.3	3.4	5.6 (Sep 08)	0.2 (Nov 08)	Chart 69
PSA.Z	(0.2)	(0.3)	2.8 (Sep 08)	(2.8) (Dec 08)	Chart 70

Extreme changes in the price relationships between the securities can be clearly seen on the charts. For instance, JPM Series J's price was at a significant discount to the Series K in September 2008, thus making it a relatively better investment choice. Another example was the very high premium that the DTE Series A was at in March 2009 versus the DTE Series C stock, thus making it less attractive for new investment.

Contrary to financial academic theory, not all preferred stocks are identical, and there are clearly times in which an investment in one security would provide a better buying opportunity than another.

CHART 68: DTE.A Minus DTE.C Ratio Chart
2005-2009

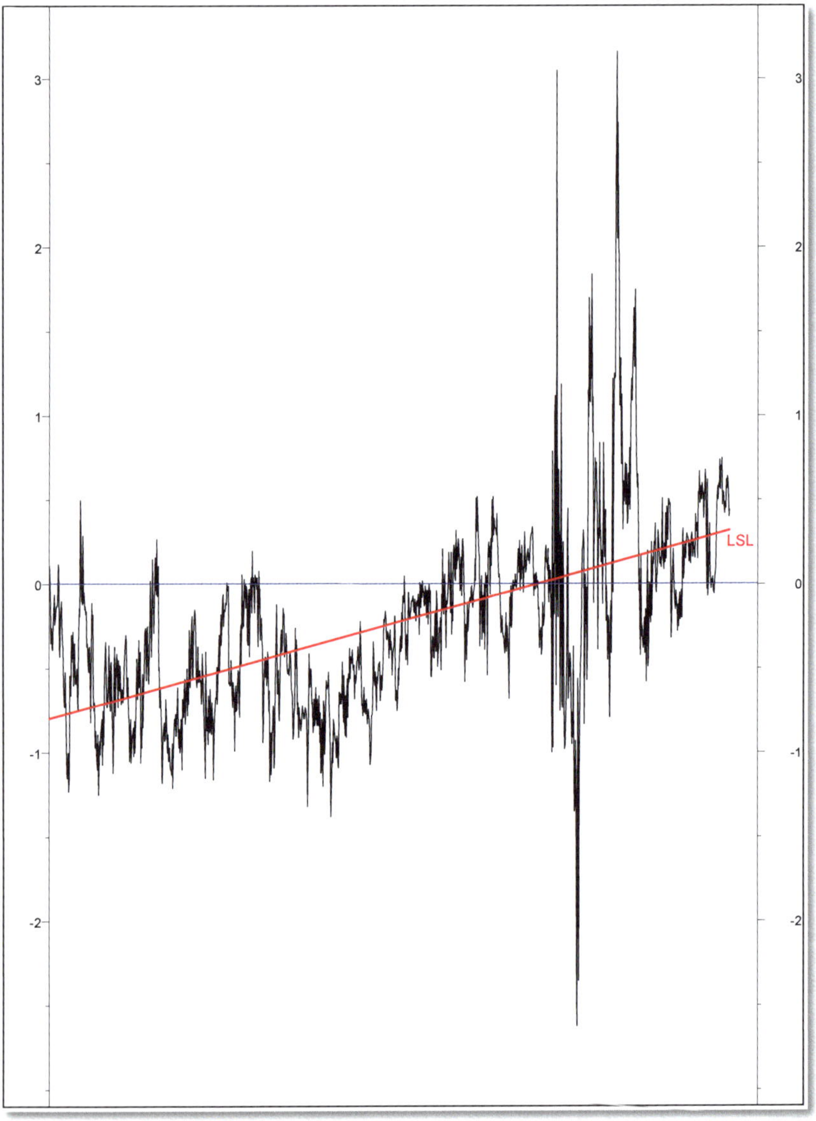

CHART 69: JPM.J Minus JPM.K Ratio Chart
2005-2009

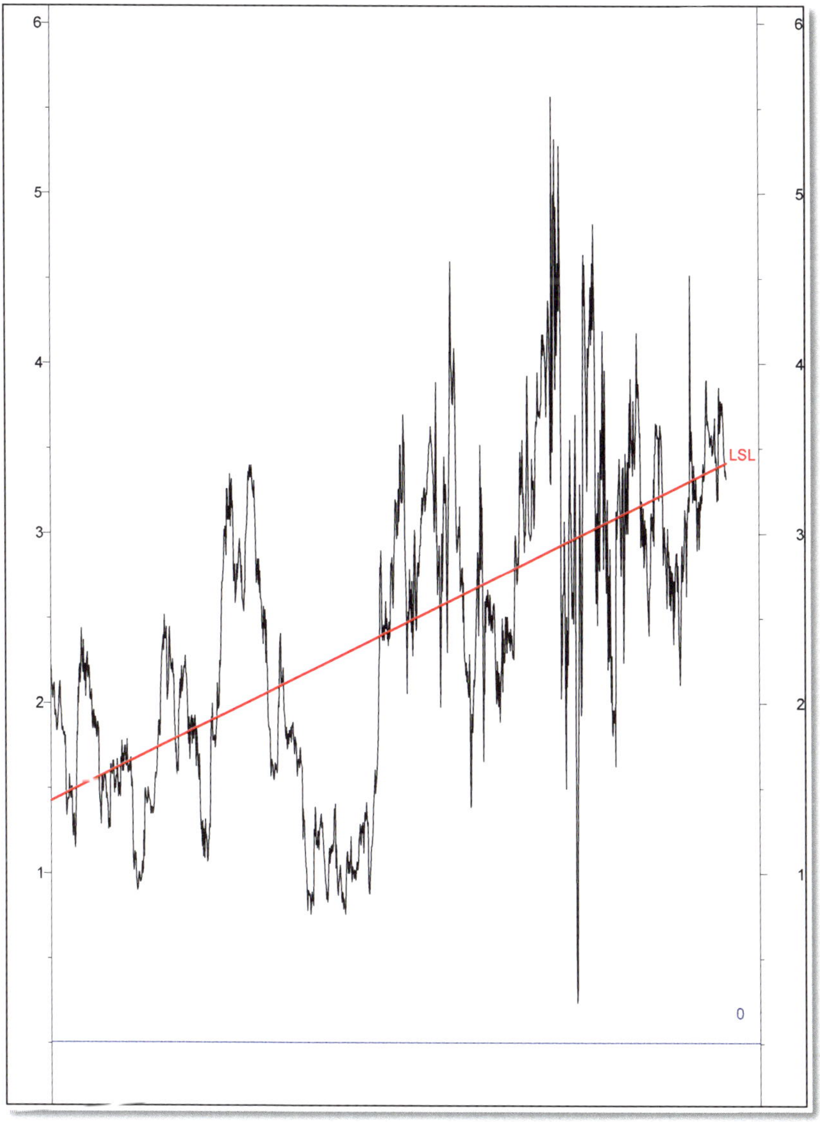

Charts created in MetaStock from Equis International

CHART 70: PSA.Z Minus PSA.X Ratio Chart
2005-2009

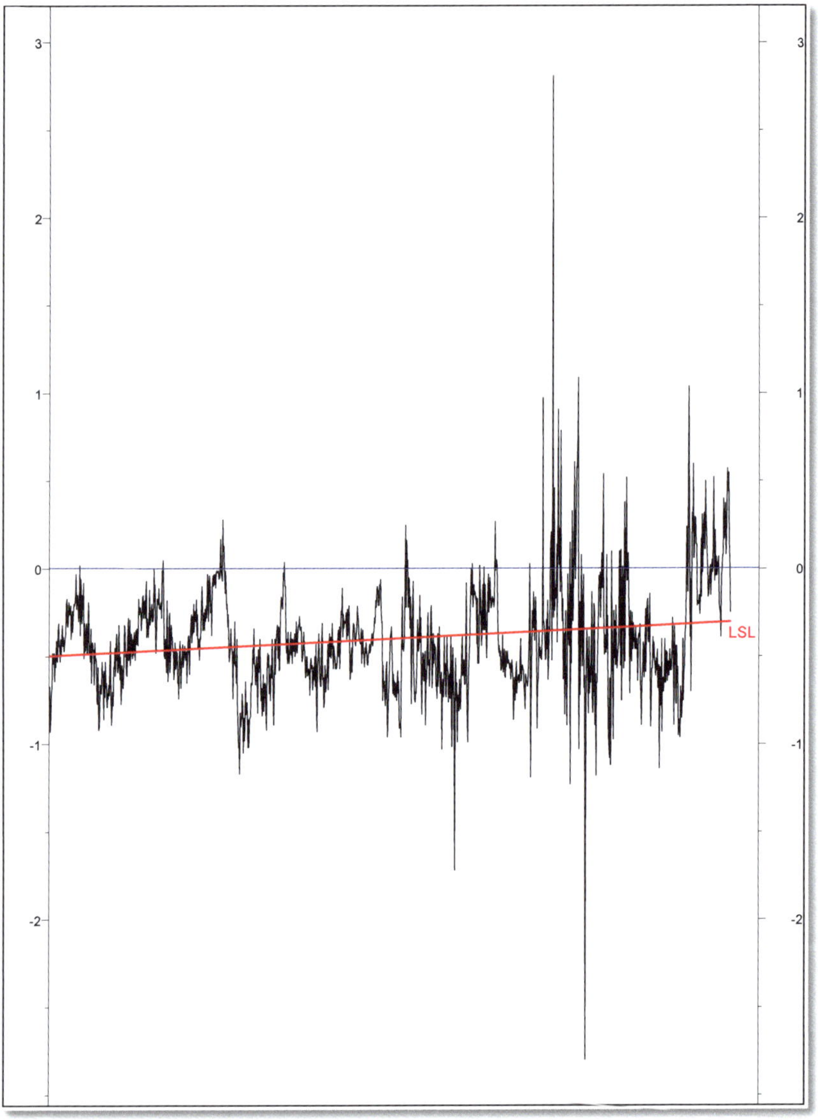

Created in MetaStock from Equis International

TECHNICAL INDICATORS

While many of the analytical tools found in Chapter 4 worked well in market analysis, they don't automatically translate into individual preferred stocks and vice versa.

The focus of this section is to use technical tools that aid in identifying changes in the intermediate trend and locate overbought and oversold points in our stocks. Of keen interest is to use indicators that performed well during the 2007-2008 bear market, as well as the frequent, volatile V- type price patterns common to preferred stocks.

To lay the foundation for future research, this analysis focused on the common interpretation of signals, default settings on indicators were used, and overbought and oversold signals from the same indicator were analyzed independently from each other. Last, each indicator was studied individually without confirmation from the other indicators examined.

DIFFERENCES FROM WIPSI

In comparing the charts of the individual preferred stocks versus WIPSI, you can quickly notice that they differ greatly in the following ways:

Trends

WIPSI exhibits well-defined up and down trends while the preferred stocks typically trade sideways. While trendline and moving average analysis was effective on WIPSI, it doesn't universally work well on individual preferreds.

Volatility

The individual stocks have regularly high levels of volatility, causing numerous V patterns and long candlestick chart shadows. This can make chart analysis difficult.

CHART 71: DTE.A Regression Lines
2005-2009

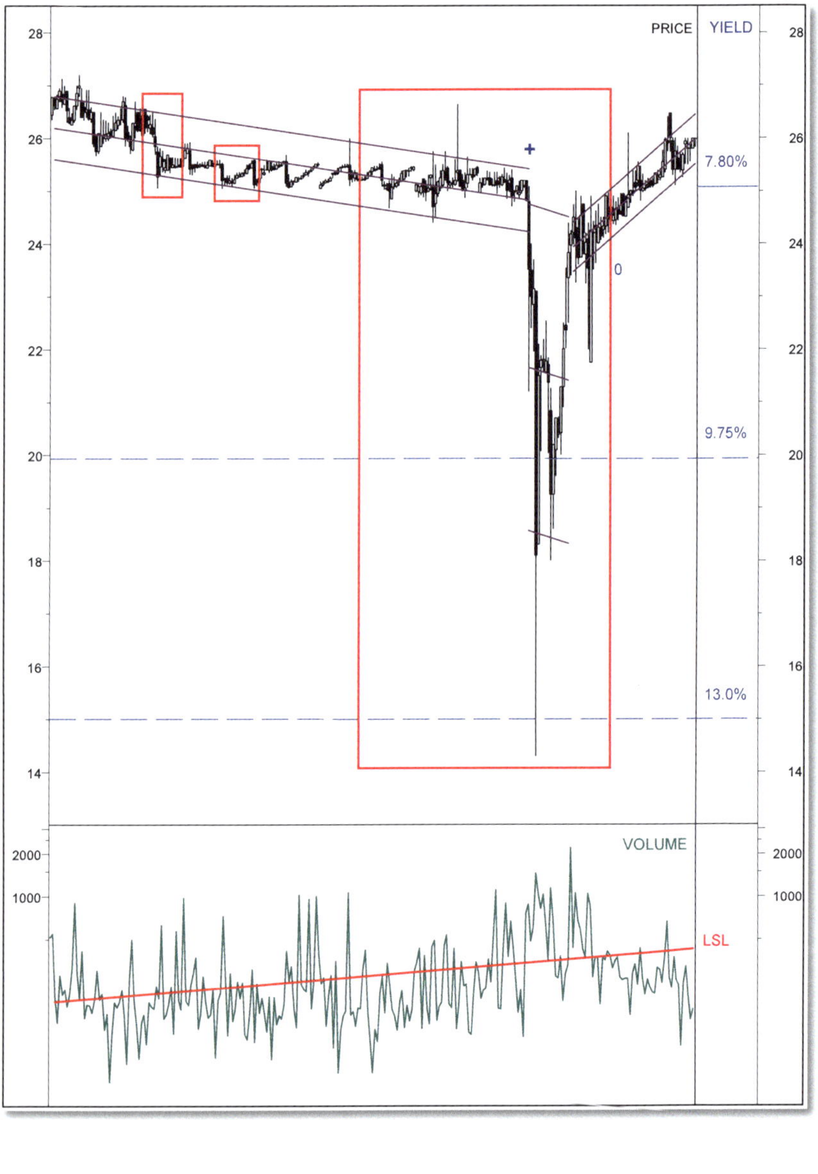

Created in MetaStock from Equis International

Regression Lines and Standard Error Channels

Since charting analysis can be very subjective, a statistical way to establish trendlines was used for identifying intermediate trends. Least squares linear regression analysis is a statistical tool that plots a line through prices so as to minimize the distance between the prices and the resulting trendlines. Standard error analysis is helpful in determining where the "extremes" lie and thus help identify trends and changes in trends.

Signal Rules

- A signal occurred at the first crossing of the standard error channel by the full body of a candlestick.
- Channels had to be at least 1 year in length.
- Repeat signals were ignored.
- The high or low of the previous move was used as the start point of the next channel.
- Both oversold and overbought signals were observed.

Conclusions and Observations

DTE.A (Chart 71) This stock traded within a narrow regression channel until 2008. On 9/19/2008 ($23.51), it gave a sell signal prior to significant decline to a multiyear low $14.30 on 10/10/2008. Once the 2007-2008 bear market was over, the stock resumed trading in a narrow regression channel.

JPM.J (Chart 72) This stock traded within a narrow regression channel until 2007. On 11/9/2007 ($23.00), it gave a sell signal on high volume and prior to significant decline to a multiyear low of $12.27 on 3/13/2009. Once the 2007-2008 bear market was over, the stock resumed trading in a narrow regression channel.

PSA.Z (Chart 73) There were six signals and at least one sell signal in each of the three downtrends in the preferred-stock market followed by excellent entry points. This indicator was effective in maneuvering through the four-year trading range of 2003 to 2006 and the bear market of 2007-2008.

CHART 72: JPM.J Regression Lines
2005-2009

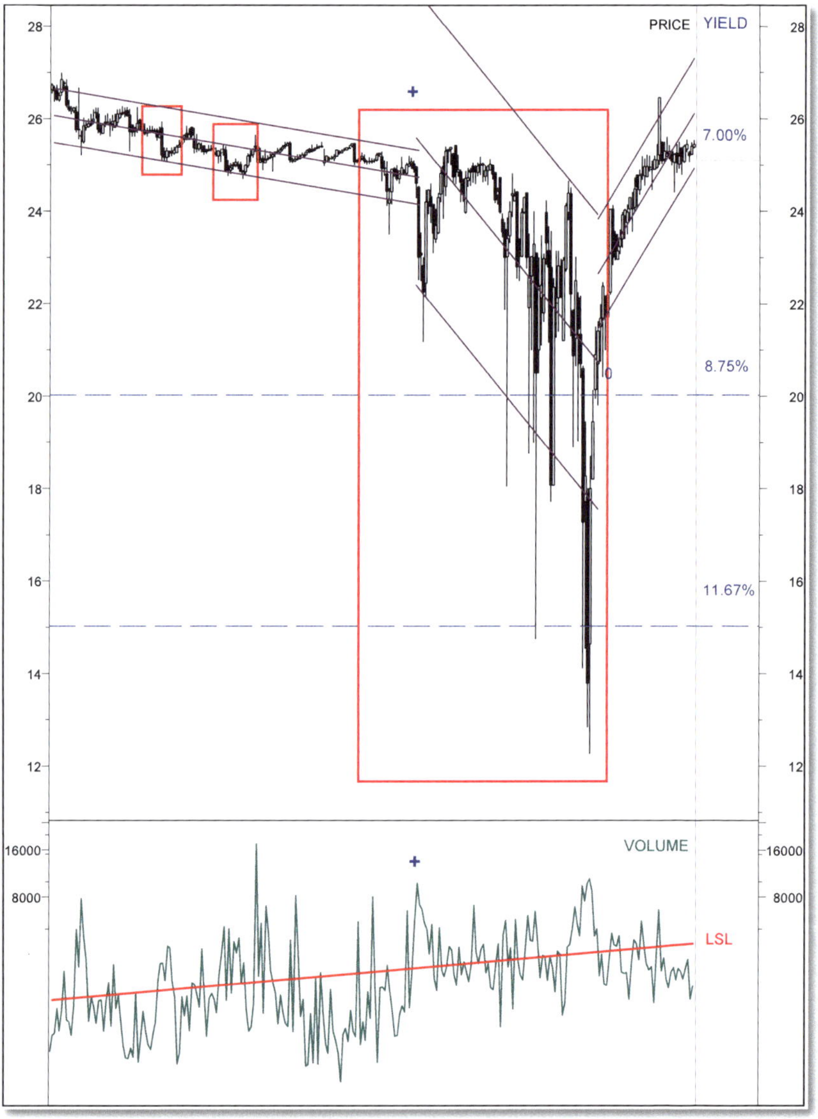

Chart 73: PSA.Z Regression Lines
2005-2009

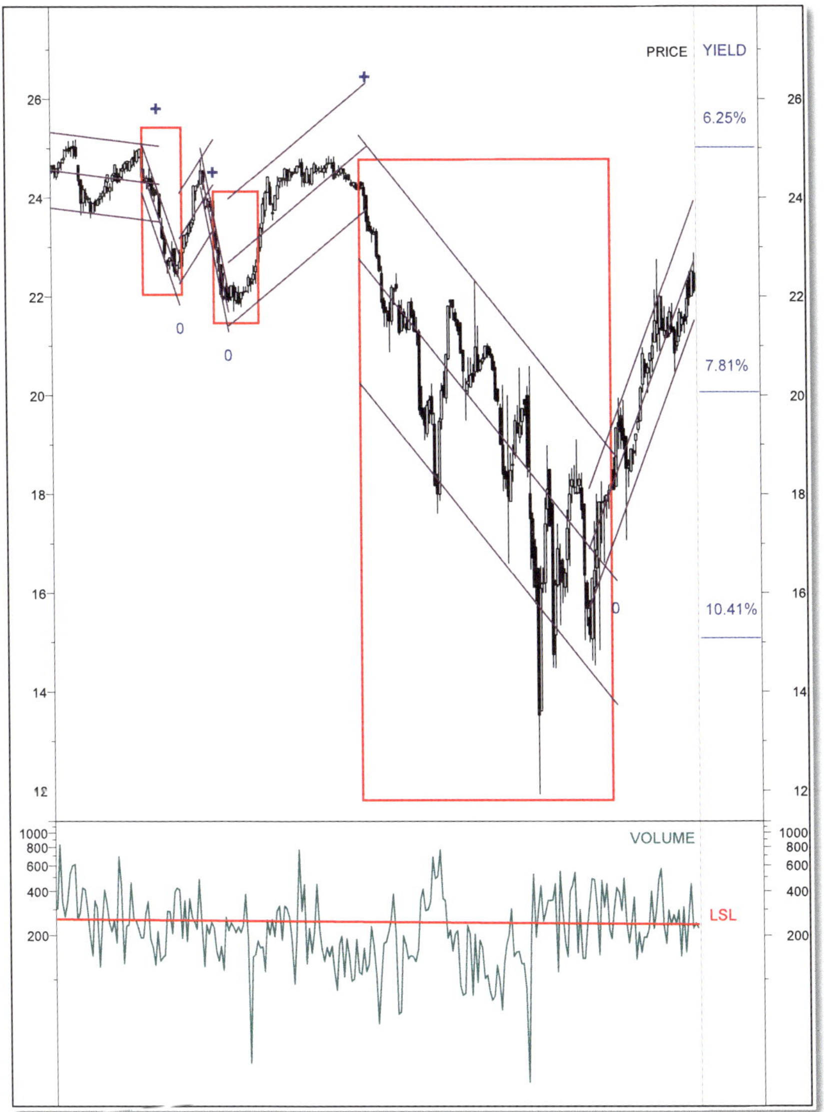

Charts created in MetaStock from Equis International

CHART 74: DTE.A Wilder RSI Oscillator
2005-2009

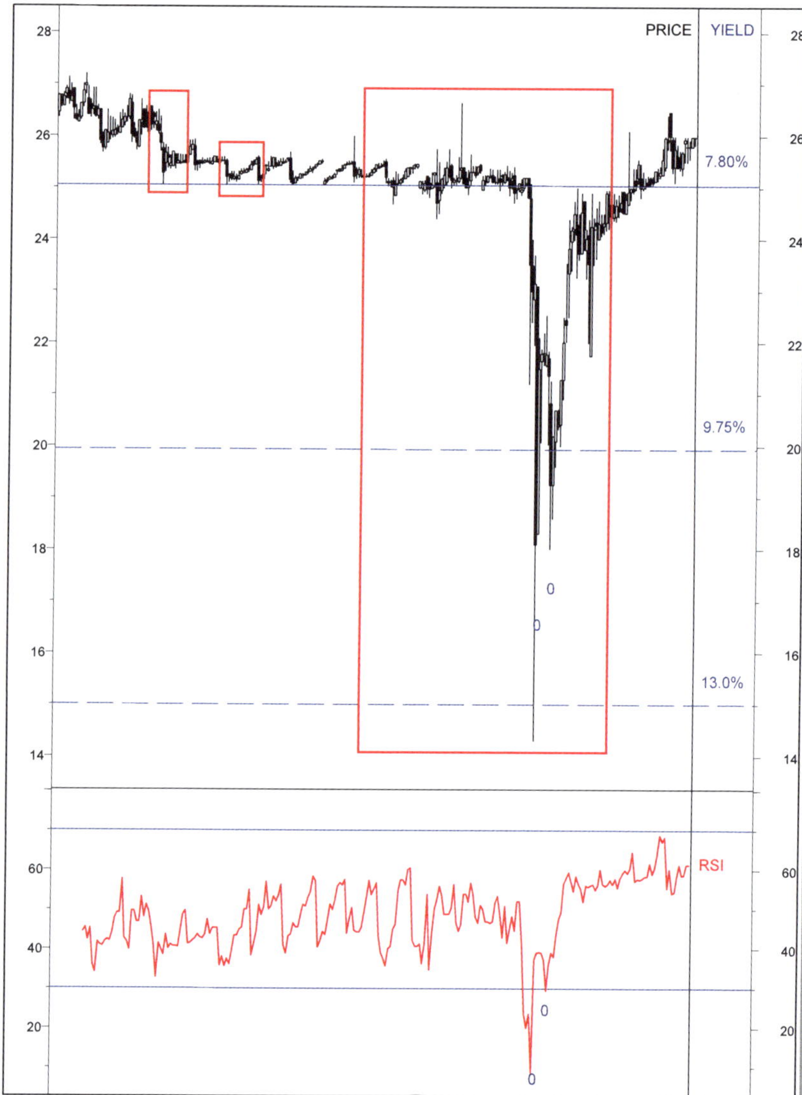

Created in MetaStock from Equis International

Wilder Relative Strength (RSI)

Oscillators are primarily used on "sideways" trading securities. The Wilder Relative Strength Indicator (RSI) was picked because of its popularity with investors. For the purposes of this preferred-stock study, the primary focus was on whether this indicator would prove useful for providing oversold signals in all market conditions.

Signal Rules

- The 14-periods calculation was used.
- The focus was placed on 70 and 30 crossover points.
- First signal was used with secondary signals only for confirmation.
- Only oversold signals were observed.

Conclusions and Observations

DTE.A (Chart 74) Throughout most of the time frame covered, the RSI indicator stayed dormant, that was until 2008. It identified two great entry points in late 2008 that preceded a powerful rally.

JPM.A (Chart 75) There were eight signals and at least one buy signal in each of the downtrends in the preferred stock market. Each signal provided a good entry point, even though some points proved to be premature.

PSA.Z (Chart 76) There were six signals and at least one buy signal in each of the downtrends in the preferred stock market. Each signal provided a good entry point, even though some points proved to be premature.

Chart 75: JPM.J Wilder RSI Oscillator
2005-2009

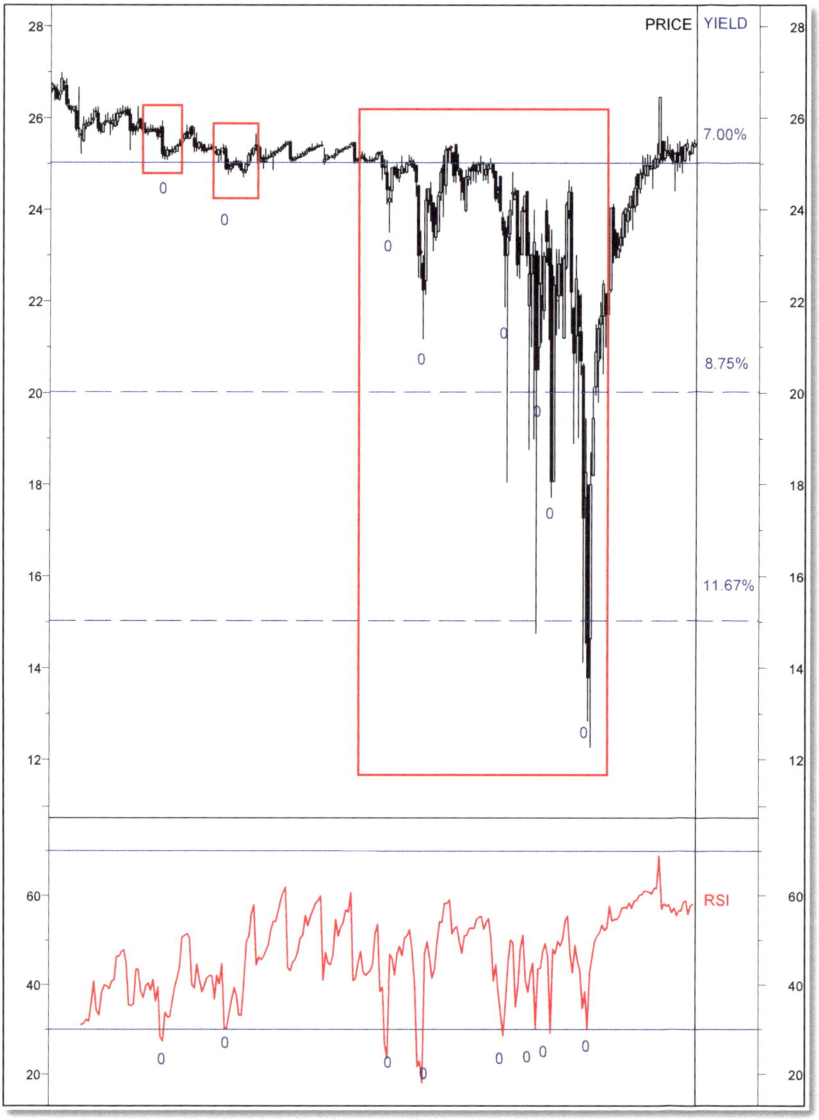

CHART 76: PSA.Z Wilder RSI Oscillator
2005-2009

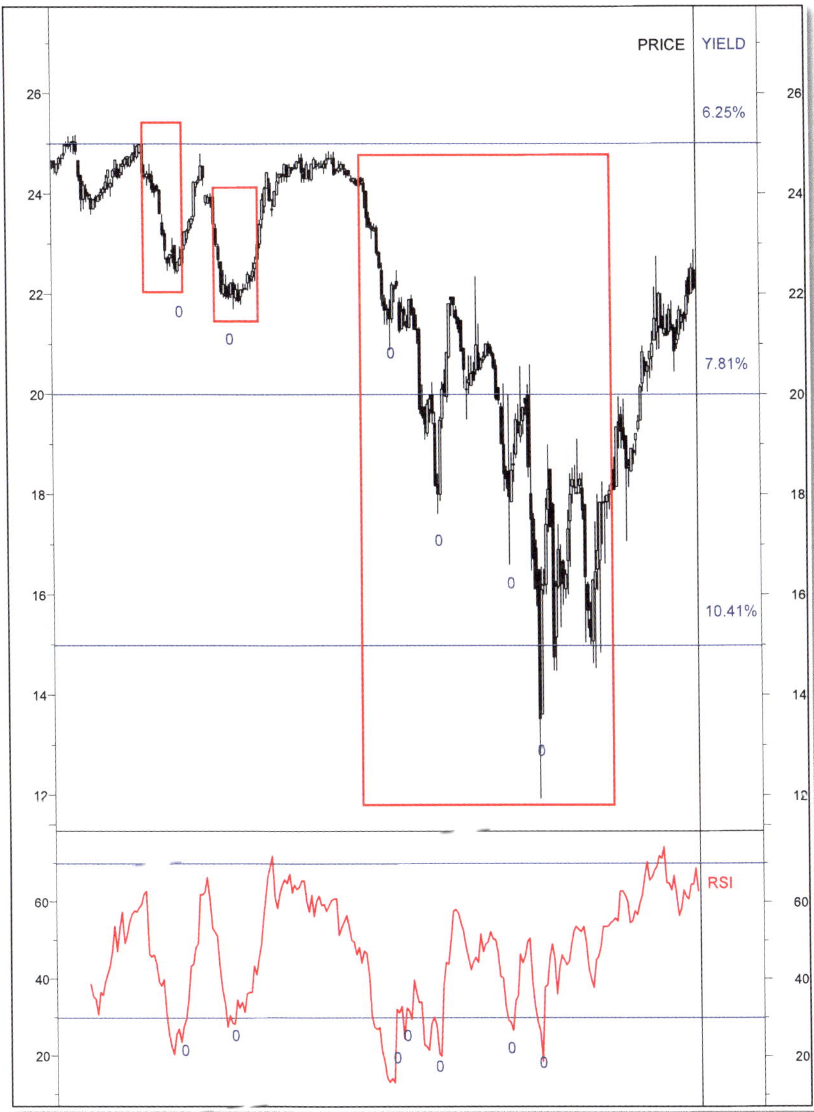

Charts created in MetaStock from Equis International

CHART 77: PSA.Z 40-Week Simple Moving Average Bands
2005-2009

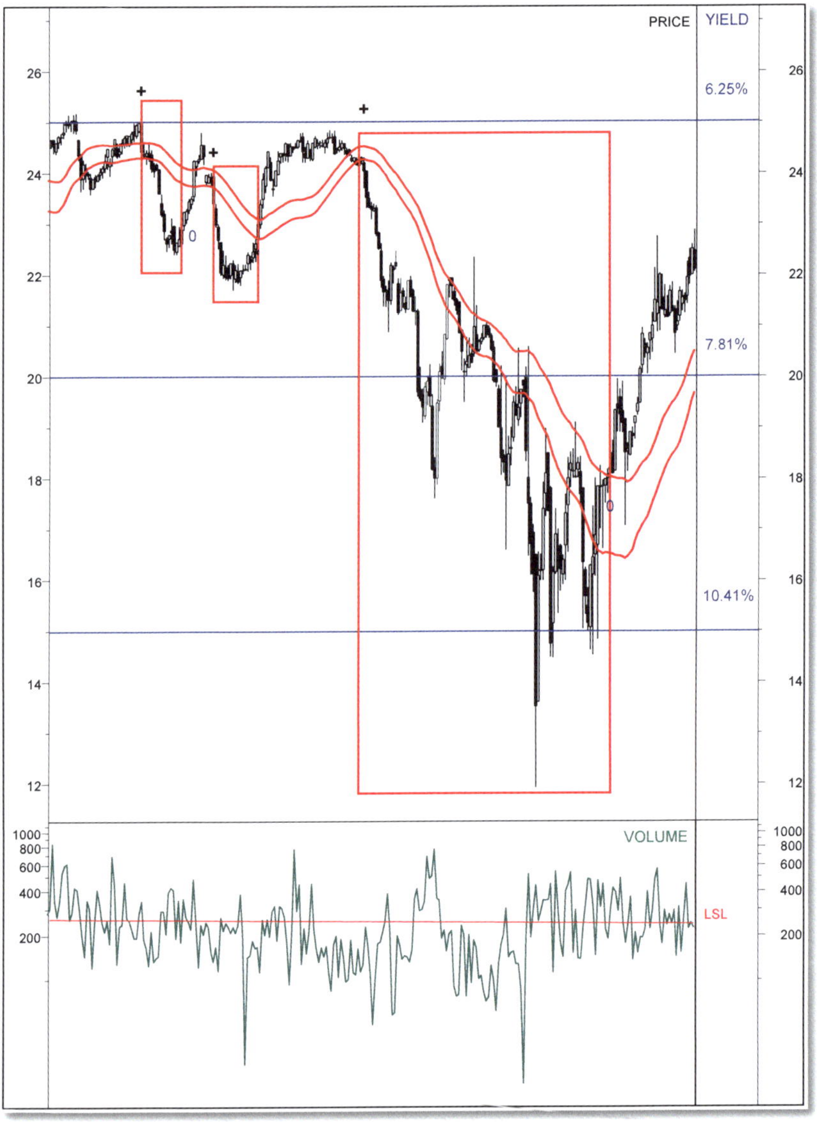

Created in MetaStock from Equis International

Moving Averages

The 40-week simple moving average (with the high-low band as a filter) was shown as an effective tool in market analysis of preferred stocks. In previous studies that analyzed the simple, weighted, and exponential moving averages for 10-, 20-, and 40-weeks, the simple moving average was found to produce fewer false signals and thus was the focus of this chapter.

Signal Rules

- A crossing of the Friday closing price above or below the simple moving average bands.
- Both oversold and overbought signals were observed.

Conclusions and Observations

DTE.A Sideways-moving price actions prove problematic for moving averages and cause false signals. The stock's trading activity was effectively flat and thus rendered MA analysis useless.

JPM.J Sideways-moving price actions prove problematic for moving averages and cause false signals. The stock's trading activity was effectively flat and thus rendered MA analysis useless.

PSA.Z (Chart 77) There were six signals with at least one point in each of the downtrends in the preferred stock market as well as the uptrend that followed. All signals provided a good entry and exit points.

Various technical tools were discovered that allow investors the means to identify general trends and effective entry and exit points for each preferred stock studied. These tools allow for a disciplined and systematic approach to buying and selling individual preferred stocks.

In the era of information overload, there is a tendency for investors to use too many indicators. Remember, the key objective of investment analysis is to identify changes in the current long-term trend of a preferred stock early enough to make timely changes to an investment portfolio. Select enough indicators to be effective, efficient, and profitable in your investment analysis and STOP!

In the next section, the market and investment analysis is summarized and prioritized in a fashion to be used in portfolio management.

Chapter 6

Coordinating Research

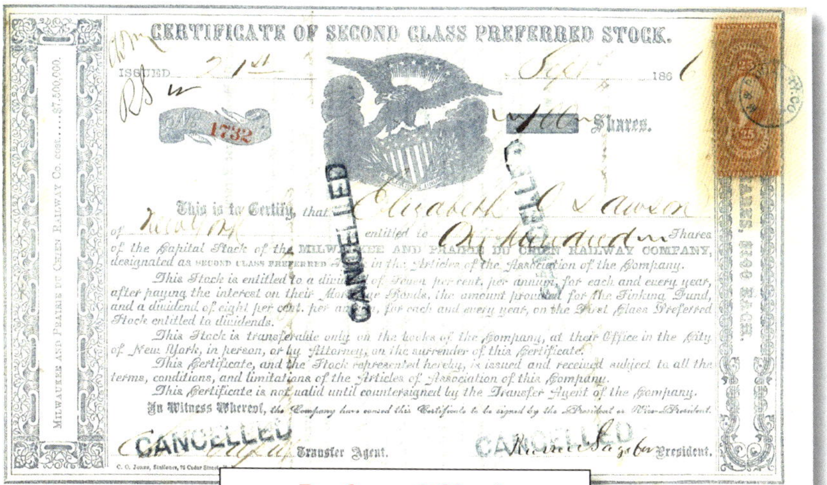

CERTIFICATE OF SECOND CLASS PREFERRED STOCK.

ISSUED ... 186

No. 1732 ... Shares.

This is to Certify, that ... of ... entitled to ... Shares of the Capital Stock of the MILWAUKEE AND PRAIRIE DU CHIEN RAILWAY COMPANY, designated as SECOND CLASS PREFERRED Stock in the Articles of the Association of the Company.

This Stock is entitled to a dividend of seven per cent. per annum, for each and every year, after paying the interest on their Mortgage Bonds, the amount provided for the Sinking Fund, and a dividend of eight per cent. per annum, for each and every year, on the First Class Preferred Stock entitled to dividends.

This Stock is transferable only on the books of the Company, at their Office in the City of New York, in person, or by Attorney, on the surrender of this Certificate.

This Certificate, and the Stock represented hereby, is issued and received subject to all the terms, conditions, and limitations of the Articles of Association of this Company.

This Certificate is not valid until countersigned by the Transfer Agent of the Company.

In Witness Whereof, the Company have caused this Certificate to be signed by the President or Vice-President.

Transfer Agent. President.

MILWAUKEE AND PRAIRIE DU CHIEN RAILWAY Co. cap. .....$7,500,000.

SHARES, $100 EACH.

CANCELLED

Preferred Stock

1866

"Market analysis is based heavily on the movement of broad market averages."
TECHNICAL ANALYSIS OF THE FINANCIAL MARKETS, JOHN MURPHY, 1999

"While preferred stocks rarely enjoy the same price gains as common stocks, these shares also are not as vulnerable to sharp declines. The average preferred stock fell only 3% in the past year versus a 21% drop in the S&P 500."
FORBES (11/18/2002)

The previous chapters examined the market analysis of the preferred-stock market, using seven different statistical tools and investment analysis of selected individual preferred stocks using eight separate aids. These results largely complement the detailed technical studies done in *Preferreds* in the Winans International Preferred Stock Index and selected stocks from 1980-2005.

This chapter focuses on how to practically use the tools to conduct effective analysis in light of managing a portfolio of investments.

It has been proven that technical analysis can be effectively and efficiently used on preferred stocks and the overall preferred-stock market to identify long-term trends, changes in long-term trends, and overbought/oversold conditions. And yet the different technical approaches studied had very different outcomes on both the Winans International Preferred Stock Index (WIPSI) and the preferred stocks selected for this analysis:

Fundamental Analysis Is the Starting Point

This analysis is the most effective, low-cost way to initially screen for investment candidates. This process also allows investors to keep apprised as to the financial strength of the preferred-stock issuers, and can be useful in confirming a technically based decision to sell an existing investment.

Yield Spread and Ratio Charts

The analysis revolves around the concept of relative change where both prices (yields) could be declining (or rising) at the same time but one price (yield) is declining (or rising) farther and faster than the other. This relative strength research is very effective and should be used by all investors. Yield spread charts help identify opportune times preferred stocks are better priced than bonds. Ratio charts are extremely effective for direct comparisons between several different preferred securities from the same issuer.

Simply put, these studies prove useful in selecting an issuer's best-priced preferred stock and timing investment between preferred stocks and corporate bonds.

Trendlines Analysis

The oldest and most commonly used type of technical analysis is charting.

Long-term trendlines were easy to identify and worked well on WIPSI. Yet individual stocks gapping and V price patterns caused by illiquidity or dividends payments make preferred stock charting more problematic.

Regression Lines and Standard Error Channels

A statistical way to establish trendlines was used for identifying intermediate trends. Least squares linear regression analysis is a statistical tool that plots a line through prices so as to minimize the distance between the prices and the resulting trendlines. Standard error analysis is helpful in determining where the "extremes" lie and thus help identify trends and changes in trends. This charting technique worked well with both WIPSI and individual stocks for oversold signals, but overbought signals tended to lag when compared to using other technical tools.

Moving Averages

An extensive study was conducted to find the best moving average for intermediate and long-term studies. In analyzing the simple, weighted, and exponential moving averages for 10-, 20-, and 40-weeks, the 40-week simple moving average filtered with high-low bands was the most effective moving average. It was significantly more effective on WIPSI than on individual stocks. It could be used on WIPSI as an independent indicator, but could be used on the individual stocks only as a secondary indicator due to their tendency to trade within narrow sideways channels during normal market conditions. This indicator would coordinate well with yield spread and regression analysis.

Oscillators

Oscillators are primarily used for extended trading ranges when moving averages are effectively flat and are ineffective. Wilders RSI and Stochastics were studied due to their popularity with investors. While Stochastic analysis proved the least effective of all studies done due to multiple false signals, Wilders RSI did prove extremely effective at identifying both overbought and oversold conditions on the individual preferred stocks. This indicator would coordinate well with ratio charts and regression analysis.

Effective research techniques were discovered that allow an investor the means to identify general trends in the preferred-stock market through the WIPSI as well as individual preferred stocks. These tools allow for a disciplined and systematic approach to buying and selling individual preferred stocks.

In the next chapter, the focus shifts to the totality of portfolio management to put this knowledge to profitable use.

Chapter 7

Portfolio Management: Seeing the Forest from the Trees

A Recommended Portfolio
in a 1928 Magazine of Wall Street

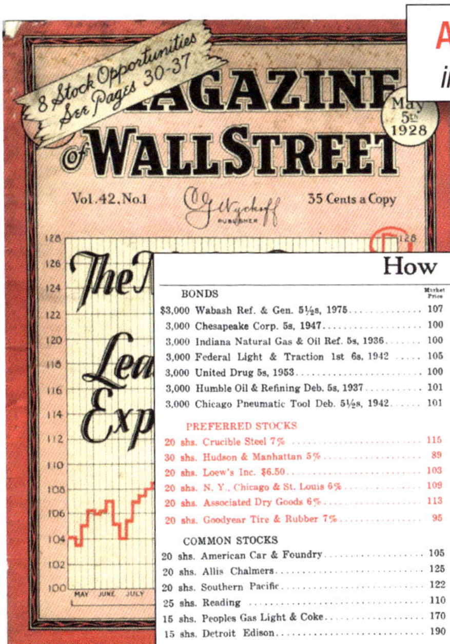

How to Invest $50,000

BONDS	Market Price	Cash Needed	Annual Income	COMMENT
$3,000 Wabash Ref. & Gen. 5½s, 1975	107	$3,210	$165	Junior mortgage but amply protected by earnings and finances of road, which, moreover, is well situated as merger prospect with some larger system.
3,000 Chesapeake Corp. 5s, 1947	100	3,000	150	Secured on Chesapeake & Ohio common stock which company was organized to hold. Dividends on stock provide ample leeway for interest. Convertible in 1932.
3,000 Indiana Natural Gas & Oil Ref. 5s, 1936	100	3,000	150	Attractive yield in view of guarantee by Peoples Gas Light & Coke, which occupies strong position among the major public utility operating companies.
3,000 Federal Light & Traction 1st 6s, 1942	105	3,150	180	Secured on first mortgage bonds and stocks of operating subsidiaries of well established public utility holding company. Interest consistently covered more than twice over.
3,000 United Drug 5s, 1953	100	3,000	150	Obligation of large and prosperous drug manufacturer and retail merchandiser. Not secured by mortgage, but interest consumes only small proportion of earnings.
3,000 Humble Oil & Refining Deb. 5s, 1937	101	3,030	150	Company one of largest and strongest of oil producers in mid-continent fields. Controlled by Standard Oil of N. J. Bonds enjoy high investment standing.
3,000 Chicago Pneumatic Tool Deb. 5½s, 1942	101	3,030	165	Only funded debt of comparatively small but well established and consistently prosperous enterprise. Interest requirements normally covered about eight times.
PREFERRED STOCKS				
20 shs. Crucible Steel 7%	115	2,300	140	Excellent progress towards greater stability and reduction in costs has placed preferred in strong position. Non-callable feature provides leeway for further enhancement.
30 shs. Hudson & Manhattan 5%	89	2,670	150	Unspectacular but steady growth in earning power has lifted this issue from semi-speculative to investment class. Convertible into common stock at 110.
20 shs. Loew's Inc. $6.50	103	2,060	130	New issue of company which has been rapidly assuming commanding position in motion picture industry. Divs. earned over 7 times. Carries common stock purchase warrants.
20 shs. N. Y., Chicago & St. Louis 6%	109	2,180	120	Strongly entrenched railroad issue. Sells on higher yield basis than others so better situated because of proximity to redeemable price of 110.
20 shs. Associated Dry Goods 6%	113	2,260	120	Senior capital issue of important department store chain. Earning power, while showing no recent growth, is well stabilized. No callable provisions.
20 shs. Goodyear Tire & Rubber 7%	95	1,900	140	Normal earnings afford ample protection. High yield predicated on unsettlement in rubber trade and, until recently, in company's affairs.
COMMON STOCKS				
20 shs. American Car & Foundry	105	2,100	120	Financially stable concern well able to maintain established dividend pending revival in railroad equipment demand. Operations becoming increasingly diversified.
20 shs. Allis Chalmers	125	2,500	120	Supplying industrial machinery to many diverse industries, earnings have achieved high degree of stability and unobtrusive growth. Dividend increase foreshadowed.
20 shs. Southern Pacific	122	2,440	120	Market for stock retarded by conservative dividend policy, but substantial equities are accruing to shareholders, which should eventually receive more tangible recognition.
25 shs. Reading	110	2,750	100	Moderate dividend does not measure road's high earning power. Likewise possesses concealed equities, as well as being strongly situated in eastern consolidation program.
15 shs. Peoples Gas Light & Coke	170	2,550	120	Supplying gas requirements of Chicago without competition, earnings are highly dependable and expanding rapidly. Yield supplemented by value of frequent subscription rights.
15 shs. Detroit Edison	190	2,850	120	One of leading operating public utilities serving important centers. Earnings currently at record proportions partly due to activity of numerous automobile plants in Detroit.
TOTAL		$49,980	$2,610	Yield, 5.2%

"If the bond market starts to diverge from the stock market, a warning is being given–the more serious the divergence, the more important the warning... the days of following only one market are long gone."
INTERMARKET TECHNICAL ANALYSIS, MURPHY, 1991

"All the market knowledge in the world will be useless without the ability to put this knowledge into action by mastering our emotions."
INVESTMENT PSYCHOLOGY EXPLAINED, PRING, 1993

"Retirement shortfalls from the stock market downturn in recent years and demographic trends are creating a longer term yearning for yield within the financial markets."
BARRON'S (4/14/2005)

The art and science of successful investing requires knowledge of history, statistics, and finance. It also needs a common-sense, disciplined approach that puts this knowledge to profitable use. This is called portfolio management.

The previous chapters focused on analyzing the preferred-stock market and selecting individual securities. And yet mastering investment analysis doesn't guarantee that an individual can successfully manage an entire investment portfolio through constantly changing economic conditions and personal financial adjustments. It's an entirely different skill set, so before you proceed, I recommend that Chapter 2 "Basic Rules for Income Investing" be reviewed again to gain a more in-depth understanding of the role of portfolio management.

Like an iceberg, the tip of the investment strategy is buying or selling securities with the real size and scale of this investment process under the waterline. The consistent implementation of the strategy is always focused on matching the investor's tolerance for financial volatility. It also governs the quick change in the allocation of assets relative to a harsh economic climate such as raising large amounts of cash during a bear market.

Investment success is much more than simply "beating the market." It requires a predetermined performance goal, a logical asset allocation, a proper investment monitoring system, and a policy for rebalancing the holdings relative to financial exposure, trading costs, and taxes.

Similar to sporting events and military operations, overall victory comes only from executing a solid strategy with a good offense AND an effective defense. The same is true of investing.

PERFORMANCE GOAL AND ASSET ALLOCATION

A good investment strategy will likely lead to profitable, long-term results. This requires establishing and adhering to a realistic performance goal based on historical facts (not media-induced financial fiction or propaganda from an investment association).

The performance goal should be a verifiable number and is the foundation on which all portfolio decisions will be made in the years to come. This discipline is truly what separates the successful investor from an individual who randomly buys investments based on "dinner party tips" (yes, people really do this).

Unfortunately, after the goal is established, it is often misunderstood. This target represents a statically relevant path to profitability over a predetermined period of time. It is not a guarantee of financial success each and every year. In fact, I have witnessed impatient people, who call themselves "long-term investors," blindly misuse the performance of market indices in quarterly head-to-head comparisons with their investments, and then rapidly make portfolio changes like it is some kind of horse race with "the market."

Quarterly comparisons of investment performance are not useful to long-term investors, and should take a minimal role in the investment evaluation process.

The simple fact is that there are going to be future bear markets that affect all investments. The investors who stay on a predetermined track have a good chance of realizing their long-term financial goals. As you read through the rest of the chapter, you will see how adhering to an investment strategy coordinates the results of market and investment analysis and provides for an actionable plan to take profits in "easy money" bull markets and to overcome unbridled fear and aggressively buy cheap investments during bear markets.

TIME FRAME USED

Assuming that there are no major changes in an investor's finances, it is common practice to set investment goals for a 5- to 10-year time horizon. Realistically, most investors don't know enough about their future finances to establish a meaningful investment strategy beyond five years. This means that an investor will establish five different investment goals over the next 25 years, where each new performance target incorporates the success or failure of the previous investment campaigns. Think of it as taking a long journey where adjustments are made for direction and speed as more information is gathered during the trip.

ESTABLISHING THE PERFORMANCE GOAL

A time-tested way to set a meaningful performance goal is to take an investment medium's average annual return from different periods of time. The first step in this process is to select periods of time that are relevant.

The following time frames were selected for important reasons:

1900-2009 This captures the investment landscape over several generations. It shows how the investments reacted in many different types of extreme situations (such as both world wars and the Great Depression) over a long period of time.

1950-2009 This time frame allows for an investment analysis without the volatile economic effects of the Great Depression and both world wars.

1990-2009 A time frame commonly used by the financial community for historical evaluations, because it captures the post-Cold War boom and the "lost decade" that started in 2000.

2000-2009 This captures the investment history since the dot.com bubble popped. This era is commonly called the "lost decade," because U.S. common stocks as a whole haven't produced any capital appreciation.

TABLE 22 provides the average annual total returns, the number of years with positive results, and income yields for common stocks, preferreds and corporate bonds since 1900, 1950, 1990, and 2000. By simply taking the average of these statistics from each time frame, a reasonable average annual return for common stocks (8.8%) and corporate income investments (7.8%) can be established.

This is a logical point to separate aggressive from conservative investment strategies. For example, if investors want an average annual return higher than 8.8% over the next five years, then they will have to accept more risks by using leverage (margin) or investing in high beta securities. On the flip side, investors who are satisfied with a goal of 7.1% can set their portfolio's asset allocation for 100% income investments and avoid the uncertainty of common-stock investing entirely.

Finally, I have found very few investors who don't make withdrawals from their portfolio at some point in time. To make long-term investment targets more realistic, do not assume reinvestment of all profits when using

TABLE 22: Historical Performance Since

Average Annual %	1900	1950	1990	2000	Average
Common Stocks	11.7%	12.3%	9.9%	1.2%	8.8%
Annual Returns > 0%	71.0%	77.0%	75.0%	60.0%	70.8%
Dividend Yield	4.4%	3.6%	2.1%	1.8%	3.0%
Corporate Income (50/50)	7.0%	7.3%	8.9%	8.0%	7.8%
Annual Returns > 0%	79.5%	78.5%	85.0%	90.0%	83.3%
Income Yield	6.0%	7.3%	7.0%	6.5%	6.7%
Preferred Stocks	7.4%	7.3%	10.2%	9.1%	8.5%
Annual Returns > 0%	75.0%	72.0%	80.0%	80.0%	76.8%
Dividend Yield	6.5%	7.3%	7.6%	7.4%	7.2%
Corporate Bonds	6.5%	7.3%	7.6%	6.9%	7.1%
Annual Returns > 0%	84.0%	85.0%	90.0%	100.0%	89.8%
Interest Yield	6.2%	7.2%	6.5%	5.6%	6.2%

the goal-setting features in investment software. In other words, stick with "average annual" versus "annualized" calculations. While both statistics are useful, the latter assumes reinvestment of all profits and thus shows a much higher rate of return than most investors will ever realize (TABLE 22).

ASSET ALLOCATION

After the five-year investment goal is established for a new portfolio, then the asset allocation is predetermined.

An asset allocation is the mix of different types of investments (common stocks, real estate, preferred stocks, bonds, etc.) within the entire portfolio, once it is 100% invested. This should encompass all securities from all the investor's accounts. The objective of asset allocation is to avoid taking more risk than required to meet the investor's predetermined objectives. It effectively sets the maximum exposure in which a portfolio should be invested in each investment medium and controls the amount and timing of profit taking and portfolio rebalancing.

TABLE 23:
Asset Allocation
2010-2015

Beginning Assets

1,000,000

Historical Average Performance		Negative Years		Taxes	
Common Stock Price Change	5.8%				
Common Stock Dividend Yield	3.0%	Growth	Income	Long Term Appreciation	Income
Corporate Income Price Change	1.1%	29%	17%	15%	30%
Corporate Income Yield	6.7%				

Asset Allocation Scale

Growth Investments	%	Income Investments	%	Investment Goal	Number of Negative Yrs	5-Year Total Return $	5-Year Cumulative Return $	Average Annual Return $	Capital Gains $	Pre-Tax Income $	Annual Taxes $
1,000,000	100%	0	0%	8.8%	29%	440,000	524,560	88,000	58,000	30,000	17,700
500,000	50%	500,000	50%	8.3%	23%	415,000	489,849	83,000	34,500	48,500	19,725
0	0%	1,000,000	100%	7.8%	17%	390,000	455,773	78,000	11,000	67,000	21,750

For an existing portfolio that is fully invested, and is at the end of a five-year investment campaign, the current asset allocation will set the new investment goal (based on projected returns over the next five years) unless the investor wants to make changes to the portfolio's holdings.

Remember, the performance goal and asset allocation have a linear relationship where changes in one will more than likely change the other.

Let's look at an example of this: TABLE 23 shows the performance projections for a new portfolio based on the statistics from TABLE 22 for common stocks and corporate income investments (50% corporate bonds, 50% preferred stocks) within a single portfolio. (In Chapter 3, it was shown that an income portfolio has historically performed better when both corporate bonds and preferred stocks are used.)

Notice how a $1,000,000 investment in each of the three different portfolios is expected to act very differently:

Portfolio 1: Capital Appreciation (100% in Common Stocks)

This portfolio is expected to achieve an 8.8% average annual return, with $88,000 in projected annual profits ($58,000 is expected from annual price appreciation and $30,000 from yearly dividend income). If all profits are withdrawn at each year-end, then the total return is projected to be $440,000. If all profits are reinvested, then the estimate is raised to $524,560. While this is the highest expected return of the three portfolios, it is also the most volatile, with annual losses expected 29% of the time.

Portfolio 2: Balanced (50% Common Stocks and 50% Corporate Income Investments)

This portfolio is expected to achieve an 8.3% average annual return, with $83,000 in projected annual profits ($34,500 is expected from annual price appreciation and $48,500 from yearly dividend and interest income). If all profits are withdrawn at each year-end, then the total return is projected to be $415,000. If all profits are reinvested, then the estimate is raised to $489,849. This portfolio is expected to be 21% less volatile than Portfolio 1, with annual losses expected 23% of the time.

Portfolio 3: Income (100% in Corporate Income Investments)

This portfolio is expected to achieve a 7.8% average annual return, with $78,000 in projected annual profits ($11,000 is expected from annual price appreciation and $67,000 from yearly dividend and interest income). If all profits are withdrawn at each year-end, then the total return is projected to be $390,000. If all profits are reinvested, then the estimate is raised to $455,773. While this portfolio is the least volatile, it also is projected to produce a significantly higher level of annual taxation ($21,750) than the other portfolios.

Other Factors

Before selecting a goal and asset allocation, other factors need to be considered:

Taxes

Historically, the government has treated profits generated by investments differently in that interest income is typically taxed at a higher level than gains realized by selling a profitable investment.

This might require corporate income investments to be kept in tax-deferred retirement accounts (e.g., IRA, 401K Plan, Defined Benefit Plan, etc.) or use some of the time-tested techniques to minimize taxes such as annual tax-loss selling, bond swaps, amortizing bond premiums, and using municipal bonds in taxable accounts.

Investment strategy and tax planning need to go hand in hand for the best investment results!

Margin Use, Aggressive Security Selection

If investors want an average annual return higher than 8.8% over the next five years, then they will have to accept more risks by using leverage (margin) or investing in high beta securities. The asset allocation should treat this as an additional investment medium and set a maximum limit relative to the size of the entire portfolio.

Remember, history has shown that investors can "blow up" a portfolio with any type of investment if they leverage it high enough or use too many illiquid investments. Such a situation will be exacerbated when a normal-to-severe bear market occurs.

> **Leverage**: Many investors have successfully used margin loans and mortgages to enhance returns and withdrawal equity from fully invested portfolios. And yet this can be the seeds of destruction for those who don't pay attention to the saying that "too much of a good thing can be bad." Repayment guarantees won't protect you if you suffer a loss in market value from highly leveraged income investments and your broker or banker forces the sale of your leveraged holdings at the worst of times.

> **Illiquidity**: Liquidity is the ability to buy and sell an investment quickly at a reasonable price. In the universe of income investments, liquidity spans from excellent to nonexistent with illiquid investments generally offering much higher yields than liquid investments.

Even seasoned investors do crazy things in bull markets. There is an old Wall Street saying worth remembering: "Don't confuse brains with a bull market." If you feel the need to gamble, then go to Las Vegas—don't use your investment portfolio!

Investor's Personality and Temperament

Many people, regardless of their age, education, and background, simply can't handle high investment uncertainty and will panic and abandon a time-tested investment strategy at the first signs of trouble. Based on the historical fact that U.S. common stocks have negative years 29% of the time, income investments (with predetermined interest payments, par values, and maturity dates) offer an attractive long-term investment choice to low-risk investors.

Income Withdrawals

For investors who need to regularly withdraw funds from a portfolio, the types of investment profit are an important consideration.

In a portfolio 100% invested in stocks, most of the expected profits are in the form of capital gains that would require selling an investment or borrowing on margin for an investor to access the needed funds. Furthermore, since stocks historically have negative years 29% of the time, there would probably be instances when stock investors would need to withdraw funds when their portfolio is at a temporary low point, thereby selling investments at less than opportune times.

As seen in Portfolio 3, most of an income portfolio's profits are in the form of income that comes in at regular, predictable intervals and can be accessed without changing the portfolio's holdings.

Which of the above-mentioned portfolios is the best? Answer: It depends on which matches the investor's needs and risk tolerance. Obviously, there is no such thing as a single best goal and asset allocation for all investors! What is ultimately most important is to set a course of action the investor can follow with confidence over the long term.

INITIAL PORTFOLIO CONSTRUCTION

Once the five-year goal and asset allocation have been set, the job of constructing the portfolio begins.

Regardless of the investment strategy used, it is important for investors to pay attention to the investment environment surrounding them. This is the job of market analysis.

Buying new investments can be like trying to cross a busy intersection during rush hour in a new car that you're not familiar with—you need to pay close attention to the traffic signals to avoid getting into a wreck.

Market analysis has to answer the question "Is it a bull or bear market?" When to buy or sell can be as important as what to buy or sell, and market analysis provides insight about the current investing climate, as well as possible economic threats in the near future.

Patience and commonsense aren't often discussed in the investment process, because they don't generate fees and commissions. Yet it's important not to rush the construction of a portfolio when market conditions are not right, and individual investment values exceed the investor's buy parameters.

Take corporate income investments. They can vary in availability and valuation, and it can take up to 90 days to finish the portfolio construction process during normal economic conditions.

An analogy I find most useful in describing the first year of owning a portfolio is like building a new apartment building:

- You have to pay to have the building built before rental income is received (i.e., transaction costs, accrued interest, etc.).
- It takes time to find good tenants, so the building is usually not 100% occupied when completed (i.e., availability of investments).
- Since tenants will be moving in at different times, they pay rent at different times and amounts based on type of rental agreement (i.e., income investments pay different amounts of interest and dividends at various times).

Keep in mind that the performance clock starts ticking AFTER the portfolio construction phase; so don't start comparing the returns of a new portfolio to a long-term performance goal until at least one full year after the portfolio is initially built or reconstructed!

It is also important to remember that investing doesn't have to be "all or none," so be fully invested only when your market analysis tools give you a green light.

MONITORING INVESTMENT PORTFOLIO

A lot of information is needed to properly monitor a portfolio of investments. Unfortunately, today's investors suffer from a bad case of "information overload" with a continuous stream of data from numerous sources.

As mentioned earlier in this book, investors should take information provided by brokerage houses and rating agencies with a "grain of salt" and will need to get additional information from other sources to properly evaluate the health and progress of a portfolio.

PORTFOLIO PERFORMANCE

As shown in Chapter 2, these spreadsheet formats (Exhibits 6, 7) can be used to accurately monitor the performance of all investments. One is only for bonds (corporate, municipal, Treasury), and the other is for equities (common and preferred stocks, real estate investment trusts, etc.). These reports are very useful and provide timely information typically not available in brokerage statements.

See Disclaimer

EXHIBIT 6: Sample Performance Report (Income Stocks)

Description	Shares	Market Value	Average Div. Yield %	Year to Date Change %	Cumulative Change $	Cumulative Income $
Equity Income						
COMMON STOCK	865	$26,132	7.9%	2.9%	$1,094	$1,603
PREFERRED STOCK 8.7%	887	$24,295	7.1%	0.3%	($2,907)	$3,647
PREFERRED STOCK 8.00%	949	$24,627	7.5%	-0.9%	($579)	$3,588
PREFERRED STOCK 8.6%	956	$24,311	8.2%	-3.6%	$897	$1,064
COMMON STOCK	221	$9,724	8.0%	14.3%	$2,143	$1,700
PREFERRED STOCK 8.765%	838	$21,646	7.9%	0.4%	($1,754)	$3,485
PREFERRED STOCK 8.3%	848	$22,345	7.3%	-30.5%	($2,994)	$2,934
PREFERRED STOCK 8.125%	919	$23,591	7.4%	-1.9%	($1,710)	$4,953
PREFERRED STOCK 7.25%	284	$7,214	6.7%	-0.5%	($414)	$1,738
COMMON STOCK	276	$9,748	5.2%	-19.0%	($2,896)	$535
PREFERRED STOCK 8%	282	$26,085	10.1%	4.3%	$1,066	$56
PREFERRED STOCK 9%	950	$24,064	8.4%	0.3%	($1,425)	$5,675
COMMON STOCK	1,335	$21,654	8.4%	0.2%	($2,255)	$1,618
Equity Income Subtotal		$265,433	7.7%	-3.8%	($13,526)	$32,596

See Disclaimer

EXHIBIT 7: Sample Performance Report (Corporate Bonds)

Description	Market Value	Par Value	Annual Yield %	Year to Date Change %	Cumulative Change $	Cumulative Income
Corporate Bonds						
CORPORATE BOND 7.5% 02/15/11	$25,470	$25,000	7.5%	-0.2%	$465	$1,808
CORPORATE BOND 7.2% 07/15/08	$15,559	$25,000	7.1%	-1.9%	$60	$7,042
CORPORATE BOND 7.75% 03/01/07	$6,053	$6,000	7.5%	-1.9%	($113)	$2,744
CORPORATE BOND 9.05% 11/15/11	$26,013	$24,000	8.1%	-2.1%	($843)	$4,630
CORPORATE BOND 7.875% 07/15/13	$11,220	$12,000	7.9%	-9.2%	($766)	$7,826
CORPORATE BOND 7.625% 5/15/0	$25,563	$25,000	7.3%	-2.0%	($723)	$7,458
CORPORATE BOND 7.75% 02/1/10	$15,000	$15,000	7.7%	-4.3%	($103)	$4,255
CORPORATE BOND 9.375% 06/01/11	$15,675	$15,000	9.1%	-0.2%	$259	$4,369
CORPORATE BOND 8.75% 07/15/07	$21,394	$21,000	8.2%	-2.0%	($927)	$15,593
CORPORATE BOND 8.25% 12/15/11	$24,750	$25,000	8.3%	2.1%	($5)	$1,712
CORPORATE BOND 10.75% 10/15/06	$8,150	$10,000	10.5%	-19.3%	($2,136)	$1,496
CORPORATE BOND 6.5% 08/15/10	$23,500	$25,000	6.7%	-1.8%	($755)	$1,345
CORPORATE BOND 7.75% 03/15/13	$45,360	$48,000	7.4%	-3.4%	($4,975)	$5,668
CORPORATE BOND 7% 05/01/12	$15,525	$15,000	6.9%	-1.4%	$380	$3,153
CORPORATE BOND 6.85% 06/01/08	$9,135	$9,000	7.1%	-1.5%	$494	$2,809
CORPORATE BOND 6.0% 01/04/14	$28,050	$30,000	6.9%	-6.5%	$1,940	$5,701
Corporate Bonds Subtotal	$326,416	$330,000	7.8%	-2.9%	($7,747)	$74,608

When reviewing these reports, there are several sets of data that are used to review the overall performance of this income portfolio:

Market (Liquidation) Value vs. Par (Maturity) Value

In comparing the market value to the par value, you will notice that the bond holdings are currently worth more at maturity than if they were liquidated today ($326,416 vs. $330,000). Remember that par value is a legal obligation that the issuer owes the holder of these bonds at maturity, so liquidation value is relevant only if you need instant cash.

Annual Yield vs. Year-to-Date Price Change

The "Annual Yield" and "Average Dividend Yield %" calculation (projected interest or dividends for the year/cost basis) shows the percentage earned on the income paid this year without the income being reinvested as done in the yield to maturity statistic. The "Year-to-Date Price Change" measures the change in the price of an investment for the current year. As can be seen, the bond investments have declined (2.9%) and the stocks have fallen (3.8%) so far during the year. It can be interpreted that the investments have caused a loss within the portfolio. But if the prices do not decline any further, the total return of the portfolio will be positive after all income is collected by the end of the year (7.8% for bonds and 7.7% for stocks).

A common mistake is to compare an income investment's annual price change to a market benchmark such as the S&P 500 Index, Winans International Preferred Stock™, or the Dow Jones Corporate Bond Average without including each investment's estimated income for the year, and thus underestimating the total annual performance of the portfolio.

Cumulative Change in Price vs. Cumulative Income Received

To measure how an investment has performed since being purchased, cumulative returns have to be analyzed. Since the investments in this portfolio have been purchased, they have declined ($7,747 for bonds, $13,526 for equity investments) in value, and yet on the positive side these investments have produced a large amount of income ($74,608 for bonds, 32,596 for income investments). In the final analysis, these investments as a group have been profitable to own.

Please keep in mind that some equity investments have dividend yields

EXHIBIT 8: Portfolio Statistics Summary (Annual)

See Disclaimer on page 216

Portfolio Performance (Year-End)					Asset Allocation		
Reporting Period (# of Years)	Cumulative	Cumulative Annual	Performance Goal	Market Benchmark Average	Growth Investments	Income Investments	Asset Allocation Changes
3	23%	8%	7%	4%	0%	100%	None

Portfolio Value and Investment Type						
Market Value	Number of Positions		Value	Portfolio Breakdown	Annual Yield	Year to Date Price Change
$977,710	37	*Bond*	$641,187	76%	7.8%	-2.9%
		Equity Income	$199,454	24%	7.7%	-3.8%

Maturity and Ratings				Equity Income Breakdown				
Average Maturity	Currently Callable	Average S&P Equivalent Rating	Financial Condition Changes		Preferred Stock	Common Stock	Real Estate Inv. Trust	Listed Partnership
Year 6	35%	BB	None	% of Port	15%	6%	1%	1%
				Value	$126,910	$51,475	$10,774	$10,295

Maturity Schedule	Year 1	Year 2	Year 3	Year 4	Year 5	Year 6	Year 7	Year 8	Year 9	Year 10	Year 11
Maturity Value	$0	$27,000	$134,600	$50,000	$40,000	$114,000	$130,000	$110,000	$30,000	$0	$231,523
% of Income	0%	3%	16%	6%	5%	13%	15%	13%	3%	0%	27%
Corporate Bd	$0	$27,000	$59,000	$0	$40,000	$114,000	$90,000	$110,000	$30,000	$0	$0
Equity Income	$0	$0	$0	$0	$0	$0	$0	$0	$0	$0	$231,523
Municipal Bd	$0	$0	$0	$0	$0	$0	$40,000	$0	$0	$0	$0
Treasury Bd	$0	$0	$0	$0	$0	$0	$0	$0	$0	$0	$0
Real Estate TD	$0	$0	$75,600	$50,000	$0	$0	$0	$0	$0	$0	$0

INDUSTRY SECTORS	Finance	Health	Retail	Service	Technology	Industrial	Staple	Energy	Utility	Real Estate
% of Portfolio	9%	0%	1%	15%	9%	36%	14%	2%	2%	12%
Position Number	3	0	1	4	3	9	5	1	1	4
Market Value	$58,219	$0	$9,000	$100,000	$60,000	$245,069	$96,829	$10,295	$15,000	$82,111

that can fluctuate over time, so the "Dividend Yield %" is an estimate based on the average of the past two years of dividend payments.

In summary, there are many ways to evaluate the overall performance of a portfolio, and while each should be reviewed, it is more important for investors with a long time horizon to review the cumulative returns annually in light of a historically significant five-year performance goal previously set.

Remember, quarterly comparisons of investment performance are not useful to long-term investors, and should take a minimal role in the investment evaluation process.

PORTFOLIO HEALTH AND QUALITY

Exhibit 8 is a copy of a spreadsheet template we use at Winans International to monitor a portfolio's overall health. It answers basic questions such as:

- How is the overall long-term performance in light of the goal previously established?
- Is the portfolio's asset allocation or investment mix the same as set in the five-year investment strategy?
- Are the income holdings properly diversified by year of maturity, investment type (government debt, corporate bond, preferred stock, etc.) and industry sectors?

Cumulative Return

Cumulative return is a more effective way to evaluate the performance of a portfolio. Notice that this sample portfolio has done very well in that it has produced a 23% total return (8% annually) over the past three years. This is currently ahead of its five-year goal and the market benchmark used. Remember that all deposits and withdrawals can affect the performance figures and need to be adjusted for.

Asset Allocation and Five-Year Goal

You can see that this sample portfolio is set up as a 100% income portfolio with a five-year annual performance goal of 7%.

Maturity Schedule

This allows an investor to track when various types of income investments will be maturing (or called early) each year and to plan future investments. This portfolio has 37 individual positions with average maturity at year six, with 19% of the portfolio's corporate and real estate income holdings coming due over the next two years. Also, 35% of the entire portfolio is callable. It means the investments could be called within the current year, which may or may not happen. Notice that investments without a due date such as preferreds are treated as long-term holdings placed at 11 years (twice the length of the performance goal time frame).

Investment Medium Breakdown

This shows how the income portfolio is invested. Notice that this portfolio is 76% in bonds and 24% in equity income investments (15% preferred stocks and 8% in various other types of investments).

Industry Breakdown

This shows how much exposure the portfolio has by industry group. Notice that this portfolio has high exposure to industrial companies and no exposure to health care companies. Future investment in industrial companies should be thought through carefully.

Financial Strength

As discussed in Chapter 5, an investor needs to watch for deterioration in the finances of the corporate issuers, and to a lesser degree, agency rating changes. Keep in mind that it is not uncommon for companies that have good financials (and have never missed a dividend or interest payment), yet receive a non-investment grade rating. On the other end of the spectrum, ratings can be "sticky" and not decline as fast as a troubled company's or municipality's financial condition warrants. It is not uncommon to see the price of a distressed investment plummet long before its ratings do.

Needless to say, I do not put much value on agency ratings! History has shown that bear markets don't discriminate between income investments of different ratings. In tough market conditions, most bonds and preferred stocks decline together regardless of their ratings.

Obviously, monitoring a portfolio involves more than simply checking the current market value or agency ratings from a brokerage statement or financial website.

Finally, I recommend doing portfolio evaluations when the investment markets are not open. It's amazing how current financial news can sway investors' perceptions of their portfolios' performance and overall quality.

PORTFOLIO MONITORING CHECKLIST

If you are planning on using investment software (or web-based services) for portfolio management, be aware they are not all the same. Get a sample report from the vendor, and see if it answers the following questions:

General Issues

- Does it list the portfolio's five-year performance goal, and provide the annual and cumulative returns to show if the portfolio is on track with the established goals?
- Does the report include all accounts that the portfolio's assets are held in, as well as all annual deposits and withdrawals made by the investor?
- Does it show the targeted asset allocation versus actual allocation?
- Does it break down diversification by investment type, issuer, capitalization and industry, maturity, and agency ratings?
- Does it show position buy size versus the actual size of each investment in the portfolio to measure individual investment exposure for rebalancing purposes?
- Does it list the total amount of transaction activity?

Bonds and Preferred Stocks

- Does it show market value versus maturity value of the bond investments?
- Does it show a schedule of maturity and call dates, so reinvestment of proceeds can be planned?
- Does it show Average Annual Yield percentages?

Leverage, Hedges, and Short Sales

- Does it show the amount of leverage and/or short sales being used, and the level of interest being paid on the margin?

- Does it show what percentage of the portfolio's market value is being hedged, and when the hedge expires?

Taxes and Costs

- Does it show the investor's annual taxes for income and capital gains?
- Does it show all portfolio-related costs (brokerage, advisory, sales loads, etc.) during the current year?

It cannot be overemphasized that monitoring a portfolio involves more than simply checking the market value from a brokerage statement or free financial website. Don't be "pound wise and penny foolish" when it comes to buying the tools needed to invest properly.

REBALANCING THE PORTFOLIO

Investment portfolios are like plants in that they are constantly changing in size and shape. Growth is considered healthy, but there are times when they both need to be "pruned" to enhance future overall growth and prevent oversize limbs from damaging the entire plant.

In the case of investment portfolios, periodic rebalancing involves selling part of a position that has grown much larger than the average-size investment, and reinvesting the proceeds into other investments to restore proper diversification in the portfolio.

If a portfolio is being monitored properly, then the larger positions should be easy to spot on a report. Rebalancing should be done in a logical, systematic fashion. For example, when a stock position becomes twice the size of an average-size position in the portfolio, it is reduced in size by 50%.

Rebalancing also involves rotating individual investment holdings by selling investments that no longer meet predetermined investment criteria and buy into new opportunities. In addition to routine portfolio adjustments, an investor must always keep an eye out for investments that show volatile price declines. Since investment price usually leads business developments, it is wise to be defensive and consider removing these investments from a portfolio. During bear markets, it is better to be safe than sorry.

Rotation is also done for tax reasons at year-end. If investors need capital losses to offset capital gains, then investments currently showing a loss are sold with new investments bought immediately. This is referred to as a tax swap.

Sadly, many investors exempt certain "pet investments" from the rebalancing process by rationalizing that they are core holdings for the long haul. Every investment should have a high price in which an investor is willing to realize significant profits by selling a portion of the position. We all love friends and family, and yet we should not love our investments!

Does the stock chart on the following page look familiar (CHART 78)?

We have all witnessed star-performing investments tank in bear markets, in which high levels of profit evaporate quickly. Proper portfolio rebalancing will help to prevent this from happening.

Remember, the key objective of rebalancing a portfolio's holdings is to keep the portfolio properly diversified and minimize the risk of large positions harming the performance of the overall portfolio. *It is not an attempt to consistently pick the elusive bull market top or bear market bottom!*

Money Managers and Their Clients

Profitable investing is hard work!

Successful investors take the task of portfolio management very seriously and know that the process of creating an investment strategy, executing that strategy, monitoring the portfolio's progress, and rebalancing to keep the portfolio diversified is time-intensive, continuous work.

Due to the time and knowledge required for investment analysis and portfolio management, many investors have elected to retain the services of a "money manager" or investment advisor to oversee the investment process. Investors must always remember that it's their money in harm's way, and they still need to be actively involved in the important process of setting a realistic goal and periodically reviewing the portfolio in light of that goal.

In the next section, the major points of this book are summarized for reflection and memorization.

CHART 78: Financial Ups and Downs!

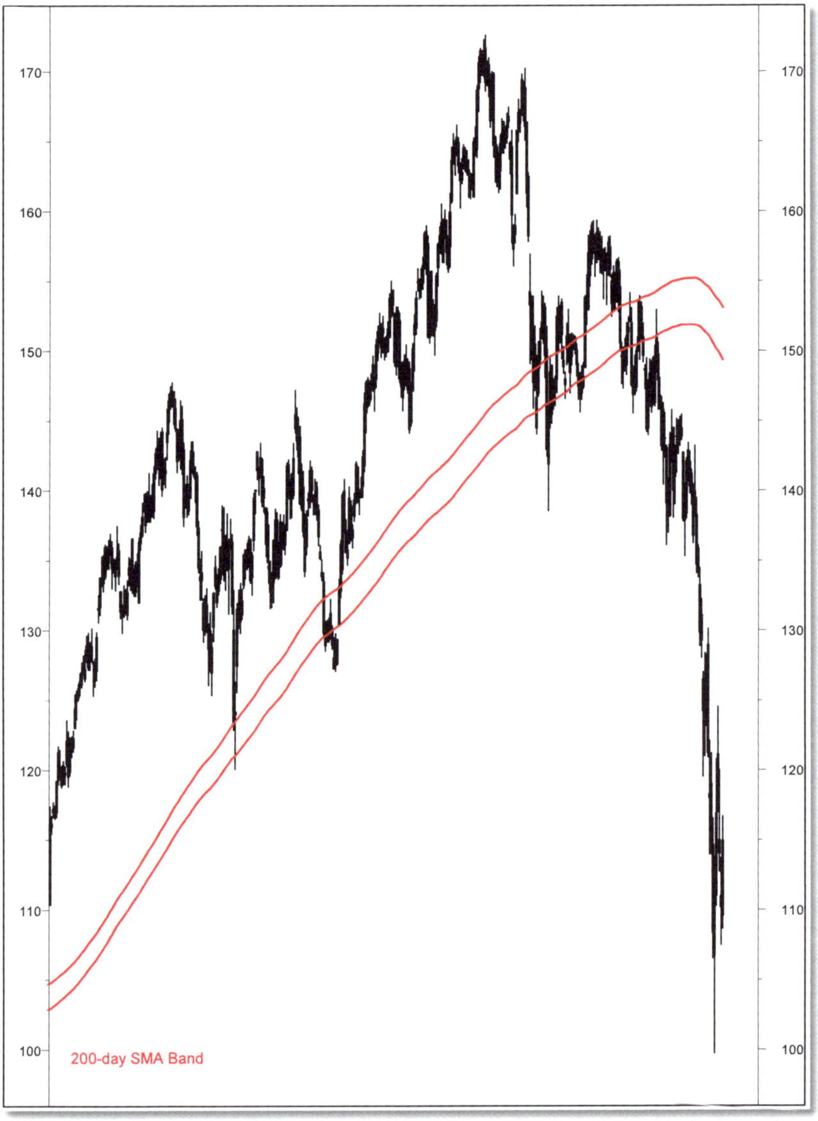

Created in MetaStock from Equis International

Chapter 8

Summary and Final Thoughts

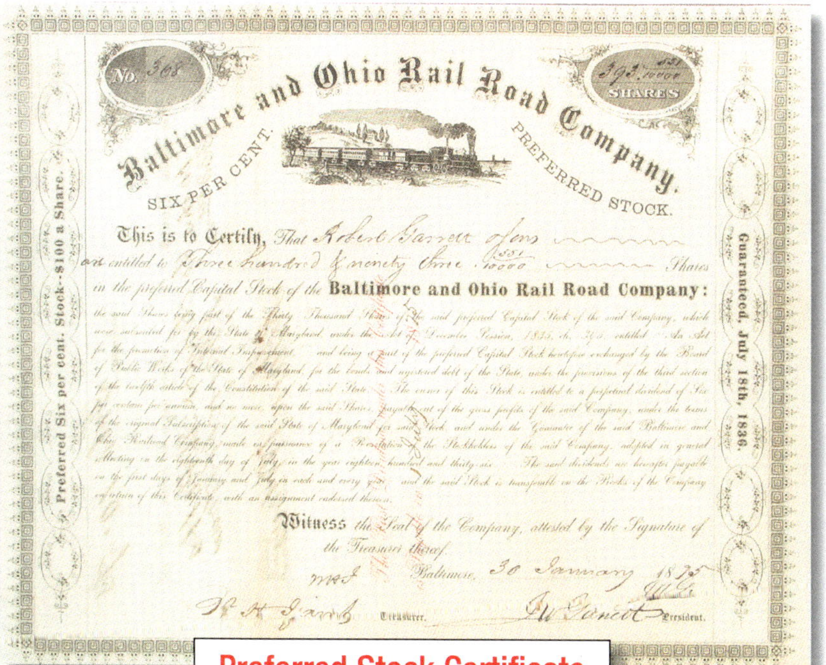

Preferred Stock Certificate
Baltimore and Ohio Railroad, 1875

"The definition of insanity is doing the same thing over and over again and expecting different results."
Albert Einstein

"Fortunate is he who has studied history."
Euripides, Greek Philosopher, 4th Century B.C.

Although not a sequel, this book is a logical extension of my first book *Preferreds: Wall Street's Best-Kept Income Secret.* When it was published in 2007, it was the first book devoted to preferred stocks since 1939 and foretold of a continuing, permanent shift of money toward "dull" income investments as the "baby boom" generation ages.

Unfortunately, many of my concerns about investors blindly buying preferred stocks came true in 2007-08.

Chapter 1
Dealt with the financial hurricane of 2008, and the mistakes made by investors such as: underestimating the risk of income investments, misusing income statistics, overrelying on agency ratings, and misunderstanding the role of market benchmarks.

Chapter 2
Reviewed the basic rules of investing in income securities that I have learned during three decades of work in the financial "trenches." The emphasis was on learning to correctly interpret and apply history's lessons as an important factor in successful investing.

Chapter 3
Focused on the uniqueness as well as the general confusion about preferred stocks and answered the questions:
"What are preferred stocks?"
"Where do I find them?"
"Have they performed well?"

Chapter 4
Dealt with effective analysis of the preferred-stock market to handle the high volatility associated with preferreds. This analysis has two purposes:

- To identify the current trend of the preferred-stock market through established technical indicators used on the Winans International Preferred Stock Index (WIPSI) from 1988 to 2009.

- To evaluate the current yields in preferreds when compared with the rates of return in other income investments such as corporate, Treasury, and municipal bonds. It answered the question "When to buy preferreds?"

Chapter 5
Focused on the tactical issues surrounding which individual preferred stocks to buy, and when they should be bought or sold. It described the issuer selection process, security screening process, and the technical analysis of selected preferred stocks over a five-year period.

Chapter 6
Coordinated the results from the analysis of the preferred-stock market and investment analysis of individual preferred stocks. It also compared these findings with those in *Preferreds*.

Chapter 7
Portfolio management brought everything together by integrating preferred stocks with other income investments by establishing an investment goal, executing the strategy, how to properly evaluate and monitor a portfolio of income investments, and how to rebalance an income portfolio.

It should be noted that the appendices in the back of this book have reference information on preferred stocks that should aid investors with preferred-stock investing. Included are:

- The Winans International Preferred Stock Index (WIPSI) specifications
- Preferred Stock Information Sources
- Data tables on the performance of preferred stocks, corporate bonds since 1900, and the 109-year yield spreads of preferred-stock yields versus common stocks, corporate bonds, T-bonds, municipal bonds, and T-bills

Final Thoughts

I am frequently asked if today's interest in preferred stocks is an investment fad that will end during the next bull market in common stocks? What these investors see as a temporary occurrence I see as the renaissance (rebirth) of income investing, where America's aging population is following the same fiscal course that its ancestors followed.

I would like to end this book with the same paragraph that ended *Preferreds*: "When investing in uncommon investment mediums, it can be unnerving if not outright scary, because Wall Street does not continuously promote them. The knowledge in this book should empower an investor to embrace preferred stocks, as they have other income investments, and thus be more successful and wealthier than the rest of the 'herd'."

These words have the same meaning today as they did in 2007.

Appendices

1907 — Business, Financial and Investment Counselors "Over Twenty One Years Of Service" — 1929
The Magazine of Wall Street
July 27th 1929
Publisher
35 Cents a Copy
10 Best Stocks To Buy Now
Selected By The Magazine of Wall Street Staff
Planting American Industrial Colonies Throughout the World
By Theodore M. Knappen
Super-Power Next Step on Pacific Coast?
By
William Knodel
Vol. 44
No. 7

Winans International Preferred Stock Index (WIPSI) Specifications (as of July 2010)

SUPPLEMENTAL INFORMATION

Industry Breakdown

Financial Services	61%
Real Estate Inv. Trusts	20%
Utilities	12%
Service	1%

Issuer Financials (average)

Revenues	$24 Billion
Earnings	$4 Billion

Dividend Cycle

91% of the issuers pay quarterly dividends in March, June, September, and December.

Agency Ratings

	Preferreds (S&P)	**Issuers (Value Line)**
Average	BBB-	B++
Range	AA+ to C	A++ to C+

INDEX TIME FRAME COVERED

1980-Present

Winans International Data and Calculations

1890-1980

Global Financial Data with Winans International Calculations

COMPONENTS OF WIPSI

Currently, WIPSI has 25 separate companies that have 100 preferred securities within the index. These are listed below in alphabetical order.

Company	Common Symbol	Number
Amerco	UHAL	1
Bank of America Corp.	BAC	5
Bank of New York Mellon Corp.	BK	2
Citicorp Inc.	C	5
Developers Diversified Realty Co.	DDR	3
DTE Energy Co.	DTE	2
Duke Realty Corp.	DRE	5
DuPont	DD	2
Ford Motor Co.	F	3
General Electric	GE	4
JP Morgan Chase & Co.	JPM	5
HSBC Holdings PLC	HBC	5
iStar Financial	SFI	5
KeyCorp	KEY	4
Kimco Realty Corp.	KIM	2
Morgan Stanley	MS	5
PG&E Corp.	PCG	5
Protective Life Corp.	PL	4
Public Storage	PSA	5
Renaissance RE Holdings Ltd.	RNR	3
Royal Bank of Scotland Group PLC	RBS	5
Southern Company	SO	5
Torchmark Corp.	TMK	1
U.S. Bancorp	USB	5
Vornado Realty Trust	VNO	5
Wells Fargo	WFC	4

The numbers of WIPSI components have gradually increased as follows:

Number	Year
13	1980
14	1986
15	1994
16	1997
19	1998
20	1999
24	2001
30	2002
92	2007
100	2010

Index Rebalancing

On June 30, 2010, six issuers were removed due to exchange de-listings or mergers with existing WIPSI components. Seven new issuers were included.

Component Weighting

WIPSI is an even-weighted index that focuses on the average price and yield of its components. This was done for the following reasons:

Due to the limited sample size of long-term, actively traded preferred securities, a data weighting could create volatility within this index that does not reflect the true trading activity of preferred stocks. For example, a high-weighted component can sway the entire index, implying that the overall market is volatile, when the price movement could be issue-specific (especially on issues being called).

Preferred stocks are issued in increments of $25, $50, and $100, and the price usually does not split. The divisors used to keep WIPSI even-weighted are easy to maintain and do not have to change. For instance, all $50 par valued preferred stocks in the index are reset to $25 par by dividing the price by two. The par value for this index is $25.

The process of weighting data is easier to apply in indices for common stocks, where a company usually has only one common stock issued. In the case of preferred stocks, a company can have multiple preferred issues, of different sizes, in the market at the same time. This raises the question

"What could be used as an effective weighting method for this index?" Do you use the capitalization for the specific preferred or do you use the capitalization for all preferreds in a company's capital structure (even though they may have been issued at different times and could have different levels of liquidity)? Unfortunately, data on most called or retired preferred stocks are not available from major data vendors, and this leaves no reliable way to back-test different weighting hypotheses over a sufficient time frame.

Other Preferred Indices with Exchange Traded Funds

Value Line's Convertible Index (ETF Sym: VALCX)
An even-weighted index that includes 63 convertible preferred securities listed since 1982. Current component turnover rate is 126%.

Standard & Poor's Preferred Stock Index (ETF Sym: PFF)
A weighted index that covers 85 preferred securities since September 2003. Current component turnover rate is 41% and is composed of 90% financial preferred stocks.

Data Release Time

The index's price and yield are calculated daily at 1:30 p.m. (Pacific Time). Supplemental information (average S&P rating, industry coverage %, company revenues, etc.) is calculated annually.

Data Source

Daily charts and data can be downloaded from Global Financial Data (globalfinancialdata.com).

Applications

WIPSI is currently formatted for MetaStock and spreadsheet software to construct charts and spreadsheet tables that can be used with the index's price, yield, total return, and supplemental data in several ways:

Charting

Price, yield, and total return charts can be used to determine long-term to short-term price trends, changes in long-term to short-term trends, and overbought to oversold market conditions. Conventional technical tools, such as chart patterns, moving averages, and relative strength indicators, can be easily used on computer charting packages.

Yield Spreads

WIPSI yield data can be combined with yield data from other investments to make yield spreads for valuation comparisons over a long time frame (see data tables on pages 206-209).

Supplemental Information

Information on the index's average ratings, industry sector breakdown, dividend cycle, and other financial information is compiled annually.

Index Use and Licensing

The Winans International Preferred Stock Index (WIPSI) is trademarked, and this report and its methodologies are copyright-protected against unauthorized duplication. Unauthorized use is prohibited.

Index Construction History

During 2004 and early 2005, the WI research staff started from scratch and developed, tested, and refined this index through the following steps:

Data Used

Data were gathered from past issues of *Barron's*, *The Wall Street Journal*, and *The Standard & Poor's Stock Guides* since 1986.

In *Barron's*, we compiled data from the Bonds, Market Laboratory on Bonds, and Preferred Stock sections, dating back to January 1986. (Please note that *Barron's* did not start listing preferred stocks until mid-2003.) To supplement *Barron's*, we also retrieved data on preferred stocks from *The Wall Street Journal* starting in 2001.

To increase the time frame studied, we also gathered the year-end issues of Standard & Poor's Stock Guide's Preferred Stock Summaries back to 1990.

Data Categorization

Please note that the data previously listed contain both preferred stocks and hybrid investment products listed as preferred stocks. Since the objective of WIPSI is to be an index for traditional preferred stocks, we excluded hybrids, floating rate, and convertible preferreds.

Hybrids are relatively new investments (most were created after 1999) and are highly invested in fixed-income investments. These include:

PINES	Public Income Notes
TRUPS	Trust Preferred Securities
SATURNS	Structured Asset Trust Unit Repackagings
QUIBS	Quarterly Interest Bonds
QUICS	Quarterly Income Capital Securities
QUIDS	Quarterly Income Debt Securities
QUIPS	Quarterly Income Preferred Securities
TOPRS	Trust Originated Preferred Securities

Data Examination

Our next task was to identify preferred securities for WIPSI. We focused on companies that normally had preferred shares outstanding during a 14-year time frame studied.

Index Composition

After identifying 57 companies that normally had preferred shares outstanding from 1986-2004, the final selection process for WIPSI's components was based on the following factors:

Issuer Consistency

The focus was on companies that have historically issued preferred stocks. Companies usually excluded from the index were those that had preferred stocks at the beginning and the end of the time frame studied, and did not have preferred stocks issued for two years within the same time frame.

To keep the index useful for long-term analysis, it is important to keep the underlying issuing companies consistently in the index.

Longevity of Issuer Itself

Preferred stocks with less than two years of trading history were usually excluded. In addition, if an issuing company had more than one preferred stock issued, the one that had been consistently traded for the longest amount of time was chosen. This rule was revised in 2007 to allow up to five securities per issuer.

Call and Convert Features

Preferred stocks, which could be called within one year, or were convertible into common stocks, were usually excluded from WIPSI. And there were some preferreds in the index whose call dates were continuous and in perpetuity. Since these securities had been traded for a long time, and there had been no corporate announcements to the contrary, it was not believed they would be called in the foreseeable future.

Trading Activity

Generally speaking, preferred stocks do not trade as frequently as their common-stock counterparts. Similar to the issues facing fixed-income indices, a minimum standard of trading activity for the components in WIPSI was established. This criterion was that the preferred securities selected need to have traded within the past week in a normal price range relative to the other components of WIPSI.

Replacement Components

Unlike most market indices, we had identified backup preferred stocks as index components. These backups were issued by the same company and had already passed our criteria to be a component of the index. In addition, these securities had similar price movements as the original selection; hence, a called preferred in the index should not have much effect on the continuity of the index.

Exclusion From Index

As a general rule, a security is removed from the index if it does not trade consistently for more than two weeks or is called by the issuer. It is replaced by a backup preferred of the same issuing company, as mentioned in the previous section. It should be noted that these securities have different symbols, and data from the removed securities will be kept in the index up to the date of removal. In other words, the new security will take over at the point where the old issue stopped.

Final Component Selection

Out of the 57 issuers selected from the preliminary analysis, 30 companies passed the selection criteria listed above and had their preferred stock included in WIPSI. Although it is believed the sample size is sufficient, an annual review of the 27 excluded issuers is conducted to see if they have met the selection criteria at that time. It should be noted that all available price, volume, and yield data for the preferred stocks of the 30 companies have been collected, and 13 companies had specific preferred stocks actively trading as far back as 1980—this became the WIPSI starting point.

Possible Component Changes

As explained above, we have backup candidates available for the called securities. The backups are issued by the same company and have a similar price movement as the original. Hence, a called preferred in the index will not have much effect on the continuity of the index. Winans International does an annual review of all preferred stocks in WIPSI for possible changes to the index.

WIPSI CHANGES SINCE INITIAL CONSTRUCTION

Data Extensions

To review the preferred-stock market prior to 1980, the percentage changes of older preferred-stock price and yield studies (Standard & Poor's 1910-1980 and Mitchell 1890-1910) were attached to

WIPSI's inception point. This provides for a continuous composite without the gapping problems associated with reviewing two separate studies.

Multiple Securities from a Single Issuer

To reduce daily price gapping of WIPSI caused by a particular security temporarily not trading, the number of index components was greatly expanded in 2007 by allowing up to five preferred stocks per issuer. This also reflects the common practice of long-standing issuers of preferreds to have multiple series within their capital structure that were originated at various times.

More information on Winans International indices and research can be found at winansintl.com or globalfinancialdata.com.

Preferred-Stock Information Sources

Preferred Stock Investment Management

Winans International Investment Management and Research (winansintl.com)

Preferred Stock Prices

The Wall Street Journal (wsj.com)
Barron's Financial Weekly (barrons.com)
Websites: PreferredsOnline.com, QuantumOnline.com

Historical Data

Global Financial Data (globalfinancialdata.com)
Winans International (winansintl.com)

Preferred Books and Published Research

Investment Atlas (amazon.com)
Preferreds: Wall Street's Best-Kept Income Secret (amazon.com)
Preferred Stock Investing (amazon.com)
Investing in Preferred Stock (amazon.com)
Market Technicians Association (mta.org)

Technical Analysis and Charting Websites

stockcharts.com
bigcharts.com
equis.com
valueline.com

Preferred Issuer Financial and Ratings Information

Websites: PreferredsOnline.com, InvestingingBonds.com, QuantumOnline.com
Value Line Investor Services (valueline.com)
Standard & Poor's (standardandpoors.com)
Moody's (moodys.com)
Bloomberg Financial (bloomberg.com)

Preferred-Stock Performance Table
1900-2009

					Inflation Adjusted		
Year	Dividend Yield	Price Change	Index 1.0	Total Return	Inflation Rate	Index 1.0	Total Return
1900	4.7%	18.6%	1.2	23.3%	1.0%	1.2	22.3%
1901	5.6%	22.3%	1.6	27.9%	1.0%	1.6	26.9%
1902	6.8%	0.6%	1.7	7.4%	1.0%	1.7	6.4%
1903	6.7%	-17.6%	1.5	-11.0%	2.9%	1.4	-13.9%
1904	7.6%	17.1%	1.9	24.7%	0.9%	1.8	23.8%
1905	6.4%	5.6%	2.1	12.0%	-0.9%	2.0	13.0%
1906	6.2%	-7.8%	2.1	-1.6%	1.9%	1.9	-3.5%
1907	6.4%	-28.8%	1.6	-22.5%	4.6%	1.4	-27.1%
1908	7.4%	30.0%	2.2	37.4%	-1.8%	1.9	39.2%
1909	6.4%	7.2%	2.5	13.6%	-1.8%	2.2	15.4%
1910	6.1%	-6.5%	2.5	-0.5%	4.6%	2.1	-5.1%
1911	6.4%	0.4%	2.7	6.8%	0.1%	2.3	6.7%
1912	6.4%	-0.4%	2.8	5.9%	2.6%	2.3	3.3%
1913	6.4%	-3.8%	2.9	2.6%	1.7%	2.4	0.9%
1914	6.6%	0.2%	3.1	6.8%	0.8%	2.5	6.0%
1915	6.6%	6.1%	3.5	12.8%	0.8%	2.8	11.9%
1916	6.2%	1.6%	3.8	7.8%	7.4%	2.8	0.4%
1917	6.1%	-12.2%	3.5	-6.0%	17.7%	2.2	-23.7%
1918	7.0%	6.9%	4.0	13.9%	17.7%	2.1	-3.8%
1919	6.5%	1.9%	4.4	8.5%	15.0%	1.9	-6.5%
1920	6.4%	-8.9%	4.3	-2.5%	15.9%	1.6	-18.4%
1921	7.1%	7.9%	4.9	15.0%	-10.8%	2.0	25.8%
1922	6.5%	8.3%	5.6	14.8%	-6.5%	2.4	21.4%
1923	6.0%	-2.3%	5.8	3.7%	2.0%	2.5	1.7%
1924	6.2%	3.2%	6.4	9.4%	0.1%	2.7	9.3%
1925	6.0%	2.3%	6.9	8.3%	2.9%	2.8	5.3%
1926	5.8%	3.2%	7.5	9.0%	0.5%	3.1	8.5%
1927	5.7%	5.0%	8.3	10.6%	-1.4%	3.4	12.1%
1928	5.4%	5.6%	9.2	11.0%	-1.4%	3.9	12.4%
1929	5.1%	1.1%	9.8	6.2%	0.1%	4.1	6.1%
1930	5.1%	0.5%	10.4	5.6%	-2.4%	4.4	8.0%
1931	5.0%	-15.9%	9.2	-10.9%	-9.0%	4.3	-1.9%
1932	6.0%	2.4%	10.0	8.4%	-10.4%	5.2	18.8%
1933	5.8%	1.0%	10.7	6.8%	-4.9%	5.8	11.7%
1934	5.8%	16.8%	13.1	22.6%	3.2%	6.9	19.3%
1935	5.0%	12.0%	15.3	17.0%	2.5%	7.9	14.5%
1936	4.4%	3.7%	16.6	8.1%	1.2%	8.4	6.9%
1937	4.3%	-4.2%	16.6	0.0%	3.6%	8.1	-3.6%
1938	4.5%	7.2%	18.5	11.7%	-1.7%	9.2	13.4%
1939	4.2%	0.9%	19.5	5.1%	-1.8%	9.8	6.9%
1940	4.1%	4.4%	21.1	8.5%	1.2%	10.6	7.3%
1941	3.9%	-5.3%	20.8	-1.4%	4.8%	9.9	-6.1%
1942	4.2%	-0.9%	21.5	3.2%	10.8%	9.2	-7.6%
1943	4.2%	1.9%	22.8	6.1%	6.2%	9.2	0.0%
1944	4.2%	7.0%	25.4	11.2%	1.5%	10.1	9.7%
1945	3.9%	8.2%	28.4	12.0%	2.4%	11.0	9.7%
1946	3.6%	-5.1%	28.0	-1.5%	8.4%	9.9	-9.9%
1947	3.8%	-8.3%	26.7	-4.6%	14.6%	8.0	-19.2%
1948	4.0%	-1.0%	27.5	3.1%	7.9%	7.6	-4.8%
1949	4.1%	7.0%	30.6	11.1%	-1.0%	8.6	12.2%
1950	3.9%	-0.9%	31.5	3.0%	1.1%	8.7	1.9%
1951	3.9%	-10.0%	29.6	-6.1%	7.6%	7.5	-13.7%
1952	4.3%	5.0%	32.4	9.3%	2.3%	8.1	7.0%
1953	4.1%	-2.0%	33.0	2.2%	1.0%	8.2	1.2%
1954	4.2%	6.6%	36.6	10.9%	0.3%	9.0	10.5%
1955	3.9%	-3.1%	36.9	0.8%	-0.3%	9.1	1.1%
1956	4.1%	-8.0%	35.5	-3.9%	1.6%	8.6	-5.5%
1957	4.6%	-0.1%	37.1	4.5%	3.4%	8.7	1.1%
1958	4.4%	-4.2%	37.1	0.2%	3.0%	8.5	-2.8%

Year	Dividend Yield	Price Change	Index 1.0	Total Return	Inflation Adjusted		
					Inflation Rate	Index 1.0	Total Return
1959	4.6%	-5.8%	36.7	-1.2%	0.6%	8.3	-1.8%
1960	4.9%	2.1%	39.3	7.0%	1.7%	8.8	5.3%
1961	4.9%	3.5%	42.5	8.4%	1.1%	9.4	7.2%
1962	4.7%	5.2%	46.7	9.8%	1.1%	10.2	8.7%
1963	4.4%	1.7%	49.6	6.1%	1.1%	10.7	5.0%
1964	4.3%	3.1%	53.2	7.4%	1.4%	11.4	6.0%
1965	4.2%	-6.2%	52.2	-2.0%	1.6%	11.0	-3.6%
1966	4.5%	-14.3%	47.0	-9.8%	2.9%	9.6	-12.7%
1967	5.2%	-11.8%	43.9	-6.6%	2.8%	8.7	-9.4%
1968	6.0%	-1.2%	46.0	4.8%	4.3%	8.7	0.5%
1969	5.9%	-16.0%	41.4	-10.1%	5.3%	7.4	-15.4%
1970	7.3%	3.6%	45.9	10.9%	5.9%	7.7	5.0%
1971	6.9%	1.9%	49.9	8.8%	4.3%	8.1	4.5%
1972	6.8%	-2.1%	52.3	4.8%	3.3%	8.2	1.4%
1973	6.9%	-12.2%	49.5	-5.4%	6.2%	7.3	-11.6%
1974	7.8%	-10.8%	48.0	-3.0%	11.1%	6.2	-14.1%
1975	8.8%	4.4%	54.3	13.2%	9.0%	6.5	4.2%
1976	8.5%	13.2%	66.1	21.7%	5.8%	7.5	16.0%
1977	7.7%	-4.3%	68.3	3.4%	6.6%	7.3	-3.3%
1978	7.8%	-11.3%	66.0	-3.4%	7.6%	6.5	-11.0%
1979	8.9%	-13.4%	63.0	-4.5%	11.3%	5.5	-15.8%
1980	10.1%	-17.1%	58.6	-7.0%	13.5%	4.3	-20.4%
1981	13.8%	-6.6%	62.9	7.2%	10.4%	4.2	-3.1%
1982	14.8%	20.3%	84.9	35.0%	6.2%	5.4	28.9%
1983	12.4%	0.0%	95.4	12.4%	3.2%	5.9	9.1%
1984	12.5%	3.0%	110.2	15.5%	4.4%	6.6	11.1%
1985	12.2%	13.4%	138.4	25.6%	3.5%	8.0	22.1%
1986	10.7%	30.3%	195.1	41.0%	1.9%	11.2	39.1%
1987	8.7%	-10.6%	191.3	-1.9%	3.7%	10.5	-5.6%
1988	9.8%	-1.0%	208.1	8.8%	4.1%	11.0	4.7%
1989	9.8%	9.6%	248.4	19.4%	4.8%	12.6	14.6%
1990	9.0%	-2.0%	265.6	6.9%	5.4%	12.8	1.5%
1991	9.1%	12.5%	322.9	21.6%	4.2%	15.1	17.4%
1992	8.1%	4.8%	364.5	12.9%	3.0%	16.5	9.9%
1993	7.7%	9.9%	428.5	17.6%	3.0%	18.9	14.6%
1994	7.0%	-16.4%	388.0	-9.5%	2.6%	16.7	-12.1%
1995	8.6%	16.1%	483.6	24.6%	2.8%	20.3	21.9%
1996	7.5%	-0.1%	519.3	7.4%	3.0%	21.2	4.4%
1997	7.5%	14.8%	634.8	22.2%	2.4%	25.4	19.9%
1998	6.7%	9.8%	739.8	16.5%	1.5%	29.2	15.0%
1999	6.2%	-14.7%	677.0	-8.5%	2.2%	26.1	-10.7%
2000	7.4%	2.1%	741.5	9.5%	3.4%	27.7	6.2%
2001	7.3%	11.5%	881.6	18.9%	2.9%	32.2	16.0%
2002	7.0%	6.9%	1003.8	13.9%	1.6%	36.1	12.3%
2003	7.0%	9.8%	1172.0	16.7%	2.0%	41.5	14.8%
2004	6.3%	4.8%	1301.8	11.1%	3.5%	44.6	7.6%
2005	6.3%	-4.3%	1327.5	2.0%	3.5%	43.9	-1.5%
2006	6.6%	2.0%	1441.3	8.6%	2.0%	46.8	6.6%
2007	6.4%	-15.2%	1315.1	-8.8%	4.2%	40.7	-13.0%
2008	7.9%	-27.3%	1059.6	-19.4%	0.1%	32.8	-19.6%
2009	12.2%	26.8%	1472.0	38.9%	1.9%	44.9	37.0%
Average	6.5%	0.9%	1337%	7.4%	3.1%	39.9%	4.3%
Median	6.6%	1.6%		7.4%	2.6%		5.3%
High	14.8%	30.3%		41.0%	17.7%		39.2%
Low	3.6%	-28.8%		-22.5%	-10.8%		-27.1%

Dividend Yields Are from Beginning of Year.
Source: Winans International Preferred Stock Index and Global Financial Data

Corporate Bond Performance Table 1900-2009

					Inflation Adjusted		
Year	Interest Yield	Price Change	Index 1.0	Total Return	Inflation Rate	Index 1.0	Total Return
1900	4.8%	6.1%	1.1	10.9%	1.0%	1.1	10.0%
1901	5.2%	4.3%	1.2	9.6%	1.0%	1.2	8.6%
1902	5.2%	-2.2%	1.3	2.9%	1.0%	1.2	2.0%
1903	5.2%	-9.1%	1.2	-4.0%	2.9%	1.1	-6.9%
1904	5.4%	12.2%	1.4	17.6%	0.9%	1.3	16.7%
1905	5.4%	-0.3%	1.5	5.0%	-0.9%	1.4	6.0%
1906	5.2%	-2.6%	1.5	2.7%	1.9%	1.4	0.8%
1907	5.4%	-10.7%	1.4	-5.3%	4.6%	1.3	-9.9%
1908	5.8%	9.2%	1.7	15.0%	-1.8%	1.5	16.7%
1909	5.7%	0.2%	1.8	5.9%	-1.8%	1.6	7.7%
1910	5.5%	-2.1%	1.8	3.4%	4.6%	1.6	-1.2%
1911	5.2%	-0.2%	1.9	5.0%	0.1%	1.7	4.9%
1912	5.6%	-2.5%	2.0	3.1%	2.6%	1.7	0.5%
1913	5.7%	-5.4%	2.0	0.3%	1.7%	1.6	-1.4%
1914	6.0%	-6.8%	2.0	-0.8%	0.8%	1.6	-1.6%
1915	5.2%	6.9%	2.2	12.1%	0.8%	1.8	11.2%
1916	4.9%	1.2%	2.3	6.0%	7.4%	1.8	-1.4%
1917	5.6%	-12.6%	2.2	-7.0%	17.7%	1.3	-24.7%
1918	5.4%	3.7%	2.4	9.0%	17.7%	1.2	-8.6%
1919	5.9%	-7.4%	2.3	-1.5%	15.0%	1.0	-16.5%
1920	6.2%	-5.8%	2.3	0.4%	15.9%	0.9	-15.6%
1921	5.5%	11.4%	2.7	17.0%	-10.8%	1.1	27.8%
1922	5.2%	6.3%	3.0	11.5%	-6.5%	1.3	18.1%
1923	5.4%	-2.7%	3.1	2.7%	2.0%	1.3	0.7%
1924	5.1%	4.5%	3.4	9.7%	0.1%	1.4	9.6%
1925	5.0%	2.7%	3.7	7.7%	2.9%	1.5	4.8%
1926	4.8%	3.3%	4.0	8.2%	0.5%	1.6	7.7%
1927	4.7%	3.4%	4.3	8.0%	-1.4%	1.8	9.4%
1928	4.9%	-3.4%	4.4	1.5%	-1.4%	1.8	2.9%
1929	5.1%	-2.3%	4.5	2.7%	0.1%	1.9	2.6%
1930	4.8%	1.5%	4.8	6.4%	-2.4%	2.0	8.8%
1931	7.5%	-18.3%	4.3	-10.8%	-9.0%	2.0	-1.8%
1932	9.1%	0.0%	4.6	9.0%	-10.4%	2.4	19.5%
1933	6.0%	8.8%	5.3	14.8%	-4.9%	2.8	19.7%
1934	4.8%	13.3%	6.3	18.0%	3.2%	3.3	14.8%
1935	4.6%	3.1%	6.8	7.6%	2.5%	3.4	5.1%
1936	4.0%	6.9%	7.5	10.9%	1.2%	3.8	9.7%
1937	5.2%	-11.9%	7.0	-6.7%	3.6%	3.4	-10.3%
1938	5.6%	-2.7%	7.2	2.9%	-1.7%	3.5	4.7%
1939	5.7%	-0.5%	7.6	5.2%	-1.8%	3.8	6.9%
1940	5.9%	1.0%	8.1	6.8%	1.2%	4.0	5.6%
1941	5.9%	-3.1%	8.3	2.8%	4.8%	3.9	-2.0%
1942	5.3%	2.8%	9.0	8.1%	10.0%	3.8	-1.9%
1943	4.4%	6.9%	10.0	11.3%	6.2%	4.0	5.2%
1944	3.4%	8.6%	11.2	12.1%	1.5%	4.5	10.6%
1945	3.0%	3.1%	11.9	6.1%	2.4%	4.6	3.7%
1946	3.4%	-4.2%	11.8	-0.8%	8.4%	4.2	-9.2%
1947	3.8%	-6.8%	11.5	-3.0%	14.6%	3.5	-17.5%
1948	3.6%	2.2%	12.1	5.8%	7.9%	3.4	-2.1%
1949	3.5%	2.5%	12.9	6.0%	-1.0%	3.6	7.0%
1950	3.3%	1.5%	13.5	4.8%	1.1%	3.8	3.7%
1951	3.7%	-5.9%	13.2	-2.2%	7.6%	3.4	-9.9%
1952	3.5%	2.1%	13.9	5.6%	2.3%	3.5	3.3%
1953	3.5%	-1.6%	14.2	2.0%	1.0%	3.6	1.0%
1954	3.2%	3.8%	15.2	7.0%	0.3%	3.8	6.7%
1955	3.6%	-2.8%	15.3	0.8%	-0.3%	3.8	1.1%
1956	4.3%	-8.7%	14.6	-4.4%	1.6%	3.6	-6.0%
1957	4.8%	-2.2%	15.0	2.6%	3.4%	3.6	-0.8%
1958	4.8%	-1.5%	15.5	3.2%	3.0%	3.6	0.3%

Year	Interest Yield	Price Change	Index 1.0	Total Return	Inflation Adjusted Inflation Rate	Inflation Adjusted Index 1.0	Inflation Adjusted Total Return
1959	5.6%	-6.3%	15.4	-0.7%	0.6%	3.5	-1.3%
1960	5.0%	4.9%	16.9	9.9%	1.7%	3.8	8.2%
1961	5.3%	-1.1%	17.6	4.1%	1.1%	3.9	3.0%
1962	4.7%	4.7%	19.2	9.3%	1.1%	4.3	8.2%
1963	4.6%	0.9%	20.3	5.5%	1.1%	4.4	4.4%
1964	4.6%	1.4%	21.5	6.0%	1.4%	4.7	4.6%
1965	4.9%	-3.0%	21.9	1.9%	1.6%	4.7	0.3%
1966	5.8%	-7.1%	21.6	-1.4%	2.9%	4.5	-4.3%
1967	6.6%	-7.7%	21.4	-1.1%	2.8%	4.3	-4.0%
1968	6.9%	-0.9%	22.7	6.1%	4.3%	4.4	1.8%
1969	8.3%	-7.9%	22.7	0.3%	5.3%	4.2	-5.0%
1970	8.4%	1.0%	24.9	9.4%	5.9%	4.3	3.4%
1971	7.7%	6.6%	28.4	14.3%	4.3%	4.7	10.0%
1972	7.7%	2.4%	31.3	10.1%	3.3%	5.0	6.8%
1973	8.4%	-3.0%	33.0	5.3%	6.2%	5.0	-0.9%
1974	10.0%	-9.1%	33.2	0.9%	11.1%	4.5	-10.2%
1975	9.9%	4.4%	38.0	14.3%	9.0%	4.7	5.3%
1976	8.0%	14.7%	46.6	22.7%	5.8%	5.5	17.0%
1977	8.3%	-2.4%	49.4	5.9%	6.6%	5.5	-0.8%
1978	9.2%	-7.1%	50.4	2.1%	7.6%	5.2	-5.5%
1979	10.9%	-13.2%	49.3	-2.3%	11.3%	4.5	-13.6%
1980	12.9%	-13.2%	49.1	-0.3%	13.5%	3.9	-13.8%
1981	14.9%	-10.4%	51.3	4.5%	10.4%	3.6	-5.8%
1982	12.0%	23.6%	69.6	35.6%	6.2%	4.7	29.5%
1983	12.3%	-1.5%	77.1	10.8%	3.2%	5.1	7.5%
1984	12.3%	4.3%	89.9	16.6%	4.4%	5.7	12.2%
1985	10.5%	15.6%	113.4	26.1%	3.5%	7.0	22.5%
1986	9.3%	11.6%	137.1	20.9%	1.9%	8.3	19.1%
1987	10.3%	-7.2%	141.3	3.1%	3.7%	8.3	-0.6%
1988	10.0%	2.2%	158.5	12.2%	4.1%	8.9	8.1%
1989	9.3%	4.9%	181.0	14.2%	4.8%	9.8	9.4%
1990	9.5%	-1.5%	195.5	8.0%	5.4%	10.0	2.6%
1991	8.5%	8.0%	227.8	16.5%	4.2%	11.2	12.3%
1992	7.3%	5.0%	255.9	12.3%	3.0%	12.3	9.3%
1993	6.6%	1.0%	275.2	7.6%	3.0%	12.8	4.6%
1994	8.2%	-10.8%	268.0	-2.6%	2.6%	12.2	-5.2%
1995	6.8%	12.6%	319.9	19.4%	2.8%	14.2	16.6%
1996	6.9%	-1.5%	337.3	5.4%	3.0%	14.6	2.5%
1997	6.5%	2.8%	368.6	9.3%	2.4%	15.6	6.9%
1998	6.0%	3.2%	402.3	9.1%	1.5%	16.7	7.6%
1999	7.5%	-9.2%	395.7	-1.6%	2.2%	16.1	-3.9%
2000	7.2%	1.8%	431.5	9.1%	3.4%	17.0	5.7%
2001	6.2%	3.4%	473.2	9.7%	2.9%	18.2	6.8%
2002	5.4%	4.1%	518.0	9.5%	1.6%	19.6	7.9%
2003	4.8%	3.5%	561.0	8.3%	2.0%	20.8	6.3%
2004	4.9%	0.2%	589.5	5.1%	3.5%	21.2	1.6%
2005	5.3%	-4.1%	596.9	1.3%	3.5%	20.7	-2.2%
2006	5.7%	-2.1%	618.3	3.6%	2.0%	21.0	1.6%
2007	5.7%	-0.9%	648.1	4.8%	4.2%	21.2	0.6%
2008	6.9%	-4.5%	663.8	2.4%	0.1%	21.6	2.3%
2009	4.3%	11.0%	765.4	15.3%	1.9%	24.5	13.4%
Average	6.3%	0.2%	695%	6.45%	3.1%	21.4%	3.4%
Median	5.5%	0.2%		5.89%	2.6%		3.6%
High	14.9%	23.6%		35.6%	17.7%		29.5%
Low	3.0%	-18.3%		-10.8%	-10.8%		-24.7%

Source: Dow Jones Corporate Bond Index and Global Financial Data

Investment Income Yields and Yield Spread Versus Preferred Stock, 1900-2009

Year	Preferred Dividend Yield	Common Dividend Yield	Preferred Spread	Corporate Bond Yield	Preferred Spread	T-bond (10 Year) Yield	Preferred Spread	Municipal Bond Yield	Preferred Spread	T-bill (90 Day) Yield	Preferred Spread
1900	4.7%	4.9%	-0.2%	4.8%	-0.1%	3.0%	1.7%	3.1%	1.6%	2.7%	2.0%
1901	5.6%	4.5%	1.1%	5.2%	0.3%	2.9%	2.7%	3.1%	2.5%	3.8%	1.8%
1902	6.8%	4.1%	2.7%	5.2%	1.7%	2.9%	3.9%	3.1%	3.7%	3.5%	3.3%
1903	6.7%	4.1%	2.6%	5.2%	1.5%	3.0%	3.7%	3.2%	3.5%	3.8%	2.8%
1904	7.6%	4.6%	3.0%	5.4%	2.2%	3.0%	4.6%	3.3%	4.3%	4.5%	3.2%
1905	6.4%	3.9%	2.5%	5.4%	1.0%	3.1%	3.3%	3.4%	3.0%	3.5%	2.9%
1906	6.2%	4.1%	2.1%	5.2%	0.9%	3.1%	3.1%	3.4%	2.8%	3.4%	2.8%
1907	6.4%	4.6%	1.8%	5.4%	1.0%	3.1%	3.3%	3.4%	2.9%	4.4%	1.9%
1908	7.4%	5.8%	1.6%	5.8%	1.6%	3.4%	4.0%	3.7%	3.7%	5.0%	2.3%
1909	6.4%	4.9%	1.5%	5.7%	0.7%	3.3%	3.1%	3.8%	2.6%	4.3%	2.1%
1910	6.1%	4.7%	1.4%	5.5%	0.6%	3.4%	2.6%	3.7%	2.3%	3.0%	3.1%
1911	6.4%	5.1%	1.3%	5.2%	1.2%	3.5%	2.9%	3.9%	2.5%	4.3%	2.1%
1912	6.4%	5.3%	1.1%	5.6%	0.7%	3.5%	2.8%	4.0%	2.4%	3.2%	3.1%
1913	6.4%	5.2%	1.2%	5.7%	0.7%	3.5%	2.9%	4.0%	2.4%	3.5%	2.9%
1914	6.6%	5.0%	1.6%	6.0%	0.7%	3.6%	3.1%	4.1%	2.6%	4.6%	2.1%
1915	6.6%	5.8%	0.8%	5.2%	1.4%	3.6%	3.0%	4.1%	2.5%	3.8%	2.9%
1916	6.2%	6.0%	0.2%	4.9%	1.4%	3.6%	2.6%	4.0%	2.2%	3.0%	3.3%
1917	6.1%	7.2%	-1.1%	5.6%	0.5%	3.6%	2.5%	3.8%	2.3%	3.0%	3.2%
1918	7.0%	7.9%	-0.9%	5.4%	1.6%	3.8%	3.2%	3.8%	3.2%	3.4%	3.6%
1919	6.5%	6.8%	-0.3%	5.9%	0.7%	3.7%	2.8%	4.4%	2.2%	4.8%	1.7%
1920	6.4%	5.8%	0.6%	6.2%	0.2%	4.9%	1.5%	4.4%	2.0%	4.5%	1.9%
1921	7.1%	6.5%	0.5%	5.5%	1.5%	5.4%	1.7%	4.5%	2.5%	5.7%	1.4%
1922	6.5%	7.0%	-0.5%	5.2%	1.3%	4.5%	2.1%	4.5%	2.0%	3.9%	2.6%
1923	6.0%	6.0%	0.0%	5.4%	0.7%	4.3%	1.7%	4.1%	1.9%	3.7%	2.4%
1924	6.2%	6.2%	0.0%	5.1%	1.1%	4.4%	1.8%	4.1%	2.1%	3.8%	2.4%
1925	6.0%	5.7%	0.3%	5.0%	1.0%	4.0%	2.0%	4.1%	1.9%	2.6%	3.4%
1926	5.8%	5.5%	0.3%	4.8%	1.0%	3.8%	2.0%	4.0%	1.8%	3.5%	2.4%
1927	5.7%	5.8%	-0.1%	4.7%	1.0%	3.6%	2.1%	4.0%	1.6%	3.2%	2.4%
1928	5.4%	4.9%	0.5%	4.9%	0.5%	3.2%	2.2%	3.9%	1.5%	3.3%	2.1%

1929	5.1%	3.9%	1.2%	5.1%	0.1%	3.5%	1.7%	3.9%	1.2%	4.3%	0.9%
1930	5.1%	4.5%	0.6%	4.8%	0.2%	3.4%	1.7%	4.2%	0.9%	3.0%	2.0%
1931	5.0%	5.1%	-0.1%	7.5%	-2.5%	3.2%	1.8%	3.9%	1.1%	1.5%	3.6%
1932	6.0%	6.0%	0.0%	9.1%	-3.1%	3.9%	2.1%	3.7%	2.3%	3.3%	2.7%
1933	5.8%	6.2%	-0.4%	6.0%	-0.1%	3.4%	2.5%	4.3%	1.6%	0.1%	5.8%
1934	5.8%	4.3%	1.5%	4.8%	1.0%	3.5%	2.3%	4.2%	1.6%	0.7%	5.1%
1935	5.0%	5.1%	-0.1%	4.6%	0.4%	3.0%	2.0%	3.7%	1.3%	0.1%	4.8%
1936	4.4%	5.2%	-0.8%	4.0%	0.5%	2.8%	1.6%	3.3%	1.1%	0.1%	4.3%
1937	4.3%	4.6%	-0.3%	5.2%	-1.0%	2.5%	1.7%	2.8%	1.5%	0.0%	4.3%
1938	4.5%	4.5%	-0.1%	5.6%	-1.2%	2.7%	1.8%	2.7%	1.7%	0.0%	4.5%
1939	4.2%	5.0%	-0.9%	5.7%	-1.5%	2.5%	1.7%	2.7%	1.4%	0.0%	4.2%
1940	4.1%	5.5%	-1.4%	5.9%	-1.8%	2.3%	1.8%	2.5%	1.6%	0.0%	4.1%
1941	3.9%	6.7%	-2.8%	5.9%	-1.9%	1.9%	2.1%	2.0%	1.9%	0.0%	3.9%
1942	4.2%	6.6%	-2.5%	5.3%	-1.2%	2.1%	2.1%	1.9%	2.3%	0.3%	3.9%
1943	4.2%	6.1%	-1.9%	4.4%	-0.2%	2.1%	2.1%	2.2%	2.0%	0.4%	3.8%
1944	4.2%	5.4%	-1.2%	3.4%	0.7%	2.1%	2.0%	1.9%	2.3%	0.4%	3.8%
1945	3.9%	4.9%	-1.0%	3.0%	0.9%	2.1%	1.8%	1.8%	2.1%	0.4%	3.5%
1946	3.6%	3.9%	-0.3%	3.4%	0.2%	1.7%	1.9%	1.5%	2.0%	0.4%	3.2%
1947	3.8%	5.5%	-1.8%	3.8%	-0.1%	1.8%	1.9%	1.4%	2.3%	0.4%	3.4%
1948	4.0%	6.3%	-2.3%	3.6%	0.4%	2.2%	1.9%	1.9%	2.1%	1.0%	3.1%
1949	4.1%	7.4%	-3.3%	3.5%	0.7%	2.1%	2.0%	2.2%	1.9%	1.2%	3.0%
1950	3.9%	8.1%	-4.2%	3.3%	0.6%	1.8%	2.1%	2.1%	1.8%	1.1%	2.8%
1951	3.9%	6.5%	-2.6%	3.7%	0.3%	2.2%	1.7%	1.7%	2.2%	1.4%	2.5%
1952	4.3%	5.8%	-1.5%	3.5%	0.8%	2.5%	1.8%	1.6%	2.7%	1.7%	2.6%
1953	4.1%	5.5%	-1.4%	3.5%	0.6%	2.5%	1.6%	2.0%	2.1%	2.1%	2.0%
1954	4.2%	6.1%	-1.9%	3.2%	1.0%	2.6%	1.6%	2.4%	1.8%	1.6%	2.6%
1955	3.9%	4.6%	-0.7%	3.6%	0.4%	2.5%	1.4%	2.2%	1.7%	1.2%	2.8%
1956	4.1%	3.9%	0.2%	4.3%	-0.2%	3.0%	1.1%	2.4%	1.7%	2.6%	1.5%
1957	4.6%	3.9%	0.7%	4.3%	-0.2%	3.6%	1.0%	2.6%	2.1%	3.2%	1.4%
1958	4.4%	4.2%	0.2%	4.3%	-0.3%	3.2%	1.2%	3.2%	1.2%	3.1%	1.3%
1959	4.6%	3.3%	1.3%	5.3%	-0.9%	3.9%	0.8%	3.2%	1.4%	2.8%	1.8%
1960	4.9%	3.4%	1.5%	5.0%	-0.2%	4.7%	0.2%	3.7%	1.2%	4.6%	0.3%

Year	Preferred Dividend Yield	Common Dividend Yield	Preferred Spread	Corporate Bond Yield	Preferred Spread	T-bond (10 Year) Yield	Preferred Spread	Municipal Bond Yield	Preferred Spread	T-bill (90 Day) Yield	Preferred Spread
1961	4.9%	3.4%	1.5%	5.3%	-0.4%	3.8%	1.0%	3.4%	1.4%	2.3%	2.6%
1962	4.7%	3.1%	1.6%	4.7%	0.0%	4.1%	0.6%	3.3%	1.4%	2.6%	2.0%
1963	4.4%	3.5%	0.9%	4.6%	-0.2%	3.9%	0.6%	3.0%	1.4%	2.9%	1.6%
1964	4.3%	3.3%	1.0%	4.6%	-0.3%	4.1%	0.2%	3.1%	1.3%	3.5%	0.8%
1965	4.2%	3.2%	1.0%	4.9%	-0.7%	4.2%	0.0%	3.1%	1.1%	3.9%	0.4%
1966	4.5%	3.1%	1.4%	5.8%	-1.3%	4.7%	-0.2%	3.0%	1.4%	4.4%	0.1%
1967	5.2%	3.5%	1.7%	6.6%	-1.4%	4.6%	0.6%	3.5%	1.7%	5.0%	0.2%
1968	6.0%	3.2%	2.8%	6.9%	-0.9%	5.7%	0.3%	3.4%	2.6%	5.0%	1.0%
1969	5.9%	3.1%	2.8%	8.3%	-2.3%	6.2%	-0.2%	4.2%	1.8%	5.9%	0.0%
1970	7.3%	3.5%	3.8%	8.4%	-1.1%	7.9%	-0.6%	4.9%	2.4%	7.7%	-0.4%
1971	6.9%	3.3%	3.6%	7.7%	-0.9%	6.5%	0.4%	5.6%	1.2%	4.9%	2.0%
1972	6.8%	3.1%	3.7%	7.7%	-0.9%	5.9%	0.9%	5.1%	1.7%	4.0%	2.8%
1973	6.9%	4.1%	2.8%	8.4%	-1.5%	6.4%	0.5%	5.0%	1.9%	5.1%	1.8%
1974	7.8%	5.7%	2.1%	10.0%	-2.2%	6.9%	0.9%	5.0%	2.9%	7.4%	0.5%
1975	8.8%	4.6%	4.2%	9.9%	-1.2%	7.4%	1.4%	5.1%	3.6%	7.2%	1.6%
1976	8.5%	4.6%	3.9%	8.0%	0.5%	7.8%	0.7%	6.2%	2.3%	5.5%	3.0%
1977	7.7%	5.7%	2.0%	8.3%	-0.6%	6.8%	0.8%	5.6%	2.1%	4.4%	3.3%
1978	7.8%	5.9%	1.9%	9.2%	-1.4%	7.8%	0.1%	5.3%	2.5%	6.1%	1.8%
1979	8.9%	6.2%	2.7%	10.9%	-2.0%	9.2%	-0.2%	5.4%	3.5%	9.1%	-0.2%
1980	10.1%	5.4%	4.7%	12.9%	-2.8%	10.3%	-0.2%	6.0%	4.2%	12.1%	-1.9%
1981	13.8%	6.7%	7.1%	14.9%	-1.1%	12.4%	1.4%	7.0%	6.8%	15.0%	-1.2%
1982	14.8%	5.2%	9.6%	12.0%	2.7%	14.0%	0.8%	9.5%	5.3%	11.7%	3.1%
1983	12.4%	4.4%	8.0%	12.3%	0.1%	10.4%	2.0%	9.2%	3.2%	8.0%	4.4%
1984	12.5%	4.5%	8.0%	12.3%	0.1%	11.8%	0.6%	8.7%	3.7%	8.9%	3.5%
1985	12.2%	3.6%	8.6%	10.5%	1.7%	11.6%	0.6%	9.5%	2.7%	7.9%	4.3%
1986	10.7%	3.4%	7.3%	9.3%	1.3%	9.0%	1.7%	8.7%	2.0%	7.0%	3.7%
1987	8.7%	3.4%	5.3%	10.3%	-1.6%	7.2%	1.5%	7.1%	1.6%	5.6%	3.1%
1988	9.8%	3.6%	6.2%	10.0%	-0.3%	8.8%	0.9%	6.9%	2.9%	5.7%	4.1%
1989	9.8%	3.2%	6.6%	9.3%	0.5%	9.1%	0.6%	7.7%	2.1%	8.1%	1.7%

1990	9.0%	3.7%	5.3%	9.5%	-0.5%	7.9%	1.0%	7.2%	1.8%	7.6%	1.4%
1991	9.1%	2.4%	6.7%	8.5%	0.6%	8.1%	1.0%	7.3%	1.9%	6.5%	2.6%
1992	8.1%	3.0%	5.1%	7.3%	0.8%	6.7%	1.4%	6.7%	1.4%	3.9%	4.2%
1993	7.7%	2.5%	5.2%	6.6%	1.1%	6.7%	1.0%	6.1%	1.6%	3.1%	4.6%
1994	7.0%	2.9%	4.1%	8.2%	-1.2%	5.8%	1.1%	5.3%	1.6%	3.0%	4.0%
1995	8.6%	2.5%	6.1%	6.8%	1.8%	7.8%	0.7%	5.4%	3.2%	5.6%	3.0%
1996	7.5%	2.1%	5.4%	6.9%	0.6%	5.6%	1.9%	5.6%	1.9%	5.0%	2.5%
1997	7.5%	1.7%	5.8%	6.5%	1.0%	6.4%	1.1%	5.5%	2.0%	5.1%	2.4%
1998	6.7%	1.6%	5.1%	6.0%	0.7%	5.8%	0.9%	5.2%	1.5%	5.2%	1.5%
1999	6.2%	0.9%	5.3%	7.5%	-1.3%	4.7%	1.6%	5.0%	1.3%	4.4%	1.8%
2000	7.4%	0.5%	6.9%	7.2%	0.2%	6.5%	1.0%	5.1%	2.3%	5.3%	2.1%
2001	7.3%	1.2%	6.1%	6.2%	1.1%	5.1%	2.2%	5.5%	1.9%	5.9%	1.5%
2002	7.0%	1.8%	5.1%	5.4%	1.6%	5.1%	1.9%	5.1%	1.8%	1.7%	5.3%
2003	7.0%	1.8%	5.2%	4.8%	2.2%	3.8%	3.1%	4.9%	2.1%	1.2%	5.8%
2004	6.3%	1.7%	4.6%	4.9%	1.4%	4.3%	2.1%	4.7%	1.6%	0.9%	5.4%
2005	6.3%	1.8%	4.5%	5.3%	1.0%	4.2%	2.1%	4.7%	1.7%	2.2%	4.1%
2006	6.6%	1.8%	4.8%	5.7%	0.9%	4.4%	2.2%	4.6%	2.0%	4.1%	2.5%
2007	6.4%	1.9%	4.6%	5.7%	0.7%	4.7%	1.7%	4.5%	1.9%	5.0%	1.5%
2008	7.9%	3.1%	4.8%	6.9%	1.0%	4.0%	3.9%	4.5%	3.4%	3.2%	4.7%
2009	12.2%	2.6%	9.6%	4.3%	7.8%	2.2%	9.9%	4.7%	7.4%	0.0%	12.1%
Average	6.5%	4.4%	2.1%	6.3%	0.2%	4.7%	1.8%	4.2%	2.2%	3.8%	2.7%
Median	6.6%	3.5%	3.2%	6.1%	0.0%	4.7%	1.1%	4.7%	2.0%	4.1%	2.6%
High	14.8%	8.1%	9.6%	14.9%	7.8%	14.0%	9.9%	9.5%	7.4%	15.0%	12.1%
Low	3.6%	0.5%	-4.2%	3.0%	-3.1%	1.7%	-0.6%	1.4%	0.9%	0.0%	-1.9%

Fixed Rates Yields Are Beginning of Year %.

Source: *Winans International & Global Financial Data, Preferred Stock, Winans International Preferred Stock Index Common Stock, S&P 500 Index with GFD Extension, Corporate Bond, Dow Jones Corporate Bond Average Municipal Bond, Bond Buyer 20 Index*

List of Charts, Exhibits, and Tables

Chapter 1

Chapter 2

Chapter 3

Chapter 4

Chapter 5

Chapter 7

Appendices

Bibliography

Books and Reports

Preferreds: Wall Street's Best-Kept Income Secret, Winans (2007)

Preferred Stock Investing, Le Du (2007)

Investing Online for Dummies, Krantz (2008)

Investment Atlas: Financial Maps to Investment Success, Winans (2008)

Investing in Preferred Stock, Josephs (2009)

"Winans International Preferred Stock Index" (Winans, Jadhav, Molakides, Gularte) 9/27/2005

"The Other Bubble" Winans 10/30/2005

"Technical Analysis of Preferred Stocks" Winans 3/20/2006

"Preferred Stock Primer" Standard & Poor's (9/25/2009)

Research Subscriptions

"Standard & Poor's Stock Guide" (January 2007, January 2008, August 2008)

"Standard & Poor's Bond Guide" (January 2007, December 2007, October 2008)

"S&P Index Directory, 2008"

Articles and Websites

2007

"Preferred Stocks Hit By Credit Crunch" *Investor's Business Daily* 8/22/07 (Emspak)

"Markets and Indexes" *Technically Speaking Magazine,* August 2007 (Winans)

"Preferred Stock Isn't Immune From Market Woes" *USA Today,* 9/3/07 (Krantz)

2008

"Preferreds Rally After a Perfect Storm" *Investor's Business Daily,* 2/6/08 (Emspak)

"You Don't Have to be a VIP to Buy Preferred Stock" *USA Today,* 2/7/08 (Krantz)

"Preferred Stocks Posting Solid Gains in 2008" *Yahoo Finance,* 3/4/08 (Winans)

"Can Other Firms Avoid Bear Stearns' Fate?" *USA Today,* 3/19/08 (Krantz)

"Bondlike Stocks Offer Decent Yields" *Kiplinger's Report,* April 2008 (Lisanti)

"Preferred Stock Can Give You Income and Appreciation" *USA Today,* 5/12/08 (Krantz)

"Preferred Stock Boom Brings New Opportunities, Questions" BoardIQ.com, 7/1/08

"Loan Costs Soar as Access Tightens" *USA Today,* 9/30/08 (Krantz)

"Preferred Stocks Have Dividend, Risk" livelongliverich.com, 10/26/08

"Recovering Fannie Mae & Freddie Mac Investment Losses" freddiefannielosses.com, 10/27/08

"Tapping Into Wall Street's Income Secret" *Barron's,* 10/27/08 (Salzman)

"Preferred Stocks Offer Best Yields in 108 Years" *Reuters,* 10/29/08 (Winans)

"Another Financial Hurricane" *Financial History Magazine*, Fall 2008 (Winans)

"The Case For Preferred Stocks" *Forbes,* 11/10/08 (Randall and Greenberg)

2009

"Preferred Stocks Outperforming Common Stocks in 2009" *Smart Money* 1/13/09 (Winans)

"Preferred-Stock Investment Paying Off" *Chicago Tribune,* 3/1/09 (Leckey)

"Takeover Deal a Mixed Bag for Investors" *San Francisco Chronicle,* 3/4/09 (Pender)

"Bonds 'a dark corner' of Market" *USA Today,* 3/10/09 (Krantz)

"Preferred Stock Showing Powerful Gains in 2009" *Yahoo Finance,* 8/18/09 (Winans)

2010

"Preferred Stocks Are 2010's Best Equity Play!" *Yahoo Finance,* 7/16/2010 (Winans)

Data Used from Following Services

Dial Data	trackdata.com
Global Financial Data	globalfinancialdata.com
Morningstar	morningstar.com
Reuters	reuters.com
Winans International	winansintl.com

Disclosure Page

Past performance should not be taken as representative of future results. Kenneth G. Winans will not be liable for any loss or damage caused by readers' reliance on the contents of this book, which is for informational and educational purposes only, and should not be considered investment advice.

These investments are not suitable for everyone, and a professional advisor should be consulted about the merits of the investments listed in this book before investing.

The contents in this book were derived from data provided by third parties. While these sources are considered reliable, Kenneth G. Winans does not guarantee or warrant the accuracy, adequacy, or completeness of the data used in this book.

The formulas and calculations used in this book are considered reliable and cannot be guaranteed. Changes can be made without notice.

All tax information provided in this book is for informational purposes only. Anything tax-related should be discussed with your accountant before it is used for tax purposes.

The amounts, percentages, and any reference to individual securities are for illustration purposes only and do not reflect actual performance or an endorsement of the company by Kenneth G. Winans.

Kenneth G. Winans and/or associates and/or employees may have an interest in the securities herein described and make purchases or sales of these securities without advance notice and at any time.

The opinions expressed in this book are solely those of Kenneth G. Winans and not those of Winans International.

About the Author

Kenneth G. Winans is a successful investment management entrepreneur, an award-winning author, and an active philanthropist.

For more than 27 years, he has conducted landmark investment research and designed creative investment strategies while serving as a portfolio manager, investment analyst, broker, and investor.

He is a regular guest on TV and radio shows nationwide and has had much of his investment research published as headline articles by leading websites, magazines, and newspapers.

Ken is president and founder of Winans International Investment Management (WinansInternational.com), which manages equity and fixed income investments for clients throughout the country and has won national acclaim for its success. In 2009, Winans International won the Small Business Commerce Association's national "Best of Business" Award. In 2008, Goldline Research ranked Winans International in *Forbes Magazine* as one of the "10 Most Dependable Investment Advisors."

He pioneered the development of several important investment indexes and technical indicators. In fact, The Winans International Preferred Stock Index (WIPSI)™ and the Winans International Real Estate Index (WIREI)™ (patent pending) are considered leading market indices in Wall Street publications and are used by major financial and academic institutions. The data are available through Global Financial Data (globalfinancialdata.com)

In 2007, Ken wrote and published the first book on preferred stocks since the 1930s, *Preferreds: Wall Street's Best-Kept Income Secret*, winner of the 2007 National Best Book Awards. Nineteen months later, he wrote and published his second book, *Investment Atlas: Financial Maps to Investment Success*. This investment history book reviews 200 years of events and how stocks, bonds, and real estate reacted. It was the winner of the 2009 Next Generation Indie Book Award's highly competitive Finance category.

He is a Chartered Market Technician (CMT), and is president of the San Francisco Chapter of The Market Technician Association. He is also a member of the Chartered Financial Analyst (CFA) Institute.

Ken has a bachelor's degree in business economics from the University of San Diego and a master's degree in finance from the University of San Francisco. In 2004, USF named him one of its most celebrated graduates.

He serves as a trustee for several nonprofit organizations such as The Museum of Finance (New York City), The W Foundation (Novato), Chabot Space and Science Center (Oakland), and the Society of California Pioneers (San Francisco).